REMEMBER ME

D0646081

REMEMBER ME

Constructing Immortality

Beliefs on Immortality, Life, and Death

EDITED BY MARGARET MITCHELL

Routledge is an imprint of the
Taylor & Francis Group, an informa business

Routledge
Taylor & Francis Group
270 Madison Avenue
New York, NY 10016

Routledge
Taylor & Francis Group
2 Park Square
Milton Park, Abingdon
Oxon OX14 4RN

© 2007 by Taylor & Francis Group, LLC
Routledge is an imprint of Taylor & Francis Group, an Informa business

Printed in the United States of America on acid-free paper
10 9 8 7 6 5 4 3 2 1

International Standard Book Number-10: 0-415-95485-1 (Softcover) 0-415-95484-3 (Hardcover)
International Standard Book Number-13: 978-0-415-95485-3 (Softcover) 978-0-415-95484-6 (Hardcover)

No part of this book may be reprinted, reproduced, transmitted, or utilized in any form by any electronic, mechanical, or other means, now known or hereafter invented, including photocopying, microfilming, and recording, or in any information storage or retrieval system, without written permission from the publishers.

Trademark Notice: Product or corporate names may be trademarks or registered trademarks, and are used only for identification and explanation without intent to infringe.

Library of Congress Cataloging-in-Publication Data

Remember me : constructing immortality / edited by Margaret Mitchell.
p. cm.
ISBN 0-415-95484-3 (hb) -- ISBN 0-415-95485-1 (pbk.)
1. Death--Social aspects. 2. Death--Psychological aspects. 3. Bereavement. I. Mitchell, Margaret.

HQ1073.R457 2006
306.9--dc22 2006021854

Visit the Taylor & Francis Web site at
http://www.taylorandfrancis.com

and the Routledge Web site at
http://www.routledgementalhealth.com

This is for James F. Darge, killed at Ypres on December 2, 1917, and for his fiancée Margaret Morrison Walker ("Mannie"), who loved him dearly until her death on September 30, 1974.

Contents

Acknowledgments

My sincere thanks go to each contributor to this volume. Your interesting work and challenging perspectives will stimulate much debate and research in this important field. I thank Mark Stoney, head of the School of Law and Justice at Edith Cowan University, for providing me with that most precious commodity—time—to get this project finished. I thank Robert Wyatt for his work in reading the text and providing excellent suggestions. Thank you, too, to my very good friend Glennys Howarth for introducing me to the study of the social context of death at the 1991 Death, Dying, and Disposal Conference in Oxford. Thanks also to the editorial staff at Taylor & Francis, especially Charlotte Roh, Dana Bliss, and Susan Horwitz for assisting the project through to completion. I thank Neil Radford for his meticulous work on the index, and for reading the book four times in the process. Finally, Robert, you are and always will be.

Margaret Mitchell
Perth, Western Australia

CHAPTER 1
Constructing Immortality
The Role of the Dead in Everyday Life

MARGARET MITCHELL

> Human beings are resourceful and every culture has attractive ways of imagining a world in which the dead are really still alive. (Merridale, 2000, p. 441)

Death is an interdisciplinary matter. This chapter and the volume *Remember Me: Constructing Immortality—Beliefs on Immortality, Life, and Death* present a very wide range of perspectives on the ways we interact with the dead in social, emotional, and practical ways. It is intended to give a broad base and add some flesh to the bones of our constructions of immortality. Its purpose is to go beyond remembering and memorializing the dead to present ways in which the dead play a lively part in our lives. But our relationship with the deceased is obviously changed (I don't need to explain why!). We may take as a metaphor Robert Wyatt's proposition, in his discussion in this volume of painting the "posthumous self," that those we keep with us after their death become "larger than life" through our attributions and activities. In a collection of essays on death and dying, Arnold Joseph Toynbee proposed a "capital fact" about the relation between living and dying: "There are two parties to the suffering that death inflicts; and, in the apportionment of this suffering, the survivor takes the brunt" (1968, p. 271). The way that the suffering referred to by Toynbee is manifested, as we will see, takes many forms. Rather than considering grief and suffering per se, however, the focus of this collection is on the creative ways that people—possibly in the face of personal suffering—continue the dead as "alive." In this chapter I discuss the private connection that bereaved individuals have with the dead, from public activism or pursuit of a cause to memorializing, and the ways people carry on physically in images and other ways such as biography.

I had difficulty at the outset of this work explaining to people that I was not talking about the afterlife, reincarnation, ghosts, or similar beliefs. Rather, my approach to "life after death" is secular and pragmatic. To me, reincarnation and an afterlife are not necessary to make things interesting. It is sufficiently interesting that we attribute feelings, desires, and emotions to the deceased, that we continue dialogues with them, that the material possessions they leave behind become imbued with potent meaning, and that we carry on public fights and pursue causes on their behalf. That the living continue to pay heed to the dead has many manifestations in our daily lives, and many functions. We might say that the "vitality" of the dead is a very real part of our lives.

Some time ago I was at a small conference on the theme of death at Glasgow University. As Monique Kornell gave her exquisite presentation on anatomical illustration and described the sixteenth-century convention of depicting the corpse as alive and told how "in this way the dead were allowed a form of eternal life," I thought it would be interesting to look at the various forms of everyday "life after death." The first chapter that I sought for this collection, from Kornell, was a literal rendition of the way that a person can continue, one way or another and in practical ways, long after his or her death. In the present volume, Kornell discusses the idea that a "second life" was given to cadavers through their use as models for anatomical illustration. In some cases these were "real," known people whose natural lifespan was greatly enhanced by their continued use by medical students and artists studying anatomy.

As I started thinking about it, many examples came to mind where the dead appear in life. An obvious example can start the discussion. A will is an instrument that a person prepares, knowing that it will be read and acted upon after they are dead. But a will is not an inert "legal instrument": the writer of the will intends to reach forward, to affect people in positive (or possibly negative) ways, and to influence their emotions. Carrying out the deceased's wishes as expressed in a will reconstitutes him or her as an active, even vital, social and political voice after biological death. In some cases the will's impact is considerable, the deceased person living on through families arguing and negotiating over inheritance, and over small and apparently insignificant items that belonged to their mother or father. Other aspects of death are also "built into" our lives, such as life insurance, death benefits, and the funeral industry. But this chapter and the collection is concerned not only with the ways death and the dead are structured into our lives, but also with our complex attributions, meanings, and explanations about the ways the dead continue to affect us.

Contemporary texts on death and bereavement, particularly since the publication of *Continuing Bonds: New Understandings of Grief* (Klass, Silverman, & Nickman, 1996), have discussed the many private ways a social relationship with close persons can continue and endure long after their death. Klass, Silverman, and Nickman questioned the idea that the "purpose of grief is to sever the bonds with the deceased in order to free the survivor to make new attachments." (p. 3) They also questioned the implied model of grief and bereavement—that is, that severing bonds and disengagement is healthy. The ideas presented in *Continuing Bonds* remain as lively and as relevant as they were a decade ago. Howarth (2000) further develops these ideas, describing the boundaries as "blurred" and breaking down between life and death. Howarth describes the many ways that the boundary between life and death can be breached, such as talking about the dead, the role of anniversaries, constructing future biographies for the dead, pilgrimage, and talking "with" the dead. Placing these ideas in a sociological context, she argues that ideas of "the continuing relationships between bereaved people and their deceased relatives and friends are not new but have been marginalized by the discourses and practices of modernity" (2000, p. 128). In the same article, she argues that the bereaved incorporate the dead person into their sense of self, and that the precise way that they do this varies according to class, gender, ethnicity, and age. The specific way that they are incorporated will *also* be influenced by the manner of death and characteristics of the relationship during life.

The psychological literature on coping with bereavement provides evidence that talking with the deceased, keeping objects that belonged to them, and frequent dreaming about them as alive are very common and can be sources of great comfort. Bennett and Bennett (2000) have studied what widows do to keep the dead person close, including using their deceased husbands' possessions and photographs of them to maintain contact and communication. Their study participants also reported the frequent experience of the deceased person being present. As Bennett and Bennett argue, the dominant scientific view is that these experiences are symptoms of "broken hearts and minds in chaos or … of looking for the deceased that characterizes the early stages of grief." But communication with the dead is common and underpins the idea that social interaction does not cease just because the person is not here. Indeed, it is not all that strange to have a conversation with someone who is not with us: witness the many muttered, admittedly one-sided, imaginary conversations we have with loved ones or adversaries who are alive and kicking but not with us.

In the same vein, spiritualist communication with the dead—or at least attempts to communicate—characterized the mass bereavement occasioned by the First World War. This led to the bereaved using any methods they felt were available to them to try to continue a dialogue with sons, nephews, husbands, and lovers killed on the Western Front. Winter (1995) explains the rise in spiritualism as a reaction to the failure of the established church to assist in such large-scale bereavement. Joanna Bourke's essay on spiritualism in this volume underlines the active participation of the dead in the psychological, emotional, and social lives of the living, particularly in response to such widespread and inexplicable loss. The title of her chapter on spiritualist communication comes from a booklet published in 1920, part of her meticulous study of original sources and extraordinary contemporaneous publications. Not all use of spiritualists and attempts to contact the dead can be relegated to the distant past. Justine Picardie's account of her attempts to communicate with her sister following her sister's death at age 33 is subtitled "Life and love after death." Published in 2001, it provides both a funny and a deeply moving account of her use of spiritualists. Of particular importance to her was her desire to hear her sister's voice—again a common and long-lasting desire among the bereaved.

Research on continuing bonds is helpful in clinical and counseling settings. That there is a blurred boundary is not only an interesting thing to know but also is useful to understand because it may inform medical, legal, and other professional (and indeed lay) approaches to people at the end of their life, the bereaved, and their families. Understanding the pervasive nature of the dead in our lives can help to explain behavior that, to outside observers and some professionals, can be difficult to explain. Despite acknowledgment of the work by Klass et al. (1996), Howarth (2000, 2006), Bennett & Bennett (2000) and others, Kübler-Ross's work (1969) has cast a long shadow on our understanding of death and grief. There remains an implicit assumption of "phases" and working toward a resolution of "letting go." Indeed, respondents in studies of bereaved persons (for example, Johnson, 2005, and in this volume) speak of friends' and relatives' expectations of an acceptable time for grieving, after which the person should be "over it." In Johnson's study, bereavement was the result of intrafamilial homicide, which is arguably a highly complex form of bereavement that is not simple to get over, yet the expectation of resolution within a time period persisted.

In some cases, the extremity of the circumstances of the death and the feelings of helplessness about it must be channeled into something positive.

In the following example we can see that the dead person, in this case the victim of a murder, has fundamentally affected the lives of the living. Ultimately the survivor attempts to achieve something good or positive from the death, in this case feelings of forgiveness for the perpetrator.

In 1994 in the United Kingdom, Frederick and Rosemary West were arrested for the rape and murder of at least nine young women, including their own daughter. The women were tortured, raped, and murdered, and their dismembered remains buried in the garden of the Wests' home at 25 Cromwell Road, Gloucester (demolished in 1996). One of those women was 28-year-old Lucy Partington, who had been missing since 1973, her remains having been identified in 1994. Her sister, Marian Partington, described the intense public exposure of her deceased sister and her family, and her pain at the negative characterization of her sister in the media. The tone of her writing is deeply distressed and angry, much of it directed at the media:

> In retrospect, it is hard to know how much of my internal feelings were scape-goated onto the media. But the intense media activity certainly contributed to the shock and sense of outrage. There was also a sickening feeling that this was going to be a long haul. Inadvertently, inexorably we were in the midst of a high profile case which had been seized on as the "crime of the century." (Partington, 2002, pp. 2–3)

Partington describes the need to "[reclaim] Lucy from the Wests and the media." Lucy, she writes, had "lost her privacy when she entered the public domain and became a 'Missing Person' after her disappearance … twenty years later the same image that had been posted on trees … was in the news again." The bones of the victims "became "exhibits for the defence" for another year, stored in cardboard file boxes in the mortuary at Cardiff Hospital. They were marked with numbers, letters, and eventually their names. "Only when Frederick West [suicided in jail] a year after the unearthing of the crime were we free to re-bury Lucy's bones, restoring her dignity in our funeral rites. As my son said, 'burying her in a nice way'" (Partington, 2002, p. 3). Marian spoke of her relief at being able to wrap the bones and make them safe, again making the inert alive and attributing feelings to the dead.

Partington's story was published in the *Guardian Weekend* (May 18, 1996). In response, she received "over three hundred letters and poems of great quality. Each communication was deeply affirming of all that is best about humanity and gives me a feeling of hope. *Lucy and I were heard, understood and honoured*" (Partington, 2002, p. 5 my italics). The difficulty of creating something good out of this damaging experience is obvious. In dealing with the horror of the murder and what it meant to her sense of self, Marian Partington, however, now participates in the Forgiveness Project specifically to work on forgiving Rosemary West. "Some people have asked whether I feel I am betraying Lucy by doing this and I say, 'No, absolutely the opposite: I feel I'm honouring Lucy.'" Partington's activities in defending her sister's characterization in the media, keeping her bones safe, and honouring her speak to the ongoing relationship with her murdered sister.

Grief and bereavement are not the main focus of this collection, although it is recognised that grief will motivate the acts of *continuance* described in this book. Grief can be channeled into activism in one form or another, which is a common consequence of experiencing the death of a loved one; people will take up causes relevant to the circumstances of the death. The motivation seems largely to ensure that the person did not die "in vain," thus rendering the death meaningful. This is even more likely when the deceased person is seen to have died under circumstances that were preventable, or where an individual or an authority can be blamed or has failed in their duty of care. The example often cited is that of Candy Lightner, the mother of a twelve-year-old girl killed by a drunk driver, who started the group Mothers Against Drunk Driving (MADD) in California in 1980. It has grown in 25 years into an influential lobby group whose aims are to "educate, prevent, deter and punish [and the organization] has caused judicial reform throughout the United States" (www.madd.org). The clever name, its acronym, and the straightforward message and purpose of this group have added to its success. The fact that MADD reflects problems in everyday life, that is drunk driving and fatal road accidents, and problems that can easily be prevented, also contributes to its longevity and success.

That these campaigns are motivated by grief and mourning, and even by the desire to maintain active contact with the deceased through *doing something for them*, seems self-evident. What may not be so evident is the almost limitless energy that is expended in the effort, and how durable it is over time. The sudden death of a loved one profoundly changes and can even consume lives. Jim Swire, whose daughter, Flora, was killed in the Lockerbie disaster of December 21, 1988 (when 259 passengers and 11 people on the ground were killed when a bomb exploded on board Pan Am flight 103), has not rested in his fight. His aim is to find out, in detail, why the disaster occurred and whether it could have been prevented, and to bring people to account. I interviewed Jim Swire on several occasions in the three years following the disaster, and he often described the clear image that he had of his daughter encouraging him to carry on, saying "Go on, Dad." In the same vein, following the conviction of Abdel Basset al-Megrahi 13 years after her death, Jim Swire is quoted as saying, "Flora would be proud of us" (Craig, 2001).

In the same year as Flora's death, Julie Ward, a 28-year-old Englishwoman, was on a photographic expedition in Kenya. In September 1988 she failed to return home to England, and some time later her remains were found in the Masai Mara Game Reserve. Her father, John Ward, has fought tirelessly to bring those responsible for her murder to justice, fighting what has been acknowledged as a cover-up and the insistence by Kenyan officials that she was killed by animals (Hiltzik, 1993). I was also able to interview John Ward and found him to be as single-minded, focused on detail, and determined to avenge his only daughter's killers as was Jim Swire. I use the term avenge advisedly; these men were on a campaign, and they were determined in their pursuits.

These are not small projects. Jim Swire has brought his fight to the U.K. government, has campaigned for airline and airport safety—indeed testing it by taking a false bomb on board a flight in 1990—and in 1998 met with Colonel Ghaddafi in Libya. John Ward, in his pursuit on his daughter's behalf, has argued with Moi's government in Kenya, police officers in the U.K., police in Kenya, has written a book, *The Animals Are Innocent* (1993), has been through two trials with no resulting conclusion for him, and reportedly has spent hundreds of thousands of dollars in his pursuit.

We can see that deaths, especially unexpected or untimely deaths, have the capacity to shape public policy through lobbying by survivors and through the public interest generated by deaths that are rendered public. In this way remembrance and memorializing are effected through creating change, especially change aimed at preventing such a tragedy's happening again. The phrase that has become almost a cliché in these situations is to try to ensure that the person *did not die in vain*. From one perspective, Jim Swire has had the opportunity for a potentially positive outcome in changing the world for the better by focusing on airport and airline safety, although subsequent events in September 2001 have demonstrated that this is a long and difficult road. John Ward's situation was different. He has not had the opportunity to try to make something good come out of Julie's death, other than his own relentless pursuit of bringing people to account. However extreme their activities over almost 20 years may appear, Jim Swire and John Ward are not to be taken lightly or dismissed as fathers incapable of "getting over it." They wish to right wrongs, and for both there is no doubt in their or indeed anyone else's mind that their daughters seem to be with them every step of the way.

On a smaller scale is what occurs when a person complains to an official body following a death. Pursuing a legal claim for compensation or even an apology for an accidental or wrongful death is a further example of how the dead continue significantly to influence the emotional life of the living and to motivate their behavior. Judith Allsop (in this volume) examines claims for medical negligence in cases of death in a particular area in England, using cases that are now closed. Allsop speaks of the need on the part of survivors not only to seek revenge but also to understand why the death happened in order for it to make sense. Such claims are particularly motivated by the survivors' need to do something for the dead, especially when the death was distressing and unexpected. As Allsop says, "There was often misunderstanding, confusion and muddle … the legacy of a death for many relatives could be a sense of unease and an obligation to the dead person to name what had gone wrong, to allocate blame … and to obtain some form of redress through the complaint." Since the time of the closed cases examined by Allsop, willingness in the United Kingdom to complain has increased over the intervening decades. Large-scale public and highly publicized inquiries have been conducted there, for example into the murder of 215 patients by the general practitioner Harold Shipman, who was convicted in 2000 and suicided in jail in 2004. For many, the political activity or legal action started and carried on in the name of the dead person *is itself* the act of remembrance and memorializing. The difficulties of pursuit, the devotion of time and energy to the pursuit, and the emotional and financial costs of pursuit simply emphasize the fact that the deceased person is still a highly active element in survivors' lives.

There are numerous other organizations, support groups, and interactive websites that are stimulated into existence by a sudden, tragic, or unexplained death. That such activity allows continued engagement with the deceased is without doubt, and it also facilitates social support and information sharing with others with the same or similar experience. However, the way in which the deceased should be remembered and how this continued attachment should take place differs among survivors, and concepts of support are far from uncomplicated. Following the Lockerbie disaster in 1988, several groups of victims' families were formed, each with a rather different agenda, and there was even some competition among them as to which was the official representative of the dead and the bereaved families. These different agendas can be explained by the markedly different reactions of bereaved relatives and friends, and also by the different meanings that are attributed to the death. Some have a desire to make good come out of bad by ensuring it does not happen again; some seek to avenge the death; and some simply seek the support of others in the same position. For some, there simply is no other way of trying to make sense of the death. In other words, the dead are attributed different social and political "voices." The relationship that people have with the deceased and the deceased's meaning to them also explains the very different approaches to making sense of the death and how the deceased continues in everyday life. This is evident in the different reactions that members of the same family will have to a death in the family.

In collecting and editing the chapters for this book, I found that family and the ongoing impact that a death of a family member has within the family is an underpinning theme. Not all responses to death are supportive and positive among family members. Indeed, death can break families apart as each responds in his or her own way and in terms of each one's relationship with and understanding of the dead person. Equally, in the challenging circumstances of a "death before death," Camilla Herbert (in this volume) describes the responses of different individuals in the family to a family member who has suffered profound brain damage through traumatic accident. The different reactions of individual family members are also seen in Lauren Breen and Moira O'Connor's research on the bereaved families of road accident victims, and in Carolyn Harris Johnson's study of families coping with intrafamilial homicide, both reported in this volume. Jenny Hockey and colleagues (in this volume) have examined family negotiations on the appropriate disposal of cremated ashes and have interpreted this in terms of a power struggle for ownership of the "memory" among family and friends. In each case desires, emotions, and choices are attributed to the dead as their negotiated memory is gently (or not so gently) argued over among family members.

We can extend this concept of the varied ways of responding to a death within a family on a wider scale into the public decisions about how particular people or events should be memorialized. Memorializing and ensuring that a memorial is fitting is a highly contentious subject among all those who have, or believe that they have, a continuing relationship with the dead, and an associated claim over how they should be remembered. This is so because memorials mean something, and they are seen to symbolize the person. A useful term for this—borrowed from the discipline of tourism studies—is "interpretation" (Lennon & Foley, 2000), which quite literally concerns how a place of death of a person will be "explained" to subsequent generations. Memorializing public figures and events will generate much debate. An example is the debate on appropriate memorializing that took place following the death of Diana, Princess of Wales, in August 1997. Public debate can parallel the fights that go on in families over disposal and appropriate memory and grieving. Following Diana's death, there were many different views about how she should be remembered and what people believed she "symbolized" (see Walter, 1999). In contrast, a *BBC News* "Talking Point" (Friday, April 19, 2002) posed the question soon after the death of the Queen Mother: "Should a statue of the Queen Mother be built in Trafalgar Square?" Among several well-intended suggestions—bronze statues, orthopedic wings in hospitals—one respondent (Keith, U.K.) said: "Oh for goodness sake, this is almost as ridiculous as the Diana fiasco that 'Gripped the Nation.' Bury the old dear and let's get on with the more important things in life, please." Because of the highly public aftermath of Diana's death and the phenomenon commented on at the time that members of the public felt they knew her (Walter, 1999), debate particularly surrounded the idea of her *continuing* through memorial. In trying to make something good out of a death—even one that became commodified to the extent that Diana's was—the rhetoric of her memorializing spoke of trying to create a living memorial. A charity to carry on her work was set up to achieve this; the Web site of the charity ("Diana: The Work Continues") states, "Even after her death … the Princess's work *lives on* in the form of commemorative charities and projects set up to help those in need."

Other examples from the many that we know of also make this point. In 1999, Jill Dando, a presenter on the British television program *Crimewatch*, was shot by a stranger. Barry George, who was unknown to Dando, was convicted of her murder. The irony of Dando's being the victim of a crime herself was lost on no one. In order to carry on the contribution she was seen to have made in fighting crime, the Jill Dando Institute of Crime Science at University College London was set up as the "first in the world devoted specifically to reducing crime." It is supported by the Jill Dando Fund as a permanent memorial. The Institute's Web site notes that this is achieved "through teaching, research, public policy analysis and by the dissemination of evidence-based information on crime reduction."

But the challenge remains of how to talk about the everyday phenomenon of the influence of the dead, in language that does not suggest something more or less than it is—that is, the very ordinary and everyday ways our dead friends, relatives, celebrities, fallen soldiers, artists, composers, and writers continue "here." It is the case that every building, photograph, song, or painting will eventually—if physically they should last so long—become the products of the dead still with us. Having said all this, it is important not to be glib. In a range of ways, as we have seen, the dead are always with us; and in another way, of course, they are not.

As we baby boomers reach an age when our bodies are informing us of our own mortality and superannuation becomes a significant matter, we may go along with Woody Allen and think: "I don't want to achieve immortality through my work; I want to achieve immortality through not dying." Beloff in this volume writes: "We do not take the absolute imperative of our morality at all seriously—if we did we could hardly go about our daily lives." Do we have, in fact, "anxieties about our own extinction," as Warner (1965, quoted in Howarth, this volume) has described, which make us interested in the dead having a social, psychological, and political voice after death? Perhaps these really are concerns about our own mortality; but this is a subject for another study.

I am going to conclude this discussion by considering some other examples of what I have been calling continuance. This part of the discussion concerns the dead as public entities rather than as the focus of private grief, through biography, obituary, and visual representation.

All of us can call up an image of Marilyn Monroe, President Kennedy, or Elvis Presley, and the older among us can remember "what we were doing when Kennedy was shot." Even though we never met them and cannot claim to know them, we have opinions about them and their memory, who they were and what they mean to us. This should strike us as surprising, since they have been dead for 30 or 40 years. Elvis Presley is alive among us through Graceland tours, merchandise, a live-cam at Graceland where we can see what is happening at this moment, and the multimillion-dollar business that has developed since his death in 1977. Visits to Graceland, which we can organize through the *All About Elvis* Web site [www.elvis.com], even bear the hallmarks of modern-day pilgrimage.

Our interest in other people's lives, whether to marvel at their achievements, empathize with them, or find out the little-known facts of their lives, has been of long standing. Samuel Johnson in the mid-eighteenth century explained this in terms of people's common interests, saying that "we are all prompted by the same motives, all deceived by the same fallacies, all animated by hope, obstructed by desire and seduced by pleasures" (quoted by Bostridge, 2004, p. ix). Mark Bostridge's collection of "biographers' tales," *Lives for Sale*, describes the many overt ways in which the dead continue to affect us, and how, for the biographer, the "biographical imagination can be aroused by a sense of place or the touch of a letter." While reading a biography we start to see the world through that person's eyes, by sharing his or her life. We might also think of obituaries as sparing biographies provided to us daily in newspapers. Reading obituaries, writes Andreas Whittam Smith, allows us into the lives of those now dead but who *live on* in these brief accounts: "Obituary notices transport you into a life you have never lived, and perhaps never could have imagined. Through these we are afforded glimpses of the twists and turns of intention and fate, culminating in the inevitable eventual, or untimely death of the subject." (*The Independent,* May 10, 1998). Obituaries may constitute an important source of reflection on our own lives and are also significant in terms of how lives and times are represented. Other researchers (e.g., Starck, 2006; Fowler, in this volume) have examined the political and other meanings of obituaries and the interpretation of memory. That there is a remarkable renewal of interest in obituaries is evident through their increase in UK,

US, and Australian newspapers (Starck, 2006). Equally, obituaries are the subject of research in a range of disciplines through content analysis of the narratives, reflecting an increasing interest in the importance of the dead in our everyday lives. As Starck has said quoting George Herbert, "Hee hath not lived, that lives not after death." (p. viii)

Ben Pimlott has described biography using the metaphor of portraiture:

> A good biography is like a good portrait: it captures the essence of the sitter by being much more than a likeness. A good portrait is about history, philosophy, milieu. It asks questions as well as answering them, brushstrokes are economical and always to the subtlest effect. Think of Velasquez, Sargent, Freud. Biography can be like that. (Pimlott quoted in Bostridge, 2004, p. 170).

Linking to this idea, I would now like to consider the literal visibility of the dead among the living. Robert Wyatt (in this volume) draws our attention to an obvious case of artists memorializing themselves through their art; Rembrandt's many portraits of himself provide an example of this artist's clear understanding of his mortality and his consciousness of his life after his death. This can be interpreted as the artist's intention to impart information about himself as he wanted it to be seen—that is, a self-presentation intended to continue after his death.

Artistic products, of course, not only represent people but can be also *about* death. Each time we go to an art gallery we are confronted with immortality, not only that of the human subjects of the paintings, etchings, drawings, or sculptures but also the immortality of the painters who—in some cases, centuries after their deaths—are still able to affect us emotionally as we respond to the narrative of the art and its aesthetic qualities. Art can also represent death as its subject. Wyatt sees Andy Warhol's images of road accidents, suicide, and electric chairs, collectively titled the *Disaster Series*, as bringing an "objective and ironic postmodern sensibility to the representation of what had previously been treated as an extremely subjective and emotional subject" (2001, p. 32)—that is, the subject of death. Wyatt also describes the imagery of the crucifixion of Christ, for example, as an early form of representation of mortality—and, thus, created immortality, because we can still look at and reflect on many of the images of this subject from the sixteenth and seventeenth centuries. As Wyatt has indicated, the "immortalisation of the death of individuals and identifiable groups [has] persisted … as a motif for painters and sculptors" (2001, p. 35).

Halla Beloff's essay in this volume on family photographs and their eventual and inevitable status as *memento mori* underlines that at an everyday level, family photographs also constitute the continuance of previous generations, and record present generations for the future as continuing images of the people in succeeding generations. In photography we have access to a medium whereby we can capture people in their contexts and keep them forever. The photographs of our smiling (or not) parents and grandparents become an important source of comfort or reflection long after they have left us. Each photograph has the potential to become a keepsake or memento; or, to put it more bluntly, will be the photograph of a dead person sooner or later. Photography is now a commonplace activity, and those images of people that are created have many functions, both intended and unintended. Images are generated for technical recording, for example by police at a crime scene or of a suspect or criminal, or by family and friends as they record a formal or casual event. Some take on significance in our lives and become icons of tragedy and death, reminding us of the deceased. One never knows when such images will be used. Photographs of people, often smiling at family gatherings or weddings, who have been killed in accidents, disasters, or murders present an incongruous accompaniment to the news text describing the circumstances of their death.

Some photographs become very well known to us, and are almost considered to be in the public domain. McKee (1997, p. 1), in his essay on images that have "assumed importance above the merely documentary," refers to two in particular—both "grainy black and white [and both] the product of the camera as a mundane documentary tool." One is the stark police photograph of Myra Hindley, convicted in 1966 with her lover Ian Brady; as the "Moors Murderers" they killed five children and buried their bodies on Saddleworth Moor near Manchester, England. The other image is the shopping center security camera photograph taken on February 12, 1993 of three-year-old Jamie Bulger being walked out of the center by the two young boys, Venables and Thompson, who would later that day murder him. They are both startling images, and as McKee notes, both seem to function as some sort of "folk representation of evil," and at the same time "discussion of the murders has become a taboo" (1997, p. 1).

These images are so well known to us and so redolent with meaning because they have been used countless times in the public print and TV media. Myra Hindley's black-and-white police portrait has been used continuously in the media since her arrest in 1966, most recently as the illustration for her obituary when she died, aged 60, in November 2002. The photograph of Jamie Bulger being led away by the two boys has also been used continuously since his murder and has been employed extensively when an image is required to denote evil.

> "This image had been used in the hunt for James Bulger and after his death this image became the icon of the story which the nation turned over and over in its mind. No image in the recent past had been reproduced so frequently nor was as immediately recognisable" (Cousins, 1996, p. 1).

The potency of the images and the degree to which they have the capacity to continue in our lives is remarkable. However, in the context of art, McKee and others have remarked that the use and adaptation of such images as an art product is seen by the public as unacceptable.

Marcus Harvey's *Myra*, a huge and now important portrait of the Moors Murderer created using children's handprints, was vandalized by outraged members of the public at the 1997 Royal Academy show "Sensation." Jamie Wagg's *History-Paintings: Cartoons for Tapestry* (large colored digital prints of the scene at the shopping mall, complete with the date and the time of the photograph—"15:42:32, 12/02/93") were required to be removed from the Whitechapel Gallery in London in 1994, after the artist received death threats and was accused of exploiting the child's murder. The deaths denoted by these photographs are still with us, and in a sense the pictures become the person(s) and the event and we must show them respect. The interesting notion of public censorship to protect the public in certain contexts following a death is, incidentally, the theme of Gerard Sullivan's research (in this volume), on the media reporting of suicide.

A similar comparison between the different uses and purposes of an image of a dead person that we can look at and respond to can be made between Joel Peter Witkin's photograph *Le Baiser* ("The Kiss") as an art product—about which Richard Read (in this volume) questions the ethical issues—and Kornell's description of efforts by an early anatomist to obtain a "a perfect profile" of a skull by sawing the "skull perpendicularly through the middle." In the former the image is created for art, while in the latter it is the innocuous and laudable modernist pursuit of good anatomical illustration. Witkin's intention appears to be to shock, and he claims that his photographs are intended to be redemptive, to challenge the spectator; but the spectator might be left with the uneasy feeling that a dead person, not only the idea of death itself, has somehow been desecrated in the name of art (Wyatt, personal communication, 2006). This may be the same argument leveled against Harvey's and Wagg's work, discussed above. The use of the dead as a concept and creating images of the dead are acceptable if they are seen as something practical, such as anatomical illustration, or if they are distanced because of being from ancient times or illustrating media stories, here their use may be thought as having some redeeming social value.

In another interesting perspective on the representation of the body, death, and immortality in art, and the artist's explanation of his sources, Ricky Swallow, Australia's representative at the 51st International Biennale of Art in Venice 2005, describes the skull, a motif that appears in much of his sculptural work, as the "ultimate used-up and independent form. Everything it needed to make sense has literally fallen away yet it remains capable of so many associations" (Day, 2005, p. 49). Swallow goes on to describe his reference:

> The skull is a familiar image from my early teens onward. My brothers always had heavy metal posters in their rooms featuring skeletons raising hell among the living. I have mentioned too many times that the skull and skeleton graphics on Powell-Peralta skateboards ... market immortality, literally taking the activity beyond the grave. (Day, 2005, p. 49)

In looking at photographs of Swallow's work—for example, the full-size skeleton that is his work, *The Exact Dimensions of Staying Behind 2004–05*—people can find the image distasteful until it is explained that the "skeleton" is actually an intricate wood carving. Their distaste is replaced by admiration for the skill displayed in the carving and relief that the skeleton turns out to be a very clever *copy*, which, barring fire, flood, or termites, will continue and be immortal. In this vein, Day (2005) writes: "[Swallow's] executions of skeletons, skulls and other symbols of death prompt a re-examination of life, while the durability … and the physicality of the artworks appear to resist impermanence."

Conclusion

This chapter has outlined some of the manifestations of the dead in our everyday lives. These vary between the intensely private and the highly public. How people are remembered and kept with us is the subject of much differing opinion, from the level of intrafamilial discussion and even fights to public debate about public figures, or figures who become public. At one level, the dead remain with us as cultural products, in art, architecture, writing, film, and other permanent records. And even here we see debate about how the person—as seen through his or her products—should be interpreted and what he or she continues to mean for us in contemporary society. With reference to these public representations of the dead, and more privately with reference to deceased loved ones and family members, we attribute meaning, emotion, and potency to them just as we did when they were alive.

It is evident that the dead do not go away but are maintained, often in an extraordinary range of ways. We have seen that this can be reflected in models of grieving and bereavement that are not based on notions of letting go and disengagement in order to get on with life.

It seems likely that the different forms of continuance serve different functions. Perhaps pursuing a claim or a campaign on behalf of the dead and keeping them alive through these means, even to the extent that it may consume one's life, can reflect a range of dynamics. Perhaps a motivation is guilt over not having prevented the death or protected the person from danger. In some ways, this can be seen as a continued caring for and nurturing the person as one did in life. In other situations, the stimulus may be a desire to exert control over a situation; in others it may be a sense that to do anything other than continue a campaign would be unfaithful to the person, or would require an acknowledgment that they have died. Careful maintenance of a gravesite or a memorial or taking care of the deceased's material possessions may serve the same function. Similarly, the idea of making something good come out of a death or tragedy maintains the person through good works, a public campaign, or a charity. In some other cases, the motivation to keep the person alive through one's actions may be attributable to seeking revenge and retribution. The incorporation of the dead into one's sense of self, as Howarth (2000) has written, is evident in all such motivations and behaviors. To let the person go would be tantamount to losing a significant part of oneself.

I recently came across an essay by Arnold Joseph Toynbee that had been written in 1968, fifty years after the First World War, and seven years before his own death in 1975. In it he described his "bonus" years and the continual memory of friends who had been killed in the war. He said:

> [Had I not been] medically disqualified for active military service … the chances are that, instead of being alive, with a pen in my hand in 1968, I should have been killed in action in 1915 or 1916. This was the fact of about half of those school-fellows and fellow-undergraduates of mine who were my intimate friends. Since that time, death has been my constant companion, for my contemporaries who were killed in the First World War have never been out of my mind from then until now. Ever since then, I have felt it strange to be alive, and have counted as a bonus all the years through which I have lived since 1916. (Most of my close friends who were killed in the First World War had met their deaths before the end of that year.) (Toynbee, 1968, p. 263)

I believe that it is almost impossible in this new twenty-first century to think about the continuance of the dead in our lives without reflecting on the impact in the West of the First World War. This has been the subject of much scholarship by many historians, including Jay Winter (for example, in *Sites of Memory, Sites of Mourning*, 1995) and Joanna Bourke (for example, in *Dismembering the Male*, 1996, and *An Intimate History of Killing*, 1999), and by cultural theorists. With the distance in time, we can examine and understand more about the continued presence of the dead of the First World War and the social meaning of the terrible carnage of that time than perhaps we could during its century.

The First World War has left its visible mark in practically every town and village in New Zealand, Australia (where there are more than 4,000 memorials commemorating 60,000 Australian deaths in the war) and throughout Britain, and in many other places far from the Western Front where men and boys were drawn to fight. This book is dedicated to one of them: Jim Darge, a young man from Glasgow who disappeared in the mud of Ypres 90 years ago.

References

Bennett, G., & Bennett, K. M. (2000). The presence of the dead: An empirical study. *Mortality, 5*(2), 139–157.

Bostridge, M. (Ed.). (2004). *Lives for sale: Biographers' tales*. London: Continuum.

Diana: The work continues. Retrieved 17 September 2006, from http://www.theworkcontinues.org/.

Cousins, M. (1996). Security as danger. Retrieved 17 September 2006, from http://hosting.zkm.de/ctrlspace/e/texts.

Craig, O. (2001, February 4). Flora would be proud of us. *Sunday Telegraph*.

Day, C. (2005). An interview with Ricky Swallow. In *Ricky Swallow this time another year* (pp. 43–53). Australia Council.

Day, C. (2005 second one) Life and death: Monuments and memories. (2005). [Media release]. Retrieved 10 November 10, 2006, from http://www.ozco.gov.au/arts_in_australia/projects/projects_visual_arts/venice_05_media_kit/files/2923/13_media_kit_english.pdf.

Forgiveness Project. Retrieved 17 September 2006, from http://www.theforgivenessproject.com.

Hiltzik, M. (1993). *The death in Kenya*. New York: Random House.

Howarth, G. (2000). Dismantling the boundaries between life and death. *Mortality, 5*(2), 127–138.

Howarth, G. (2006). Death and Dying: A sociological introduction. Cambridge: Polity.

Howarth, G., & Leaman, O. (Eds.) (2001). *Encyclopedia of death and dying*. London: Routledge.

Johnson, C. A. (2005). *Come with Daddy: Child homicide-suicide after family breakdown*. Crawley: University of Western Australia Press.

Klass, D., Silverman, P.R. and Nickman, S.L. (1996). *Continuing Bonds: New Understandings of Grief.* Washington, DC: Taylor & Francis.
Kubler-Ross, E. (1969). *On death and dying.* New York: Macmillan.
Lennon, J. J., & Foley, M. (2000). *Dark tourism: The attraction of death and disaster.* London: Continuum.
Merridale, C. (2000). *Night of stone: Death and memory in Russia.* London: Granta.
McKee, F. (1997). A touch of evil. *Variant, 2* (pp. 1-4). Retrieved 17 September 2006, from http://www.variant.randomstate.org/2texts/Francis_McKee.html.
Mothers Against Drunk Driving (MADD). www.madd.org.
Partington, M. (2002). If you won't tell us, we'll have to make it up. Paper presented at the Centre for Studies in Crime and Social Justice, Economic and Social Research Council (ESRC) Research Seminar "Disasters: Origins, Consequences and Responses," June 11, 2002, Edgehill. Retrieved 17 September 2006, from http://www.edgehill.ac.uk/cscsj/seminarreportssessions.htm.
Picardie, J. (2001). *If the spirit moves you: Life and love after death.* London: Picador.
Pimlott, B. (2004) Brushstrokes, In M. Bostridge (Ed.) Lives for Sale: Biographers' Tales, Continuum, London, pp. 165-170.
Starck, N. (2006). *Life after death: The art of the obituary,* Melbourne: Melbourne University Publishing Ltd.
Swire, Jim. Retrieved 17 September 2006, from http://www.lockerbietruth.com/.
Toynbee, A. J. (1968). Epilogue: The relations between life and death, living and dying, In A. J. Toynbee et al., *Man's concern with death* (pp. 259–271). London: Hodder & Stoughton.
Walter, T. (Ed). (1999). *The mourning for Diana.* Oxford & New York: Berg.
Ward, J. (1993). *The animals are innocent.* London: Trafalgar Square Books.
Warner, W. L. (1965). The city of the dead. In R. Fulton (Ed.), *Death and identity.* (pp. 360–382) New York: John Wiley & Sons.
Whittam Smith, A. (1998, May 10). Follow me into the living world of obituary reading. *The Independent.*
Winter, J. (1995). *Sites of memory, sites of mourning.* Cambridge: Cambridge University Press.
Wyatt, R. (2001). Art, death of, In G. Howarth & O. Leaman (Eds.), *Encyclopedia of Death and Dying* (pp. 31–33) London: Routledge .
Wyatt, R. (2001). Art History, In G. Howarth & O. Leaman (Eds.), *Encyclopedia of Death and Dying* (pp. 31–36) London: Routledge.

CHAPTER 3

Sustaining Kinship

Ritualization and the Disposal of Human Ashes in the United Kingdom

JENNY HOCKEY, LEONIE KELLAHER, AND DAVID PRENDERGAST

Cremation is now the most common form of disposal in the United Kingdom, yet although it was legalized in 1884, it did not become a popular form of disposal until after the Second World War and it surpassed full body burial as the most common preference only in the late 1960s. Since the early 1970s, however, two-thirds of all annual disposals have been cremations, rising to an average of 71.54% since 2000 (Pharos 2004, p. 20), making this the customary choice in the United Kingdom. This surprisingly recent development can be seen to have rendered the dead mobile, unlike the fixed location of a whole body burial; ashes can be distributed according to the needs and desires of those who succeed the deceased person. Up to 60% of ashes are now being removed from crematoria rather than being left behind for scattering at the crematorium's Garden of Remembrance. The question we address here, however, is how the needs and desires of those involved in a death are identified, how they represent themselves in particular practices or items of material culture, and most crucially, whose needs and desires are expressed in any one instance of disposal and subsequent memorialization.

The data we present here are drawn from a 30-month ESRC (Economic and Social Research Council) funded study that has explored this trend via ethnographic work in the four sites in England and Scotland used by Davies and Shaw (1995) in an earlier study of attitudes to death and disposal: these are Barking and Dagenham, Nottingham, Sunderland, and Glasgow. In each of the four areas, in-depth interviews, followed by focus groups, have been conducted with a minimum sample of seven professionals. Fifteen bereaved people who have chosen to remove a relative's or friend's ashes from a crematorium for disposal elsewhere have also been interviewed in each city.

Consensus?

The project receives requests from media to describe exotica within our data, yet the practices described in our data usually reflect the following:

Traditional sites of disposal (family graves)
Domestic locations (house and garden)
Natural landscapes (mountains and rivers)
Urban landscapes (pubs, football grounds)

What is interesting is the way in which these apparently mundane locations can represent the outcome of complex social negotiations, careful reflection, and meaning making. In addition, there is evidence of a reenchantment of the everyday world. So while it seems unlikely that firing the dead into space and turning them into diamonds are anything more than minority activities, our data suggest a growth of practices that do contrast quite starkly with the material culture of modernist rationality—for example, the lawn grave and the perfunctory crematorium ceremony. What we are seeing now is much more elaborate informal memorialization. But since such practices and items of material culture often share the same cemetery landscape as lawn graves and 1970s modernist crematoria, it can be a confusing environment both to read and to engage with in some form. It is one that gives choice, but not obvious guidance as to what is appropriate.

Thus, we have an apparent lack of any consensus as to how ashes should be dealt with or what they represent. We also need to bear in mind that over 40% of ash remains are still left behind at crematoria. When sets of ashes are removed, what people do with them may seem relatively unambitious, compared with sensational media stories, yet these are innovative strategies—for example, keeping the remains of the dead in the house or garden, or taking personal responsibility for their disposal rather than employing an officiant. Yet after this relatively innovative act of removing ashes from crematoria, we also find that the forms drawn on may evoke very *traditional* practices or sites of disposal, such as the interment of ashes in mini-versions of traditional graves (Kellaher et al., 2005). This has caused us to ask how individuals are managing this range of choices and associated practices, and particularly to consider the repertoire of beliefs and values that they draw on in evaluating a form of disposal and memorialization that they are either contemplating, have carried out, or have participated in.

"Doing it Properly"

In this environment of choice—and therefore uncertainty—interviewees often discuss their concerns about "doing things properly." As Moore and Myerhoff (1977) point out, "beneath all rituals is an ultimate danger … the possibility that we will encounter ourselves making up our conceptions of the world, society, our very selves. We may slip in that fatal perspective of recognizing culture as our construct, arbitrary, conventional, invented by mortals" (Moore & Myerhoff, 1977, p. 18). Taking matters into our own hands can evoke precisely this concern, as one of our interviewees described. Ida Cole is a Glaswegian woman in her seventies. If we examine the range of reservations she expresses about the disposal that she found herself undertaking, we begin to get a picture of an ideal type, Ida's conception of a proper or authentic ritual. Her concerns hinge on two issues: *Who should participate in the disposal of ashes, and how should this be carried out?*

Ida Cole

When a lifelong friend of Ida's died, the son asked her if she would take the ashes along to a reunion of friends who had been evacuated together to a boarding school during the Second World War. Ida's friend always participated in these reunions, and her son wanted Ida to scatter the ashes at the hotel where the gathering would take place. Ida begins by talking about her journey up to the hotel:

> I had picked up two other people who are older than me … it's a hundred miles or so, down on the Solway coast. And I had picked the [ashes] up but I didn't say anything to [my friends] about, I mean they knew her, they were more her age, they would sit in classes with her.

When asked why she didn't say anything, she replied:

> 'Cos even at that stage I didn't, I wasn't quite sure in my mind what I was going to do, and then once I was there and we'd all met up and we were altogether I thought "I don't think, I don't think I want to make a ceremony of this." 'Cos it would probably have fallen to me to do it and I don't think emotionally it would have upset me but I

> just didn't, they might have wondered why her sister, 'cos they knew her sister, they know her sister, they might have thought how is her sister not here?

So Ida was reluctant to undertake any form of ceremony, feeling that she was not the appropriate person to perform it. Not only did she find it impossible to tell the group of friends, but when she did dispose of the ashes, she chose to do so secretively, under cover of darkness. Rather than taking them up to her room, she left the ashes hidden in her car.

> I was a wee bit unhappy, so … the night after we arrived, it was darkish and I went out round the lawn, took the lid off and started scattering the ashes and then just came in and put the urn in my car … it has big lawns … and I just went in at the end nearest to the sort of front entry and went round the lawn and I could look to the hotel with all the lights on it, there were no lights coming from the side of the building down onto the lawns … I wasn't being overlooked by anyone, there would be nobody looking, you don't see looking out from light into the dark really do you?

Ida clearly felt very uneasy about the whole thing—particularly when the ashes were still visible on the lawn the following morning—and throughout her interview she reflects on whether she had somehow done the wrong thing. For example, she didn't feel able to ask the hotel manager if scattering was allowed:

> I thought it's not fair, you know, am I overstepping the mark having done this? I don't, and I didn't ask because awkward for [him].

Her primary need for secrecy stemmed from her belief that only family can carry out a proper ceremony, an authentic ritual. So if she had told her friends at the reunion what she was doing, the dead friend's sister would have found out:

> and that would have been the way her sister would have heard and that might have upset her sister, who would have been angry with her nephew. So there were sort of family ripples that could have been caused, and her own brother was still just nearby too and he had been at the same school so I felt I couldn't really talk about it to others when the nearer relations hadn't been consulted.

What Moore and Myerhoff (1977) describe as the "ultimate danger" that lurks beneath all rituals, the fear that their made-up quality will be revealed, is very evident in Ida's account. Compared with her "ideal type" model of independent ash disposal, Ida was the wrong person in the wrong place, hence her furtive nocturnal activity out on the hotel lawn. Both the who and the how of a proper ritual had somehow gone awry.

This raises the question of what people are trying to achieve when disposing of ashes. If Ida was unhappy with what happened, as she clearly was, what would have satisfied her? And had she felt happier about the way her friend's ashes were disposed of, how would we make sense of a more positive response? Moore and Myerhoff (1977) may note the inevitably made-up quality of all rituals, but we can still draw on anthropological conceptions of what constitutes ritual and think about their salience in situations such as Ida's. We can ask, for example, whether our interviewees believe that conducting a ritual or series of ritual activities has some kind of transformative effect. Does it make change happen, whether in terms of focusing and thus amending the emotions of those who survive deceased people, or in terms of ensuring that deceased people have been given peace, or that their memory has been shaped and stabilized in a particular way? In the case of Ida's friend, it would seem that any transformation of status or memory had somehow been aborted, and her friend was left marooned in the liminal space of the lawn. Equally, we can ask whether in fact an interviewee is simply seeking to create a ceremony, a social occasion that marks the death of a family member or friend and the changed status of those associated with the deceased person, but this ceremony does not in itself produce those changes. We also need to consider the possibility that interviewees may be constructing a sequence that has ritual and ceremonial components.

The key to much of what we describe here is the issue of power. Radcliffe Brown (1964) represents ritual as a series of practices that produce particular emotional orientations, and in so doing create a sense of collectivity. However, ethnographic sources, including our own, demonstrate that the authenticity of particular ritual practices is not simply a given but stems from their rhetorical or persuasive potentiality. If we consider ritual as the materialization of a set of metaphors—for instance, the wine that stands for the blood we can then imbibe, or the watery immersion that stands for the purification we can receive—then we can bear in mind Lakoff and Johnson's statement that "whether in national politics or in everyday interaction, people in power get to impose their metaphors" (1980, p. 157). What the data that follow describe are the ways in which power is ascribed or assumed during the period that ensues once a corpse has been cremated. As we demonstrate, relatedness is often the key to power: some participants have power or at least responsibility thrust on them; some make ruthless claims for power; and some are left awash in uncertainty, metaphorically and perhaps literally scratching their heads.

We begin, however, one step back, by considering the cultural resources drawn on by those faced with this very recent opportunity for choice—recent in that the practice of removing ashes from crematoria has not been normal practice until the 1990s. In many cases, it is recent too in that most people encounter a close bereavement with little prior experience, having grown up in a time in Western history when proximity to death is the exception rather than the rule.

One resource we can turn to is the therapeutic bereavement literature that grew up particularly in the second half of the twentieth century. During the 1970s this literature was much taken up with a post-Freudian emphasis on letting go of the dead, confronting their loss with unrestrained emotional expressiveness and then reinvesting, emotionally, in a new life and set of relationships. In the 1990s this was challenged by new models of grief that identify ways of establishing "continuing bonds" between the living and the dead through narrative biographical reconstruction, through forms of material culture such as photographs, benches, or grave gardening, and through private or domestic memorialization (see Klass et al., 1996).

To what extent, then, are our interviewees conceptualizing their activities as a way of continuing their relationships with the dead and, in a sense, keeping up with the latest trends in the successful management of bereavement? Certainly it is the case that this recent turn in the bereavement literature's emphasis *legitimates* this kind of activity; this is not to say, however, that prior to the 1990s many individuals and families did not somehow maintain the dead as a part of their everyday lives, but simply that they might have done so in a more private or perhaps covert fashion.

Indeed, if we examine the social science literature on death, the notion of a continuing bond between the living and the dead has a much longer history. While many anthropologists have focused on a death as a form of disorder that puts systems of meaning under threat, the tracing of how the dead are categorized and how they are located, both spatially and temporally, often reveals a continuing relationship with the living. Hertz's (1960 [1907]) study of the Dayak of Southeast Asia differentiates among the deceased, the bereaved, and the corpse but then draws them into line with one another as they proceed from liminal disarray to reintegration within separate but *associated* domains. More recent sociological work has examined the relationship between the living and the dead within a shared *domestic* environment. For example, Howarth's interviews with older widows revealed their experiences of their dead partners' persistent presence, which was not just accepted but welcomed (cited in Hallam et al., 1999, pp. 142–159). How the living make sense of a relationship that runs counter to modernist rationality is explored in Bennett and Bennett's (2000) work, which presents evidence that the bereaved interviewees experienced a tension between supernaturalist and materialist interpretations of their experiences. In the authors' view, while materialist accounts may be mustered for an interview, supernaturalist interpretations are often closer to respondents' everyday understandings of where the dead might be located. The prevalence of experiences of the presence of the dead is also evident in more recent anthropological work, for example, Davies and Shaw's (1995) exploration of attitudes to death and disposal, and Francis et al.'s (2001, 2005) accounts of the relationships between the living and the dead that unfold via cemetery visits and the materialities of grave tending and gardening practices.

This work suggests to us that people disposing of ashes may be seeking to position the dead in a material and a *social* sense. Relatedness is therefore likely to feature among the beliefs and values that underpin their choices and the ways in which they evaluate their choices, both in prospect and in retrospect. This includes the issue of relatedness as Ida understands it—that is, the issue of *who* should be undertaking the disposal and, from the therapeutic and social science literatures, the issue of *how* the living and the dead might relate to one another when they are no longer both alive. It is within these two often intermeshed realms that conceptions of relatedness are asserted, resisted, contested, and renegotiated. And it is through such interactive processes that relatedness itself comes into being.

Our dataset includes people who have disposed of the ashes of different family members—elderly parents, partners, young and older children, siblings—and of friends. Drawing on this repertoire of relationships, we now want to consider how relatedness might operate as both a concept and a practice. Given the sometimes unexpected nature of the circumstances in which many of our interviewees found themselves, we need to draw on perspectives that are theoretically adequate to help make sense of highly fluid and contingent thought, actions, and events. In work on family, Morgan (1996), for example, has argued that familial relatedness is the outcome of family practices, and that family should not be seen as a stable or fixed entity. Rather, it is constantly produced, reproduced, recast, and renegotiated within the flow of everyday life. If, as in the example of our own data, family members contest one another's conceptions of an ideal type or authentic ritual, Morgan argues that such contestations need to be seen "not simply to arise out of family relationships; they also and simultaneously constitute or reconstitute those relationships" (1996, p. 141). Anthropological work on family—traditionally located within kinship studies—has similarly shifted its focus from the study of structure to the investigation of practice and in so doing has redefined this staple area of the discipline. Hutchinson (1996) draws on ethnographic accounts of the Nuer to examine what she calls the *media* of relatedness—in their case, blood, food, and cattle—arguing that such media are not only interchangeable but also convertible. During periods of war, which Hutchinson calls times of profound social and political upheaval, money, paper, and guns can be made to stand in for blood, food, and cattle as the media through which relatedness is produced. This insight is suggestive when it comes to relationships between the living and the dead and how the media of relatedness might change or be converted once death has profoundly transformed the embodied practices of relatedness that previously defined and connected the living and the dead. While evidence of continuing bonds between the living and the dead suggests that these relationships can have a material grounding of some kind, the bodies of the dead *have* been incinerated or interred. So while the widows interviewed by Bennett and Bennett (2000) did report sensory experiences—they saw, smelled, heard, and felt the touch of the dead—we do need to acknowledge that something has happened to change the body. What we are suggesting, however, is that while the media of relatedness between the living—financial support, physical love and care, practical help—cannot easily be sustained with the dead, they *can* be converted into different media that express the same idiom. For example, another interviewee, Carol Devon, had cared for her father on a daily basis while he lived in a flat opposite her marital home. This very practical medium of relatedness was no longer possible once he had died. However, Carol described how she and her daughter had interred his ashes under a birdbath in her daughter's garden; the entire rationale for this disposal choice is framed in terms of care, the idiom through which she had always understood their relatedness. In her view, he would be warm and safe down there in her *daughter's* garden: the birdbath couldn't be knocked over; everyone could be around him as the children played in the garden; and the ashes would have a permanent home. The last was important because Carol and her husband were themselves considering moving house.

What people choose to undertake on behalf of deceased people, and their relationships with them—whether at the time of disposal or during a more extended process of memorialization—is therefore potentially an extension of precisely the practices through which relatedness was constituted in life. What we are particularly interested in is how conceptions of genealogical relationships constrain or enable bereaved people, and the extent to which individuals might resist or indeed draw on particular idioms of relatedness in contesting the expectations of others, whether family, friends, or professionals. This means looking not only at how relatedness is brought into being through disposal and memorialization strategies, but also at people's reflections on what they *might,* or what they *have* carried out—and here the research interview needs to be recognized as yet another site at which relatedness is brought into being. Thus, people tell us not just about what they did but also about how they thought and how they negotiated with other individuals in the process.

At a superficial level, it might appear that Ida Cole simply believed that ties between family members were of a different order than those between friends, and therefore family rather than friends should dispose of the ashes of a relative. However, as already indicated, her friend's son opted for a different idiom of relatedness—the long-standing, uncomplicated relatedness of old school friends, rather than the complexities of the relatedness that constituted his family. And indeed, Ida herself recognized and therefore went some way toward affirming this conversion when she said:

> I could see why her son wanted that, that seemed quite appropriate because we were all very happy at that school, you know, it was a happy place.

Even so, while recognizing the grounding of his decision, she still felt uneasy with it and told him so:

> I said to him on the phone, it came as such a surprise to me that he phoned and asked this, I did have the presence of mind to say 'well have you spoken to your aunt and your sister about this?' and he said 'och no we don't, we don't … ,' he said 'a multitude of counsellors there would be confusion' and he had obviously made up his mind.

So, to use Carsten's (2000) word, from the perspective of the friend's son, family ties were "optative"; and, as Ida understood it, he opted out of them for the sake of family harmony.

We can also compare the kinds of conversion in which Ida and the son were involved—that is, out of family and into the long-standing relatedness of friendship—with conversions that occurred *within* a family. As Morgan has argued, out of the *differences* between family members, family relationships are "constituted and reconstituted." However, the possibility of "latent social identities" lends a fluidity to such processes, to conceptions of who might or might not have the power of decision making, who might or might not participate. When Urry refers to the notion of "imaginary co-presence" as a key constituent of family relatedness (cited in Morgan 1996. p. 144), he is referring not just to those individuals who interact face to face, but also to those who may be physically distant or indeed dead. However, the processes of imagining that co-presence need to be seen as potentially unstable, and family members may choose to reconfigure co-presence according to their own agendas.

Turning to another interviewee, a member of the Smale family, we find an extended network of kith and kin participating in an increasingly long sequence of ash disposal ceremonies after a young male relative died in a skiing accident. Thirty-five-year-old Louise Smale, the young man's sister, described the process. Having initially planned to dispose of the ashes at two separate sites, his relatives became involved in a complex set of negotiations that culminated in four separate ceremonies at four different sites. In retrospect, Louise noted, "I do feel it's really emotionally draining, having four different events." Each ceremony involved a large number of relatives and friends, and here Louise describes the first gathering after his death, identifying each individual by his or her family position rather than simply saying that a lot of the family was present:

> there was me and my husband and Samuel, there was my other brother and his girlfriend and my sister and her partner, and there was a cousin, my brother's, you know my cousin, my cousin and his girlfriend and then another cousin and then an aunt, my dad's sister-in-law, so all people who knew him quite well.

Louise also describes the complexities of agreeing on the *appropriate* idiom of relatedness when it came to the challenge of innovating at a time of intense emotional trauma. Indeed, she explained these difficulties in terms of family relatedness—that is, the assumption that strategies for managing emotion are learned and passed on within families:

> there's a pattern in our lives as a family … I've got another brother and a sister. I talked to my sister quite a lot. My other brother I never really ask him, you know about things like you know his, partly … not succeeding, never asked him about it, because it's a sort of pattern that we're in really.

She goes on to substantiate this claim by noting that like her brother, her mother and father are "very much from the put up and shut up culture." Her mother especially is one to bottle up emotion; this, Louise suspects, is as a result of losing her own mother at fifteen whilst she was at boarding school, yet being kept in the dark about the death until after the funeral had taken place. Louise argues that this was a terrible way of handling the situation and suggests that this, combined with the later loss of another close family member a few years later, had "partly ruined" her mother's life.

Having now lost one of her sons and this time being in control of proceedings, Louise's mother, with her family, gradually began to devise an appropriate series of ash disposal events. While her mother had initially wanted them simply to be interred in a family plot in Wales, this emphasis on family as the key idiom of relatedness also came through strongly when she later laid personal claim to the ashes and chose to inter a portion in her own garden, under a tree. When Louise describes the planning of this later ceremony, she says:

> I wanted it to be more than just immediate family there, because it makes the loss greater when there's just you know me and my brother and sister and our partners and children, no one else. I find it easier, I personally find it easier when there's my aunt or other people around and I personally like the sort of more communal events. I don't just think its family only and I, you know I wasn't that close to him ... didn't spend that much time with him. Other friends of his spent a lot more time with him than I did. And this girl … he sort of got together with … he was a consultant, he worked for Barclays … I think that he was really keen on her and she was keen on him … and I felt that you know she should have been invited … you know other people who spent a lot more time with him than I, I, I did, so just because I was his sister it didn't mean that I should have exclusive right over.

Thus Louise, abetted by her sister, sought pretexts for inviting her brother's friends along. However, her mother made it clear that she felt strongly about the ceremonies being just family—especially those within the more private precincts of the home and family grave.

> For [Mum] it's always the thought of having other people around that is really hard … because she doesn't, can't let go in front of other people. But I think if other people are not there, she still finds it very hard letting go … Maybe she has got a real reason that she can only really grieve properly if it's just us and her, but I mean there was just us, the immediate family and Steve and Ann, on the twenty-ninth [earlier ceremony in mountains] and she didn't, wouldn't, she was bottling up. She would not let herself weep, at all. Some tears came to her eyes but she, she wouldn't, you know she can't, she can't let herself go. I haven't once seen her let herself go, you know I saw Dad more than her, so you know but that's, that's years of controlling it I think, but I mean it's, it's tragic in a way.

At the time of the interview in January 2005, the family was beginning to plan the fourth and final disposal ceremony, in the family plot in Wales. Louise described the complex and ongoing negotiations within the family on the subject of inviting friends along. Her mother continued to maintain that she would prefer only family to be at the ceremony, while Louise and her sister remained convinced that it would be wrong to exclude friends.

These data exemplify a set of tensions that contrast with those identified by Ida Cole. For Louise, when it comes to her dead brother, family does not form the basis of relatedness. Friendship, instead, is the appropriate idiom, one that evokes the man she imagines he had become. For her mother, family constitutes the appropriate set of relationships—and here, again, we return to the issue not just of who should participate but also of how the ceremony should be conducted. In Louise's view, her mother sees the question of emotional expressiveness as key to ritual's satisfactory nature, its authenticity. Without interviewing her mother, we cannot, of course, make sense of whether it is the opportunity to *show* feelings that her mother feels is important, or whether her concern is the *inappropriate* expression of emotion within a group made up of both family and friends.

In terms of issues of power, then, we can see Ida as someone who has power imposed on her—or maybe *responsibility*, in that it was her friend's son who laid claim to decision-making rights but failed to empower Ida, so she felt at odds with the idiom of relatedness he was asserting. By contrast, Louise Smale describes a situation where low-key contestation characterized the negotiations surrounding the sudden and entirely unexpected death of a young family member. Claims to power emerge during the processes of disposal, and events take shape in ways that reflect individuals' capacity to assert particular idioms of relatedness in a persuasive manner.

We move on from these more detailed discussions to present additional data that describe much more hotly contested power claims; and again, it is wrangles over idioms of relatedness that provide the bases of these struggles. Thus, our Glasgow ethnography describes the marriage of two gay men by a humanist officiant. Both partners had alcohol dependency problems, and when the first died, prematurely, his family of birth laid claim to his ashes and yielded up only a tiny portion of them to the surviving partner after the intervention of a third party. So small was the portion that the partner felt compelled to burn some of the deceased person's effects to augment the remains; yet as our interviewee, the humanist officiant, noted, even the ashes he was given were suspiciously unlike human ashes, and the natal family may well have fobbed off the partner with some other kind of incinerated material. This amalgam of ashes was scattered in a ritual event at Loch Lomond, and the surviving partner expressed the wish to be scattered in the same location when he died. This expression of relatedness was, however, denied him as well: the officiant reported that when he too died not long after, *his* natal family also laid claim to the ashes, and the officiant was unable to act on his behalf and carry out the scattering at the site of his partner's disposal. This example demonstrates the powerful way in which what Morgan describes as "latent social identities" can be asserted, with the customary privileging of the marital bond being usurped by the latent identity of son or brother—one of an implicitly heterosexual us.

To be excluded from planning a funeral or deciding the fate of the ashes has emerged as a commonly recurring theme within our whole data set, and a source of potentially great distress. One woman from Nottingham wished to be interviewed so she could tell us how her estranged sister had taken away her father's ashes after his funeral and scattered them in Hastings without either inviting or consulting her. In a different interview in Glasgow, Keith, a middle-aged ex-boxer turned student, described how he had fallen out with his father and avoided seeing him for many years until he was contacted and told that his father had died. The wider family, well aware of the rift, took it on themselves to arrange the funeral, though Keith only recognized the extent of his exclusion as he sat at his pew and noticed his father's coffin being borne into the church not by the funeral directors, but by several of his cousins and uncles. Soon after the funeral he inquired about the ashes, to find his father's brother had picked them up from the crematorium. Seething with anger, he went to his uncle's house and demanded the ashes, claiming relatedness on the basis of his right of blood as sole son. Once these were handed over, the informant took them home to his living-room mantelpiece; for the first few weeks, he felt he was "confronted" by his father because of their presence. This led to his spending the next month meditating on where the problems had lain in their relationship and what pitfalls he might avoid with his own children. Two years later, the ashes are still in his house, but they have now been moved to a less public but still auspicious place in his record collection cupboard.

For some interviewees, the struggle for control of both the ashes and the decisions of other family members arises not from the imposition of responsibility on them or from an urge to act as a primary decision maker, but as a *response* to the unwanted or unilateral efforts of another family member. This was certainly the case for the Kirksall siblings, who could not agree on what to do with their mother's ashes after her death in 2003. As a middle son in a sibling group of seven, our interviewee William Kirksall, a community center manager, says he felt uncomfortable having to act as a primary decision maker in his extended family. However, because his elder brother is disabled and easily upset and his eldest sister is prone to be domineering, he often feels it necessary to speak out strongly. This feeling was particularly acute during discussions about the disposal of his mother's ashes because, though his mother had indeed stated that she wanted to be cremated, she had only flippantly said that she would be content to have her ashes scattered in the rose bushes on an island where one of the youngest daughters lives. The children themselves are united in feeling that this is not a suitable option, however—first because it is too far for most of them to visit, and second because they feel their mother just suggested this option in order to prevent them from spending money on her, something they certainly would like to do. In the resulting context of uncertainty, the eldest sister therefore announced, and consistently repeated, that she would take the ashes and scatter them on a grave she and her husband had bought for their own ashes and those of her husband's parents. Highly irritated at this suggestion that the remains of his mother be moved into a shared grave belonging to *another* family, William has vetoed this idea and is angry about his sister's claim to ownership of the ashes simply on the basis of her "seniority." He recalls telling her: "You know, I'm fifty years old, you may have got away with that when I was seven or eight but you're not getting away with it now, you know." When asked about his objections he explains:

> I just, well two things. I think one: I kind of felt like cheap. It's like with all this family we couldn't afford to buy a plot you know? and that was part of the argument, it was part of the argument, but the ones who were there were saying well that's not a problem because I'll pay for it, my sister will pay for it, my other sister will pay for it, you know so don't use the cost of it. But there was also an element of I think from theirs which, that family is my oldest sister's family so therefore it was kind of felt they were almost like taking it over to that side, you know, there's all kinds of things, there's all kind of things that were being verbalised but at the same time you could feel the feelings underneath and what it was about. There was almost a bit like who possesses mother …

Eventually it was decided that a new grave for the ashes would be bought, one with a Kirksall headstone that would provide a focus for visiting and a permanent memorial that the scattered siblings and their children could visit on their periodic return trips home.

All these examples return us to Moore and Myerhoff's (1977) warning that danger lurks beneath all ritual: when the idiom of relatedness fails to persuade, the ritual process itself stands revealed as a distressing fabrication. Our informant Ida, mentioned earlier, provided an account of another ash disposal ceremony that embodied the riskiness of innovation. It had been relayed to Ida by another friend and concerned a request for ashes to be scattered on the deceased person's favorite golf course:

> when this request came through, and this person had evidently wanted her ashes scattered on the sixteenth, which is a short hole crossing a burn … apparently this lady had great memories of that and she thought that's where she would like her ashes or her relations,

> I don't know which, well it was a windy, stormy day and I think they were straddling the burn and trying to do things when one of the folk involved slipped in, I'm not saying she needed resuscitating or anything and the ashes were also blowing around, so it wasn't a very reverent sort of demise for her in the end but it caused a great deal of glee, and those of us who were hearing the story thought well that's a place we're not going to ask for ashes to be scattered.

Such anecdotes are common and seem to form a mythology that has grown up around independent ash disposal, a popular culture associated with this new practice. Throughout the life of this project such stories have been relayed to us—the humorous turn of events when the ashes, most typically, blow back all over the family. The popularity of these anecdotes illustrates the delicacy of creating and enacting ritual in the semipublic environment of a gathering of family or friends who are "trying to do things," as Ida puts it. Clearly the notion of reverence that she evokes can be a central element within an authentic ritual, and the arbitrariness or slipperiness of reverence preoccupies the popular imagination.

Conclusion

Our chapter has addressed the theoretical question of what it is that constitutes family, or appropriate relatedness, when it comes to independent ash disposal. We argue that the shift from a focus on structure to a concern with practice has generated anthropological and sociological accounts of relatedness that help make sense of how the choices surrounding ash disposal *are* being made. Ida's experience clearly left her feeling she had "overstepped the mark." As a result, we have begun to explore the ways in which survivors implicitly recognize "the mark" and so attempt to remain within bounds that produce authentic ritual behavior. If we draw on the notion of ritual as essentially rhetorical, then we begin to understand how particular idioms of relatedness, when asserted by particular individuals, potentially persuade participants that they are "doing it properly." In many of our accounts that rhetorical process has been only partially successful, at times because the wrong person finds himself or herself in or lays claim to a position of power, and at times because the material practices of disposal and memorialization are somehow ineffectual in evoking transition, closure, fond memories, or newfound peace. When ashes blow back over the mourners or lie in a damp, visible heap on a hotel lawn, then the ritual process can be seen as aborted and its made-up quality can stand revealed. This is not to say, however, that *certain* randomly occurring events cannot take on symbolic power, when framed within ritual time and space.

One final extract from Louise Smale's account of an incident during her brother's funeral illustrates this point:

> … and then one of my uncles saw a butterfly during the service which is amazing for January, so you know you can, you can, some people believe that that might be the spirit coming back, you know it's difficult, it was quite amazing.

References

Bennett, G., & Bennett, K. M. (2000). The presence of the dead: An empirical study. *Mortality, 5*(2), 139–157.

Carsten, J. (Ed.). (2000). *Cultures of relatedness: New approaches to the study of kinship.* Cambridge: Cambridge University Press.

Davies, D., & Shaw, A. (1995). *Reusing old graves: A report on popular British attitudes.* Kent: Shaw & Sons.

Francis, D., Kellaher, L., & Neophytou, G. (2001). The cemetery: The evidence of continuing bonds. In J. Hockey, J. Katz, & N. Small (Eds.), *Grief, mourning and death ritual.* Buckingham, UK: Open University Press.

Francis, D., Kellaher, L., & Neophytou, G. (2005). *The secret cemetery.* Oxford: Berg.

Hallam, E., Hockey, J., & Howarth, G. (1999). *Beyond the body: Death and social identity.* London: Routledge.

Hertz, R. (1960 [1907]). *Death and the right hand.* New York: Free Press.

Hutchinson, S. (1996). *Nuer dilemmas: Coping with money, war and the state.* Berkeley: University of California Press.

Kellaher, L., Prendergast, D., & Hockey, J. (2005). In the shadow of the traditional grave. *Mortality, 10*(4), 237–250.

Klass, D., Silverman, P. R., & Nickman, S. L. (Eds.). (1996). *Continuing bonds: New understandings of grief.* Washington, DC: Taylor & Francis.

Lakoff, G., & Johnson, M. (1980). *Metaphors we live by.* Chicago: University of Chicago Press.

Moore, S. F., & Myerhoff, B. G. (Eds). (1977). *Secular ritual.* Assen: Van Gorcum.

Morgan, D. (1996). *Family connections.* Cambridge: Polity.

Pharos International. (2004). Disposition of cremated remains in Great Britain. *Pharos International, 70*, 20.

Radcliffe Brown, A. R. (1964). *The Andaman Islanders.* New York: Free Press.

CHAPTER 4

"Rachel Comforted"

Spiritualism and the Reconstruction of the Body After Death

JOANNA BOURKE

Tragedy struck Edith Cecil-Porch Maturin four times between 1900 and 1917. First, her twelve-year-old son died in 1900, followed five years later by her nephew. Another nephew and son were killed during the First World War. When, in 1920, she decided to publish the words her first son had spoken to her immediately after his death, she dedicated her book, *Rachel Comforted: Conversations of a Mother in the Dark with Her Child in the Light*, to "other Rachels still uncomforted." The Rachel she was referring to figures in the Old Testament story of a woman who "mourned for her children and refused to be comforted, because they were not [alive]." Despite Maturin's conventional religious beliefs, neither the Bible nor the consolations of the established churches soothed her anguish over her child's death. In contrast, her experiences with spiritualist communication (using a planchette, a small, heart-shaped board supported by two casters and a pencil which, when a person rested her fingers lightly on the board, traced letters without apparent conscious direction) had provided comfort—and she wanted to share this release with all the mothers recently bereaved in the carnage of the First World War. There were two ways in which communicating with her child "in the light" helped: it convinced Maturin of an afterlife, and it reassured her that this afterlife was familiar and thus not to be dreaded. Maturin described how her "wounded mother-heart" was relieved to discover that her son had not become a "far-away, unapproachable angel" but possessed a body almost identical to the one she had hugged, and that he was residing in a place where there were cottages covered with roses, cricket courts, electric lights, motor-cars and trains, pets, furniture, songbirds, flowers, and class differentials. When she asked her son whether he was happy, he replied that only her grief marred his pleasure: "Are you happy, Sunny?" she asked, to which her son replied via her planchette, "Yes, yes, yes, Mother. Quite, quite, quite. Kisses 12,000" (Maturin, 1920). Rachel was comforted.

Mrs. Maturin was no crank. She was an active feminist and suffragist, an adventurer, and a prolific writer of novels, essays, and accounts of her treks in exotic places. Her experiments with spiritualism were shared by a wide range of working-class and middle-class people in the late nineteenth and early twentieth centuries. (The best histories of the movement are Barrow, 1986; Brandon, 1983; Cerullo, 1982; Homer, 1990; Oppenheim, 1985; Owen, 1989; Shortt, 1984; Walkowitz, 1988; and Winter, 1995.) Spiritualism catered for people disillusioned with traditional Christianity and claimed that the established churches not only had "no new message" but even failed "in the presentment of the old" (Tilby, 1918, p. 253; also see Ward, 1920, p. ix). Spiritualist movements flourished not only within an increasingly secular culture, but also during certain periods. In particular, they grew when the level of extraordinary deaths soared (as in wartime), as opposed to the ordinary deaths of the elderly or the very young. Although its history is generally traced to 1848—when two sisters, Maggie and Katie Fox, started communicating with spirits from their house in Hydesville, New York—spiritualism flourished immediately after the devastation of the American Civil War (which saw half a million men killed) (Kerr, 1972, p. 108), and its heyday was during the First World War and immediately afterward. During a war as devastating as the First World War, spiritualists were used to trace men who had been reported missing in action or killed. This function was described by one officer, Brigadier General C. R. Ballard, in a letter to his mother on March 1, 1915. He wrote:

> Capt. Mosley has had some very curious news; his sister was married to an officer in the Guards who was wounded and missing at the Chateau in August; she of course made all sorts of inquiries, and went to a clairvoyant who told her that her husband was lying badly wounded in a hospital in Munster. After that very contradictory reports came in—first it was officially reported he was dead—then the Geneva Red Cross people told her he had been picked up alive on the field—then a man of his own Regt. turned up who declared he was dead and brought a dying message—which seemed quite conclusive. Last

week, however, she got a letter from him himself saying he was badly wounded and had been in Munster all the time. (Ballard, 1915)

Ballard professed not to believe such spiritualist communications, although he admitted that the spiritualist message had been "an infinite comfort" to the sister. Ballard's example was unusual in one respect: the loved one being sought turned out to be alive. More usually, spirits communicated with their loved ones in order to persuade them of their death. Thus, one mother received (in Morse code via the wireless) a message from her son, who had been posted as missing. Her son told her: "Mother, be game. I am alive and loving you. But my body is with thousands of other mothers' boys near Lens. Get this fact to others if you can. It is awful for us when you grieve, and we can't get in touch with you to tell you we are all right" (Rutherford, 1920, p. 24). Sons, lovers, and husbands were "all right" in the afterlife.

This revival of spiritualism around the time of the First World War did not surprise spiritualists. After all, they wisely observed, there were "so many hands thrust back to clasp our own here, so many hearts eager to tell us that they are yet near us and alive" (Glenconner, 1920, p. 135). Yet the spiritualist phenomenon was a very diverse one, and the ways in which spirits communicated with earthbound people were numerous. Spirits guided the hands of mediums, their words automatically appeared on slates, tables danced, strange tappings were heard, and pianos began playing significant tunes. Physical phenomena included the materialization of the dead person (or a part of the dead person), movement of objects, psychic lights, and spirit photographs, while mental phenomena include telepathy, clairvoyance, spirit healing, and thought transfer. If the range of methods used to communicate was wide, spiritualism contained an even more bewildering diversity of belief. However, central to all spiritualist beliefs were the ideas that the human personality or soul survived the death of the body and that communication was thus possible. Through an analysis of the writings between the bereaved and the spirits, this chapter examines one component of this movement: the function of these writings for the bereaved around the time of the First World War. The purpose of their communication was multifarious, but managing grief and enabling the bereaved person to forget the departed loved one were always central. Paradoxically, this process of forgetting was achieved by reassuring the bereaved that the loved one continued to exist in a recognizable form.

Spiritualism provided a way for people to stop being distraught about a special death and to reinvent their lives. In almost all accounts, spirits explicitly instructed the bereaved to cease mourning. For instance, S. O. Cox had become interested in spiritualism after his daughter, Ella, died at the age of fourteen. In their communiqués, Ella repeatedly scolded Cox for excessive grief. Cox's dead father even made an appearance to reinforce the message. "Be happy. Cultivate a sense of humour," his father's spirit commanded him, before threatening him with the question, "What is the good of coming to see you unless we bring a little of the happiness from up here?" (Cox, n.d., pp. 26–27; for similar messages, see Barker, 1918, pp. 61–65, and Downs, 1920, p. 21). "Every tear tortures the dead," wailed one dead soldier. This soldier continued:

> Tell the mothers and fathers and sisters and wives to stop crying. No man can stand the sight of tears, the sound of sobs. They feel it much worse here, because they can't get in touch to comfort. It's awful. ... We are still capable of mental anguish. That is the hell material. And every tear shed on earth falls on a heart here. (Rutherford, 1920, pp. 33, 36; cf. p. 39)

In particular, it pained the spirits to be thought of as dead. As one spirit insisted, the so-called dead actually possessed "more life than ever. If the bereaved and sorrowful could only realize that, the pain of parting would be greatly alleviated" (Lodge, 1916, p. 24; cf. H.M.G. & M.M.H., 1920, pp. 7–8). Indeed, bereaved people were doing no one any good by grieving. Grief could artificially attach spirits to the earth, hindering their progress and "casting a shadow over the brilliant outlook of eternity" (dead father speaking to Winifred Graham, in Graham, n.d., p. 217; cf. Heslop, c.1915, pp. 12–13). Inordinate grief was "really selfish on the part of those who indulge in it" (Business Man, 1927, p. 17). In the words of an airman killed during the Second World War, speaking through the famous medium Estelle Roberts: "Father, don't look back; look forward ... we are still alive. I will be all right so long as you do not grieve" (Barbanell, 1944, p. 46).

Spirits were fighting a losing battle, though, and they had a duty to comfort those relatives and friends who insisted upon (or were incapable of resisting) their sorrow. They did this in two ways. First, they comforted the bereaved by telling them that death had been painless. In the words of the spirit of Charles Dickens, the "pillow of death" was "smooth" (Melbourne Medium, 1873, p. 5). One spirit, known only as "A Soldier Doctor," had been talking to a young man killed in the First World War. This soldier-spirit had described how he had been struck by shrapnel during battle and, while still running, "came over." In the afterlife, the soldier

> continued his flight toward the enemy, who he soon met coming toward him in the same aggressive way—two combatants met and thought they were in deadly battle when they discovered they had

> lost earthly bodies. Each made the discovery about the same time. Their astonishment caused a cessation in hostilities, and I met them looking at one another in a bewildered sheepish manner. (H.M.G. & M.M.H., 1920, p. 44)

The "sheepish" looks of two noble warriors (engaged not in anonymous artillery barrages but in the "fair" bayonet struggle) underlined the surprising painlessness of dying in battle. For other soldiers, the emphasis was more realistic, focused rather on escaping the "awful holocaust, the carnage and the slaughter which the Hun has brought into Europe." This was the view of the "new correspondent" communicating to earthly men and women on June 25, 1916. He stressed the "the immediate *relief* this is the saving thought,—Release!!" (Recorder, 1916, pp. 45–46). There might be a brief period of "sharpness" as the spirit was released from the body, but it was a fleeting moment. Thus, the spirit of Private Dowding reassured his readers:

> Physical death is nothing. There really is no cause to fear. ... Something struck hard, hard, hard against my neck. Shall I ever lose the memory of that hardness? It is the only unpleasant incident that I can remember. I fell, and as I did so, without passing through any apparent interval of unconsciousness, I found myself outside myself. … You see what a small thing is death, even the violent death of war! … no horror, no long-drawn suffering, no conflicts. Dowding, 1917, pp. 6–8)

A mother was told by her son that there was "no horror in death. I was one minute in the thick of things, with my company, and the next minute Lieutenant Wells touched my arm and said: 'Our command has crossed. Let's go … Bob, we're dead.' I didn't believe it at first. I felt all right" (Rutherford, 1920, p. 25). As in many of these examples, the shift from the earthly to the spiritual plane was often so slight that it took a while for men to recognize that a radical change had taken place. "Many people do not realise that they are dead," exclaimed "A Business Man," "They have been very ill, and in great pain, and passing over, find themselves free of pain and think that they have recovered" (Business Man, 1927, p. 17). Men were quite cheery in the afterlife: "It's a lifelong holiday, day and night … everything is delightful!" enthused the spirit of one man killed at Neuve Chapelle in 1915 (dead soldier called H***** in Recorder, 1915, p. 37). Or, as another explained to his mother, "the soul leaves the body as a boy jumps out of a school door. That is suddenly and with joy" (automatic writing from a spirit, in Rutherford, 1920, p. 28; see also Kelway-Bamber, 1918, pp. 1–2).

Second, spirits reassured the bereaved of their continual presence. The dead are all around us, they asserted (Kennerley, 1939, p. 7). This could be proved through the use of photographs taken in spiritualist studios throughout the country, but most famously in the photographs of spirits hovering above mourners during the armistice celebrations in 1918 (see photos in Barlow, c. 1930; also see Stead, 1925). As numerous spiritualists shouted loudly, "Love bridges the chasm" (Barker, 1918, pp. 61–65; Bazett, 1931, p. 26; Dyke, c. 1922, pp. 9, 28, and 38; Glenconner, 1920, p. 46; Heslop, c. 1915, pp. xi, 14–17; Lodge, 1918, p. 83; Stead, 1925, pp. 10–13, 16–17). Such love brought peace to women like Pamela Glenconner and Violet Prattley, who had a son and a husband, respectively, killed in the battle of the Somme, 1916. They both sought and received comfort from spiritualist communication with their loved ones. In the words of Glenconner, who spoke to her son in her sleep: "So great was the sense of consolation after one of these dreams, that the fact of his having died would on waking seem almost negligible; for hours after I was lapped in a sustaining sense of joy" (Glenconner, 1920, p. 102; also see a letter from Violet Prattley to Clive Chapman after attending a seance in his home, in Chapman & G.A.W, 1927, p. 110). What did these spirits tell people? As we have already seen, they provided homely reassurances and exhortations to "carry on." In addition, however, the message of spirits was often highly prescriptive. They frequently lectured their listeners about appropriate behavior, including warning soldiers against going to prostitutes. They admitted that they would

> shadow those evil creatures who try to tempt men to obsess. As soon as one of these harpies gets hold of a young fellow, and begins to suggest that he should obtain earthly pleasures … our spirit warns him against doing so. (Ward, 1920, p. 66)

Spirits also attempted to influence behavior more directly through moral instruction. Suicide, capital punishment, and cremation were strongly disapproved of (Business Man, 1927, p. 42). During a war that seemed to represent the opposite of progress and human goodness, they recited slightly old-fashioned, even childish morality tales stripped of philosophical modernism. From the Other World, S. O. Cox's daughter informed her father that she was growing pansies in her garden, and that when he did good works her pansies "look up, nod, and smile," but when he had selfish thoughts they became faded and marked. "My garden reflects the work you do," she lectured in a sweet, high-pitched voice, which was probably as effective in influencing behavior as the more gruff commandments issued by God the Father (Cox, n.d., pp. 25–26). The reasons for leading a "good and moral" life here on earth did not include the threat of hell. In an article published in *The Spiritualist* in 1873, entitled "How Do the Spirits Live?" readers were assured that "the better lives men live on earth, by doing good to everybody and everything, the happier they will be in the hereafter. … The angels in heaven and upon earth are happy in proportion to the goodness and usefulness of their lives" ("How Do the Spirits Live," 1873, p. 195). Goodness was clearly ascribed to the spirits: they were clothed in colors depending on their deeds on earth. Thus, red indicated that they had performed more than their share of evil deeds; blue signaled a life of good deeds; and pale blue marked out the holiest spirits (Gorer, 1955, p. 259). In the words of the spirit of Charles Dickens, communicating in 1873, "knowing and feeling" that "holy and innocent" spirits were always watching "binds you up in faith, establishes you in hope, and gives you strength to battle with the temptations of the soul" (Melbourne Medium, 1873, p. 4).

The nature of the spirits' lives in the afterlife also preoccupied people on earth. In many ways, the bereaved discovered, the afterlife was remarkably similar to life on earth—or, at least, similar to *idealized* life on earth. Ideal gender relations, for instance, were maintained in the other world. Death relieved the individual of his or her body, but gender was located in the "soul" rather than the body (Ashby, 1915, p. 7). Thus, in spiritual communication with his father, the young soldier Raymond Lodge admitted that there were men and women in the other world and, although they did not have children, they still fell in love with each other (Lodge, 1918, p. 197). Of course, there was something pure and virginal about love in the spiritual realm. Spiritualists evoked the Victorian concept of chastity as an ideal for both men and women, even within marriage. No woman was going to be "bothered" by her lover in the spiritual world! In the words of the spirit simply known as M. A.: "We have sex in the highest sense, but free from bodily lusts and passions" (M.A., 1930, p. 13; see also Laelia, 1939, p. 111; Lawrence, 1921, pp. 9–10). There was "no sexuality in the grosser sense and no childbirth," swore the writer and enthusiastic spiritualist Arthur Conan Doyle in his *The New Revelations* (1918, p. 98).

The other world was free of other anxieties as well. It was a dirt-free zone where there was no decay and no excrement. Although the spirits often claimed to be able to eat and drink (indeed, they gave extravagant and sensual descriptions of such pleasures), they did not defecate. One Victorian lady recounted a discussion with a spirit in which she gave him an apple to eat, then asked him "What became of the apple?" The spirit, Joey, told her that it had simply been "dispersed into the air" (*Echoes of the Eighties*, 1921, chap. 20). More bluntly, another spirit informed his listeners that they ate only fruit and vegetables and this food was "entirely burnt up in our bodies, there is no sewerage" (M. A., 1930, p. 13).

There was another form of purification that occurred after death. The body survived the afterlife—but in a slightly different form. Because of "the sin and sorrow of our race," the future body was a "glorified likeness" of what it was on earth, spiritualists discovered. All blemishes would be removed. The Rev. D. M. Lamont admitted that some bereaved people wanted to "see their friends after death just as they saw them on earth." "The very blemish on that dear face had become endearing to me," they told him. Lamont reminded such people that "it was the love behind the blemishes that endeared them. When that same love will translate itself into the features of the glorified countenance, those longings for defects shall vanish." The body would retain its unique identity, but its beauty would be "enhanced." The "victory of Christ over sin and death cannot be complete except He restored the whole man body and soul," Lamont explained (Lamont, 1920, pp. 51, 58–60, 63). Arthur Conan Doyle provided another explanation for the retention of individual likeness (albeit without unsightly scars and suchlike) after death. In 1918 he asked, "Are we to be mere wisps of gaseous happiness floating about in the air?" He provided his readers with the answer:

> If there is no body like our own, and if there is no character like our own, then say what you will, *we* have become extinct. What is it to a mother if some impersonal glorified entity is shown to her? She will say, "that is not the son I lost—I want his yellow hair, his quick smile, his little moods that I know so well." (Conan Doyle, 1918, p. 105)

But spiritualism did promise a "wholeness," which must have been reassuring to many bereaved parents, wives, and lovers after the First World War. Men did not bleed in the other world; gaping wounds left by bayonets or shrapnel were instantly healed; limbs ripped off by bombs were replaced (Chapman and G.A.W., 1927, p. 64; Lawrence, 1921, pp. 9–10; Lodge, 1918, p. 195; Ward, 1920, p. 185). Such processes did not benefit only the young men mutilated in battle. Congenital deformities slowly disappeared in the other world (Kelway-Bamber, 1918, p. 11; Lodge, 1918, p. 195). Teeth that did not fit were replaced (Lodge, 1918, p. 195). Even older men or those who had undergone a long sickness prior to death rejoiced that their bodies after death reverted to their prime: "I am now hale and hearty, looking a young man in the prime of life," boasted one spirit to his earthly son (Thomas, 1928, p. 107; see also Conan Doyle, 1918, p. 85).

The comfort provided by such reassurances was not concerned only with the corporeal survival of the individual. In a world where the sacrifice of the dead was being demeaned, the spirit world insisted on honoring their sacrifice. In a session of automatic writing from a "new correspondent" just before the battle of the Somme, the message is clear:

> They [the dead soldiers] are splendid but there are thousands of them. ... Heroes! gods! if devotion and bravery are worth Divine attention! Your *duty* is to give this assurance (these letters) to the mourners of the men who have fallen in battle. (Recorder, 1916, pp. 45–46; see also Stead, 1925, p. 15)

The spirits never ceased asserting that the war was a "righteous" one that really would "clear away some old evils and prepare the ground for the building up of a better civilisation" (Ward, 1917, pp. 25–26). The enemy simply "*must* be fought to the death" (letters by a dead soldier called S****, 11 May 1916 in Recorder, 1916, p. 15). Heroism and self-sacrifice were back in fashion among the spirits, who rallied against a culture that seemed to value only place and power, gold and greed. Remember, they cried, self-sacrifice and love prepared men and women for the spirit life (automatic writing by S****, 7 May 1916, in Recorder, 1916, p. 7). Spirits during the Second World War also took up this refrain, reassuring their listeners that what they were doing to "put the world right" was valuable: "It's a great task you have set yourselves," one spirit urged (Barbanell, 1944, p. 48).

The spirits also persuaded people back on earth that their struggle on the Western Front was a holy one, fully supported by hosts of angels and spirits who hovered over the battlefields, unwilling to desert their comrades in their valiant fight (Bere, letter to his wife, March 29–30, 1917; automatic writing by S****, May 7, 1916, in Recorder, 1916, p. 6). Some spirits even formed "relief battalions" to bring comfort to wounded men (automatic writing from "Bob," killed in France, to his mother, in Rutherford, 1920, p. 40; cf. Downs, 1920, p. 11). Furthermore, it was easy for these spirits to identify the "good" from the "evil" dead because the auras hovering above the German soldiers spelt "grossness, bestiality, cruelty, and absolute cur-rish [sic] fear," while the auras hovering over British troops were "bright with hope, love of country, of fellow-soldier, of home, and all that is beautiful and bright" (automatic writing by S****, May 7, 1916, in Recorder, 1916, p. 26; cf. Barker, 1918). In the afterlife, the two types of souls obviously could not mingle. The German dead were "too brutal for our gospel, they go to their own place—attracted thither by a wonderful law of attraction, which is to be the extension and fulfilment of the same law of like, or repulsion, which we went through on earth" (message from S****, June 4, 1916, in Recorder, 1915, p.26).

This chapter has concentrated on only one aspect of spiritualist communication: its function in comforting, reassuring, and making the sacrifice of death a worthy one. Clearly, however, spiritualism was not only about bereavement, or even death. For many it was a livelihood or a light-hearted form of recreation; others were merely indulging an intellectual curiosity about the other side. Whatever the motives, however, tens of thousands of bereaved parents, spouses, siblings, and friends found in the often unbelievable descriptions of the other world a belief system that comforted them and enabled them to rebuild their lives. The visionary world described by the spirits held much in common with earthly life, except in a number of areas (particularly those aspects of modern life considered to cause anxiety), and their message was often highly prescriptive. Much of their communication consisted of morality tales, a repudiation of the gross dismemberment of war, and a devastating critique of modernism. The power of the medium over his or her customers cannot be doubted, but many bereaved people found through spiritualism a direct route of their own to their loved ones in the afterlife. Through molding their vision of the afterlife, they created a space within which the dead could be both honored and put to one side. In this way, Rachel was comforted.

References

Ashby, J. (1915). *Death: The gate of life*. Manchester.

Ballard, C. R. (1915). Letter to his mother, March 1, 1915. In file "Letters, mainly to his family 1874–1916," Liddell Hart Centre for Military Archives.

Barbanell, S. (1944). *Some discern spirits (the mediumship of Estelle Roberts)*. London.

Barker, E. (1918). *War letters from the living dead man*. London.

Barlow, F. (c. 1930s). A collection of psychic photographs, with a catalogue by E. J. Dingwall. British Library, CUP.407.1.1.

Barrow, L. (1986). *Independent spirits: Spiritualism and English plebeians 1850–1910*. London.

Bazett, M. (1931). *The broken silence*. London.

Bere, M. A. (1917). Letter to his wife, March 29, 1917 and March 20, 1917. In file "Letters," Imperial War Museum 66/96/1.

Brandon, R. (1983). *The spiritualists: The passion for the occult in the nineteenth and twentieth centuries*. London.

Business Man, A. (1927). *A common sense view of religion*. London.

Cerullo, J. J. (1982). *The secularization of the soul: Psychical research in modern Britain*. Philadelphia.

Chapman, C., & G.A.W. (1927). *The blue room: Being the absorbing story of the development of voice-to-voice communication in broad light with souls who have passed into the great beyond*. Auckland.

Conan Doyle, A. (1918). *The new revelation*. 2nd ed. London.

Cox, S. O. (n.d.). *Talks with immortals*. London.

Downs, T. (1920). *The way, the truth and the light: Spiritual philosophy and phenomena; positive revelation*. Sydney.

Dyke, P. H. (c. 1922). *Seeing through another's eyes*. Huntingdon, U.K.

Echoes of the eighties: Leaves from the diary of a Victorian lady. (1921). London.

Glenconner, P. (1920). *The earthen vessel: A volume dealing with spirit-communication received in the form of book-tests*. London.

Gorer, G. (1955). *Exploring English character*. London.

Graham, W. (n.d.). *My letters from heaven: Being messages from the unseen world given in automatic writing to Winifred Graham by her father, Robert George Graham*. London.
H.M.G. & M.M.H. (Eds.). (1920). *A soldier gone west*. London.
Heslop, F. (c. 1915). *Speaking across a border-line: Being letters from a husband in spirit life to his wife on earth*. 2nd ed. London.
Homer, M. W. (1990). Sir Arthur Conan Doyle: Spiritualism and new religions. *Dialogue, 23(4)*, 97–121.
How do the spirits live? (1873, May 15). *The Spiritualist: A Record of the Progress of the Science and Ethics of Spiritualism*, p. 195.
Kelway-Bamber, L. (1918). *Claude's book*. London.
Kennerley, J. B. (1939). *The story of "Ken": The way of bereavement*. London.
Kerr, H. (1972). *Mediums, and spirit-rappers, and roaring radicals. Spiritualism in American literature, 1850–1900*. Urbana: University of Illinois Press.
Laelia. (1939). *Life … past, present and future*. Sydney
Lamont, D. M. (1920). *Our friends after death*. London.
Lawrence, E. (1921). *Spiritualism among civilised and savage races: A study in anthropology*. London.
Lodge, O. J. (1918). *Raymond or life and death with examples of the evidence for survival of memory and affection after death*. 10th ed. London.
M.A. (1930). *From world unseen*. London.
Maturin, E. C.-P. (1920). *Rachel comforted: Conversations of a mother in the dark with her child in the light*. London: Dodd, Mead and Co.
Melbourne Medium (1873). *Spiritual communications and the comfort they bring; by the disembodied spirit of Charles Dickens, through a Melbourne medium*. Melbourne.
Oppenheim, J. (1985). *The other world: Spiritualism and psychical research in England, 1850–1914*. Cambridge.
Owen, A. (1989). *The darkened room: Women, power and spiritualism in late nineteenth century England*. London.
Private Dowding: A plain record of the after-death experiences of a soldier killed in battle, and some questions on world issues answered by the messenger who taught him wider truths. (1917). 2nd ed. London.
Recorder. (1916). *Do thoughts perish? Or the survival after death of human personalities*. London.
Rutherford, J. F. (1920). *Talking with the dead?* London.
Shortt, S. E. D. (1984). Physicians and psychics: The Anglo-American medical response to spiritualism, 1870–90. *Journal of the History of Medicine and Allied Sciences, 39*(3), 339–355.
Stead, E. W. (1925). *Faces of the living dead: Remembrance Day messages and photographs*. Manchester.
Thomas, C. D. (1928). *Life beyond death with evidence*. London.
Tilby, A. W. (1918). The riddle of after-life. *Edinburgh Review, 227*(464), 253.
Walkowitz, J. R. (1988). Feminism and spiritualism. *Representations, 22*.
Ward, J. S. M. (1920). *A subaltern in spirit land*. London.
Wilberforce, B. (1916). *After death what?* London.
Winter, J. M. (1995). *Sites of memory, sites of mourning: The Great War in European cultural history*. Cambridge.

CHAPTER 5

Collective Memory and Forgetting

*Components for a Study of Obituaries**

BRIDGET FOWLER

I am immersed in a problem: What are newspaper obituaries, sociologically speaking? Why do we choose to remember these lives and what do they tell us about those whom we respect in capitalist modernity? I shall start by seeing these brief biographies in terms of social or collective memory, convinced that they are more than a series of recollections about random individuals.[1] But the concept of collective memory also has a certain contemporary seductiveness. I shall pose a sceptical question about whether this is an intellectual tool which is really good to think with, or whether it is merely an empty, but fashionable, phrase. Refuting the latter argument, I shall explain why by first introducing the *fin-de-siècle* concept of memory, with Bergson in 1896. I shall then explore the role of collective memory in the theory of two canonical interwar and wartime writers, Halbwachs, on the social frameworks underpinning memory, and Benjamin on the decline of traditional memory. This clarification completed, I shall return to the problem of the obituaries as collective memory and offer a theory of their social determinants, meaning and types.

It is impossible to analyse social memory without alluding to the philosopher and psychologist, Henri Bergson. His *Matter and Memory*

* Originally published in *Theory, Culture & Society* 2005 (Sage, London, Thousand Oaks and New Delhi), 22(6), 53–72 (2005). Reprinted with permission.

introduced a genuinely new way of thinking at a period when the sciences of memory were being founded in late 19th-century Paris. Bergson is important for challenging the early medieval notion of memory as a storehouse or a great central depository of ideas and impressions.[2] Instead, he advanced a model more adequate to modernity: the mind is like a telephone exchange in which nerve cells in the entire body play a key role (1991:30). Memory, for Bergson, derives from the necessary interaction of mind and matter (1991:13). Perception is itself inseparable from memory images, despite the fact that it is geared principally to the requirements of practical action (1991:73-4). The entire processing of perceptions depends on a complex selection, in which nerve-cell information from the outside world is sieved or filtered through memory-images of the past, within the visual centres of memory in the brain: "[I]n all psychical states", Bergson argued, "[…] memory plays the chief part" (1991:43).

However, and here I agree with Lawlor, Bergson should not be understood as a subjectivist (2003:29). He also thought that such perceptions—filtered through memory images—just fit the test of externality: that is, they must be adequate to the object that is perceived. Memory then, was neither a container nor a camera (1991:38-9), but made up a circuit, rather like an electrical charge, between mind and matter.

Bergson also made a key distinction between two kinds of memory, voluntary memory (or motor-memories)—as when we learn our tables by heart—and involuntary memory-images, which acquire the form of crystallized, sensual impressions (1991:80-1, 88). This second form of memory-image emerges uninvited, as in dreams, but enriches each everyday act of perception. Indeed perception, Bergson strikingly remarked, is "like an immense keyboard on which an external object executes at once its memory of a thousand notes" (1991:128).

Although Bergson was one of those thinkers whom Durkheim regarded as making a great leap forward in psychology, he discussed only individual representations or memories. What, then, are collective representations? In Durkheim's view this term was used to denote those categories and systems of classification which are fixed or carefully delimited, due to the long and steady influence of the collectivity (Stedman-Jones, 2001:70). Only in individual representations are signs and symbols elective or chosen (Durkheim, 1965:25). Of course, collective representations can exist only through the medium of individual interaction, but they are socially situated and are thus 'social facts'. In the case of fields such as religion or metaphysical beliefs, they are conditioned by other representations as part of a wider grammar of ideas; they are thus to a certain degree independent of socio-economic structures (1965:31).[3] How do we recognize collective representations apart from this quality of obligation? First, simply by their proliferation: we have *more images* of the great, those at the centre of sacred cults. Second, collective representations are often learnt by heart, as in catechisms of the Ten Commandments. They are thus transmitted to the body, whilst individual representations, in contrast, relate only to each person's own memories, hopes, and dreams. In short, for Durkheim, memory-images, like other forms of collective representations, only have resonance and authority because they are attached to social and group realities. Such patterns of collective consciousness might be attenuated in modernity, but they were never entirely forgotten (1964:166-168).

Two Pioneers of Collective Memory: Halbwachs and Benjamin

Halbwachs's 'path breaking' (Coser, 1992:21) concept of collective memory is profoundly influenced by two sources: the Durkheimian arguments above and the notion of collective *mentalités* (or structures of feeling) developed by the Annales historians, Marc Bloch and Lucien Febvre. Halbwachs takes issue with Bergson's individualistic conception of memory, however dynamic and interactive the latter's model of the mind. Yet Halbwachs also goes beyond Durkheim's periods of 'collective effervescence': an intensified set of sentiments and creativity which emerges from great conferences, demonstrations and gatherings (Durkheim, 1964:99). As in Marxists' conceptions of concerted revolutionary action and its re-enactment in popular festivals of liberty, such collective effervescence serves to revitalize the social in the minds of individuals (Marx: 1852; E. Bloch, 1986). However, in between these periods, Halbwachs suggests, collective memory acts to recreate events, for example, imaginatively re-embodying the past within a whole topography of sanctified places. Indeed, it is collective memory itself which enhances the depth and clarity of certain individual memories:

> One cannot in fact think about the events of one's past without discoursing upon them. But to discourse upon something means to connect within a single system of ideas our opinions as well as those of our circle [...] the framework of collective memory confines and binds our most intimate remembrances to each other (Halbwachs quoted in ed. Coser, 1992:53)

Halbwachs' most sensational proof of the power of the social is that we only exceptionally remember our dreams because the dream has too much purely individual content:

> No memory is possible outside frameworks used by people living in society to determine and retrieve their recollections. This is the

> certain conclusion shown by the study of dreams ... (Halbwachs quoted in ed. Coser, 1992:43).

For Halbwachs, collective memory is actively sustained through place memory, especially through the social construction and reconstruction of sacred group landmarks (1980, p. 140; see ed. Coser, 1992:193-235). For example, Halbwachs discusses 'walking a city' such as London, accompanied, on different occasions, by an architect, surveyor and painter. These representative figures allow him to enter temporarily into their social circles, so as to grasp their different ways of seeing London's history (1980:22-4). Thus there are different collective memories, which mutually illuminate a scene, crisscrossing it from their different perspectives.

Collective memory also has a certain distance from public memory or history. Deploying Halbwachs' own imagery, it can be said that while history fixes dates and places precisely on the banks, collective memory flows in a social current within which we 'bathe midstream' (1980:50-60). In the same vein, collective memory often possesses a certain fuzziness, as in the child's evolving views of their father. Only in the day after the father's death is a clearer focus gained, argues Halbwachs (1980:72). I would argue, similarly, that the death of those we know crystallizes within the obituary into individual memories of their presence, structured by a group framework. Such memories, often poignant, may be recalled within these columns by friends, colleagues or even journalists. Yet in this obituary context, the theorized rupture between public history and collective memory is too total. We might accept Halbwachs' point that the former has more rigorous procedures. Nevertheless, collective memory imperceptibly influences the problematic of all historians to some degree, whilst having its most notable effect on the new historian of mentalities (Hutton, 1993:77). Does not the collective memory encompassed within these miniature biographies—the obituaries—feed back and shape public historical assessments?

Halbwachs extended his concept of collective memory from family memories and religious groups to the new phenomena of bourgeois society, identifying certain *mentalités* and cultural inheritances with specific social classes. Thus he writes of the transformation of the aristocracy from the 'nobility of the sword' to a nobility of public service, or of bourgeois lawyers' adaptations to the once aristocratic Inns of Court. He also focuses on the co-operative project, which, through the medium of shops, building societies and temperance hotels, had become part of everyday life for millions of British working-class people (Halbwachs, 1958:88). Here, collective memory incorporates the rational foundations of group experience into new traditions (Coser, 1992:183–184).

However, Halbwachs' outstanding strengths in the study of groups' collective memories do not transfer easily to the concept of national collective memory; nor are all his views persuasive. Schwartz notes acerbically, yet convincingly, that Halbwachs adopts an extreme historical perspectivism at this level, in which the needs of the *present* entirely colour the collective memory of the past (Schwartz, 1982:375). Schwartz's own studies address issues such as the specific choices of American leaders for commemoration via statues in the Capitol at different times. These studies provide impressive evidence for at least *some* historical continuity rather than constantly renewed choices according to the latest fashion. Schwartz plausibly argues that, despite a perennial, present-oriented revaluation of values, the past always imposes a set of determining limits (1982:395-396).

The Halbwachsian antithesis between collective memory and history (1980:52) has rightly been criticized for adopting, as absolute and unchanging truth, a positivist conception of history (Hutton, 1993:xxv, 77, 97). More tendentiously, Halbwachs has been depicted in some quarters as a Burkean conservative whose concept of collective memory bears considerable resemblance to the organic notion of collective traditions branching out from the tree of order (Osiel, 1997:213-214; cf Ricoeur, 2000:146-151[4]). Halbwachs' theoretical ordering of the memories of different groups is argued to be too closely integrated with the memory of the powerful (Misztal, 2003:55). He has been held to have been overly influenced by Durkheim's notion of 'mechanical solidarity' and by the importance of a solidarity based on emotional and moral consensus rather than reasoned argument (Osiel, 1997:213–214).

However, these interpretations are coloured too exclusively by his guiding concept of the social framework of memory, ignoring Halbwachs' further emphasis that "everyone does not draw on the same part of this common instrument" (1980:48). Antagonistic critiques of Halbwachs as a regressive Romantic forget his inconvenient recognition that some groups, such as newly formed families, possess an innovative turn towards the future. They neglect, too, the stress in his thought on the *rational* principles underlying group ideas (see Halbwachs, 1958; also Coser, 1992:81-83, 44-45).

This being said, the greater complexity of national or international memory necessarily engenders important new concepts in the writings of a later generation. Foucault, for example, proposes the idea of 'counter-memories'—oppositional memory—as a distinctive, if unelaborated, feature of his thought. His counter-memories are comparable to Bourdieu's 'worlds in reverse,' such as that of 1850s bohemians (Foucault, 1977:160-161, 206-211; Bourdieu, 1993:39).

Alongside Halbwachs, the second great interpreter of collective memory is Walter Benjamin. His most accessible and compelling account of collective memory is perhaps *The Storyteller*, in which he links the flourishing of the story-telling tradition to two conditions, both disappearing in contemporary societies (Eiland & Jennings, 2002:143-166). The first is the link between the story and lived experience, which always has its roots in the past. Soldiers returning from the First World War could not tell stories to communicate the qualities of the war; so unimaginable was the nature of the reality that had greeted them at the front. Virtually all were condemned to silence.

The second condition for storytelling is epic wisdom, which, once again, is based on tacitly accepted moral assumptions. Yet these are shared by progressively fewer people in societies dominated by Taylorist production and the allure of fashion. Thus the storyteller, with his funds of wisdom, hangs on only in less developed areas. Here he derives his acceptance either from being a long-settled inhabitant, with years of untended observation or from the more variegated experience of the seaman or traveller. In both cases, the stories told are fed by collective memory.

In contrast, the main cultural source of the modern, deskilled city dweller is the newspaper. Now, in Benjamin's view—with which I shall disagree—the newspaper cannot be the vehicle for collective memory. Rather, newspapers merely process information, governed by 'evident verifiability': 'Every morning brings us news from across the globe yet we are poor in noteworthy stories' (Eiland & Jennings, 2002:147). The only exception is the Soviet newspapers of the 1920s where an attempt was being made, via readers' letters, to make a collective product by collating the old form of the story with the medium for the new literacy.

Benjamin's masterpiece is his extraordinary sociological analysis of the modern city in *The Arcades Project* (1999). This focuses on the city of Paris to reveal the vicissitudes of collective memory. Benjamin's method lies in a demystification of the new 'religions' that emerge in the capitalist city, including that based on commodity fetishism. It also lies in the exploration of the accompanying utopia which go hand in hand with these social transformations: the technological utopia of Fourier and the progressive bourgeoisie, so ironically treated in Offenbach's operetta (e.g., *La Vie Parisienne*, *Orphée aux Enfers*) (Benjamin, 1999:4-5, 8) or the revolutionary utopia of Blanqui, which ended with the Commune (1999:26).

Writing in 1936, amidst the shabby decay and destruction of the *quartiers* of the modernist city, Benjamin's archaeological exploration is intended to reveal the contrasting newness of the material and symbolic culture of the mid-19th-century city, particularly the architecture that shaped its iron-and-glass arcades and great boulevards. For Benjamin, such physical forms went hand in hand with the unprecedented social relations of the modern metropolis. No longer shaped by feudal hierarchies but by invisible differences, these social relations were founded increasingly on both the social levelling and the new divisions of the money economy, as well as in the stratification created by fashion: 'The phantasmagoria of capitalist culture attains its most radiant unfolding in the cycle of fashion…' he argues (Eiland & Jennings, 2002:37).

Benjamin proceeds to link these new sources of collective elation to the collective memory of past utopia (2002:34). His words still have the power to startle, when he writes of: '[the religious] intoxication of the great cities: the department stores are temples consecrated to this new intoxication' (1999:61)—as though the commodity were the hash available in Indian temples for spiritual exaltation. He displays from angle after angle the impact of the commodity on collective memory, as in the new umbrellas or the elegant cashmere shawls woven with French flowers (1999:46, 34).

Yet Benjamin is most prescient in formulating his distinctive notion of the 'cultural inheritance', which acquires its salience for him as a form of collective memory. Now, on the surface, the standard process of consecration or canonization of a body of national works seems innocuous enough. Benjamin disagreed, partly because his immediate problematic was more harsh than ours. He was witnessing the mid-1930s appropriation of all cultural goods for administration by the German state, a process in which any 'unselected' intellectual property was exposed to destruction. His response was incisive: thinkers should distance themselves from "the idea of a stock of cultural goods inventoried and available once and for all. Above all, they should strive to form a critical concept that will counter the 'affirmative concept of culture'" (Eiland & Jennings, 2002:312). This affirmative concept was the stance that divorced culture from any practical significance. It thus segregated it, in particular, from collective memory, which historically has had its forms of remembering focussed on solving dilemmas of action (Halbwachs). Indeed, for Benjamin, a 'genuine tradition' would perform this function better, since it would be organized to focus on defamiliarising techniques of cultural production and would be alive to issues of cultural reception (Eiland & Jennings, 2002:312).

Despite its seeming resonance in terms of social memory, Benjamin sees the implementation of cultural policies around the concept of 'cultural inheritance' as fraught with difficulties. For a start, he emphasizes the danger that only those works narrowly defined as 'art' (consecrated or fine art) will become part of such an inheritance. Thus against the bureaucratized procedures of rationalized museums, he places the insightful expansiveness of collectors who pursued a personal vision, such as Eduard Fuchs. Fuchs had gathered together objects such as *unsigned* pots, despite narrow contemporary concerns revolving mainly around individual authenticity in the artist's work (2002:283). Moreover, at odds with the then current contemplative awe towards artworks supposedly embodying the great tradition or national inheritance, Benjamin emphasizes a wider body of work. Famously, he was one of the first to draw attention to those films and plays that were intended to galvanize the minds of those watching, even if in a distracted mode: Chaplin's cinema, for example (2002:141). Indeed, Benjamin's sociological gaze taught him that the transient tastes of museum directors, pursuing 'showpieces', or the consumption patterns of a polite elite might all too easily be *substituted* for the collective inheritance (2002:282, 284).

To sum up, Benjamin associated the switch to more impersonal, urban forms of narrative—such as the novel—with a *decline* of storytelling and collective memory, which I have disputed. Everything that he wrote about the city in modernity suggests that disparate elements of collective memory still persist within the new context, although in both estranged and utopian forms. His critique of the 'bourgeois literary-artistic apparatus' shows that he is implicitly concerned with literature or cultural production as part of a tradition of collective memory. He usefully expands such production beyond the restricted channels of a formalist aesthetic to redeem it for this purpose.

We have so far introduced a notion of collective memory that we have distinguished from (official) history and from newspaper information. Since the interwar writing of Halbwachs and Benjamin, further intellectual developments have been made, some wrapping the topic in chic cultural pieties, others advancing into important new terrain. New dangers have been cited: '[w]e have forgotten our own forgetting' remarks Casey (1987:2 see also Ferguson, 2004:26-27). More specifically, memory has further fragmented, alongside modernity itself (Frisby, 1985; Matsuda, 1996; Nora et al, 1992, 1996). In the context of these multiple realities, the conception of 'counter-memory' has been introduced and, indeed, has become vital within the field.

Memory Crisis and Fission: Counter-Memory

The social frameworks for memory in capitalism become fractured by rival constructions of the past (Popular Memory Group, 1982:211). Indeed, public memory has sometimes been subject to a politics of spectacular fission, as in the case of the destruction in 1871 of the Vendôme Column, the official commemoration of Napoleon I. The Communards' counter-memory of the First Empire fuelled their anger against the second emperor, Louis-Napoleon III (Matsuda, 1996: chap. 1). Here remembrance led not to enduring memorials, but to the toppling of monuments, a graphic enactment of the limits to usurped power.

Such "counter-memory" evokes symbolic struggles over the meaning of events in which the leadership of the subordinated people actively contest the dominants' coding of historical acts. But memory, as has been pointed out dramatically by Foucault, is also a control over those whose practices and knowledges do not fit taken-for-granted historical assumptions:

> Memory is … a very important factor in struggle … If one controls people's memory, one controls their dynamism … It's vital to have possession of this memory, to control it, to administer it, tell it what it must contain. (quoted Osiel, 1997:210)

Paul Connerton has similarly linked various forms of memory with economic and political power, including war memorials and poetic odes. He argues that when a dominant group wants to remove another from power, it does so by refusing that group access to social memory (1989:1). Here we have the "structural amnesia" that Misztal has so illuminatingly researched (2003:30)[5].

Despite Foucault's later 'discursive inflationism',[6] his enduring early importance is in having reinstated various forgotten others—homosexuals, the mad, prisoners, inhabitants of work-houses—whose voices had been systematically silenced, misheard or neglected (1977:160-161, 206-211). When such marginalized others confront their atomized condition, it is only with an impoverished memory of different or earlier voices. Certainly they possess a counter-memory, but only the imperfect resources of the 'reverse discourse' guide it. Yet this can still be a powerful social technology for repudiating official control.

For Halbwachs, memory operates imperceptibly and can never be totally expropriated. Yet for him, collective memory, as the historical glue of groups' lives, is gradually declining (1980:79). For Benjamin, in contrast, an 'archaeological' project can discover hidden caches of older cultural forms to inform memory. In particular, traces of the earlier city of modernity remain, partly in old architecture, partly also in literature and art. From these we can gain unexpected insights, even 'epiphanies'. Cultural documents are the repositories of tradition, but they can register also types of oppositional consciousness (or counter-memory), which might otherwise be expunged.

It is in this context that Paul Ricoeur (2000) has tellingly expanded the Freudian notion of memory-distortion at the individual level, to embrace the concept of memory-clarification and distortion at the social level. In this way, the active shaping of collective memory becomes a stake in a wider enquiry into ideological mystification or Orwellian history-control.

Following Ricoeur, I want to delineate 'blocked memory', 'manipulated memory' (on a practical plane) and 'memory abusively commanded' on the ethico-political plane (Ricoeur, 2000:83-111). Such wounded memory is a fundamental component of ideology.

For many late-Foucauldian texts, only a fragmentation of memory is apparent, promoting a retrospective view of incompatible pasts. Yet recent enquiries have argued that, for the most important issues, fragmentation is not enough (Ricoeur, 2000:Osiel, 1997). Indeed, Osiel contends that vis-à-vis the 'large-scale administrative massacres' which make up the grand narratives of history, we cannot simply let a 'hundred interpretative flowers bloom' (1997:265; Winter, 1995:5). Instead, we seek in major trials to found both legal processes and subsequent collective memory on careful witnesses and reliable testimony. Thus he accepts that in key events such as the legal action against Argentinean army officers following the 'dirty war' it is possible to found a genuine resolution on adequate witnessing (Osiel, 1997:7).

This need to evaluate a record accurately is also an element that characterizes the obituaries (Bytheway & Johnson, 1996). Admittedly, there are limits to the obituary as a form of witnessing, due to constraints on critical openness at the time of death and the conflicting perspectives of different newspapers. In compensation, obituaries also supply evidence for a higher Brechtian resolution of clashing viewpoints (Osiel, 1997:251, 290-292). Admittedly, such truth effects are reduced where power interests mould how a story is told (see Osiel, 1997:245). This is particularly apparent where various 'voices' conflict, as when one or a few newspaper authors offer resistance to the dominant representations of an individual. Yet in supplying factual materials that can be read in terms of a wider relational perspective, the obituaries contribute a vital resource for actively shaping and demystifying collective memory (see Ricoeur, 2000:381-382, 450).

The Obituary as a Repository for Collective Memory

What, then, is the obituary, sociologically speaking? It is like Borges' mythical animal, a hybrid breed made up of various elements. Struggling against its earlier euphemistic conventions, the national newspaper obituary could be seen as a semi-ritualized nexus of ethical, political and professional worlds. Like the memorial service, it is a secularized rite de passage, to help the bereaved; it is also a verdict, derived from professional peers, about the worth of the dead person's contribution.[7] Finally, despite conflicting interpretations vying for authority, it aims to provide the last judgement about their personalities. Lacking the emotional intensity of the shared memorial service, the newspaper obituary is, nevertheless, a major form of collective memory within modernity (Casey, 1987; Connerton, 1989:chap. 3). Now that it is throwing off its earlier chrysalis of rigid aristocratic formulae, the obituary as a newspaper genre is becoming less coded, more subtle and more weighty.

The obituary was prefigured in a secular literary form like Aubrey's *Brief Lives* (1669-1696), although stripped of Aubrey's elaborate portrayals of astrological conjunctures and his subjects' bodies. Introduced into magazines and newspapers in the mid-18th century (Houlbrooke,1998:329-330), the obituary has been undergoing a gradual internal transformation. It contributes to a collective memory that is bursting out of its old, 18th and 19th-century form (cf Hume, 2000:50-51). In 1900, this was still an elite mould, shaped by the worldview of the aristocracy. The 1900 obituaries of noble soldiers and clergymen were broken up only with an occasional colossal 'prophet' like Ruskin, who was the closest these obituary columns came to a dissident intellectual.

Even now, the obituary offers a paramount occasion for remembering the dominants. In this respect, it contributes significantly to "the inertia of social structures" (Connerton, 1989:5). The 'great and the good' subjects subtly shape 'society in the mind', well after their deaths (Ricoeur, 2000:580). Within these columns are represented subjects whom every obituary editor feels compelled to feature, possessing as they did recognized temporal or intellectual power (Princess Margaret, Lord Hailsham, John Gielgud and others). Paradoxically, the editors express clear national or public obligations towards such representations of the public sphere, even at a time when 'information packages' are becoming increasingly individualized.

Despite exceptions, the obituary still mainly derives from a bourgeois world. The career as a steady mountain climb ascent, which is its pervasive and yet *tacit* assumption, has its roots in the meritocratic aspirations of the new middle class, as in the novels of Stendhal. Its typical concealment of any assistance from kin contributes to an illusion of distinctively individual achievement. It removes from view those strategic acts on the part of families to prevent their children from falling economically into the abyss.

The obituary's 'model' is of purely individualistic success. Yet a systematic study shows that as many as 77 percent of the contemporary British obituary subjects within British newspapers have had an education at fee-paying public school or academy.[8] This reveals the continued roots of such individual achievement in social privilege. The figures are not much lower for the radical newspapers. Certainly, the highest figure—80 percent—appears for *The Times*, but 61 percent of *The Guardian* obituary subjects were also public school educated. Moreover, subjects who have been to these schools extend across virtually every obituary field.

The British subjects of obituaries in 2000 lived through a time when only a tiny fraction of the age group acquired higher education. Yet a very high proportion (56 percent) of the obituaries' subjects had been to university. The persistence of privilege again is telling, with the presence of a particularly large minority (35 percent) who have been to Oxford or Cambridge (38 percent in *The Guardian*). Of course, by 2000, a small minority of the Oxbridge-educated had possessed working-class origins. Nevertheless the important phenomenon is that the two universities operated as a deep structure within these obituaries. It has been Oxbridge, I would argue, that has shaped the self-image of an educationally selected elect and empowered them for further achievement. Rather like the state nobility, this is an elect which is found cross-nationally in the obituaries: the *grandes écoles* in France and the Ivy League in the States play a similar, extraordinary role. Studies—such as Bytheway and Johnson's (1996)—which emphasize the shift from 'the great and good' to 'the ordinary and eccentric' in current obituary subjects, neglect this continued role.

Today's obituaries are less likely to be of the military, clergy or elite civil servants than in 1900. Despite salient variations according to the specific newspaper, they are much more likely to be cultural producers—artists, writers, musicians and actors—or academics or politicians. Yet despite this historic shift towards the arts, as many as 71 percent of the obituary subjects can be cast under the heading of social 'reproduction': that is to say, their fathers (sic) had themselves possessed similar well-placed occupations. Since only 6 percent of the whole obituary sample were from small farmers', working-class or petty bourgeois origins[9], most cases of 'reproduction' were from positions within the dominant class.[10] Little more than a quarter, (28 percent), had arrived at their positions of power or status by either a major (16 percent) or a minor (12 percent) ascent. Surprisingly, whereas we might have expected the obituaries featuring *popular* culture to be exclusively from upwardly mobile individuals, this is by no means always the case. The actors, cartoonists or romance-writers who have most shaped popular culture have not always shared the material position of their publics—Barbara Cartland is a case in point (see her obituaries in *The Times* and *The Guardian*, 22 May 2000). There is only a very narrow band within the obituaries of 'working-class biographies', composed of individuals "reproduced" within the lower class, whose position as political, union or cultural activists might be said to constitute one strand of today's exemplary heroes. In this respect, obituaries in late modernity still feature disproportionately the lives of the great families within collective memory (Bourdieu, 1984:72).

The obituary has gradually become more universalistic in other respects. As a record of achievements in the public sphere, it now features figures such as literary critic Lorna Sage (*The Guardian*, 13 Jan. 2001) or the philosopher Elizabeth Anscombe (*The Guardian*, 11 Jan. 2001). Yet it also comes as something of a shock to discover the tiny minority (19 percent) of women in the obituary portraits—not much of a change from the 10 percent who were featured in *The Times* in 1900.[11] Certainly, there is some democratization in the *mode* of representation of women: they are no longer featured as adjuncts to a distinguished 'family' but, as in the bourgeois model, as individuals in their own right. Yet there are remarkable discrepancies between the structural conditions of men and the women, not least the fact that in 2000, the few women who attained obituaries tended more often to be single, divorced or widowed than in the case of men.

In a world where international influences are more evident, the obituaries of the year 2000 are notably more cosmopolitan than in earlier periods. Whether in British, French or American newspapers, the obituary no longer inhabits an age of nationalism. We begin to see not just a cross-national business elite, but also a wider, more diverse body of writers, artists, sportsmen and politicians. The Third World, especially, although only making up a small minority, is no longer the absent 'other' it once was.

The greater hybridity of origins of today's obituary figures in British newspapers is also reflected in the relatively high minority who have been migrant (40 percent) (30 percent in *Le Monde* and *The New York Times*). If, again, this is a telling feature of so many obituaries, we should also note that the rationales for these subjects' experiences of migration are varied. Amongst them are portraits of exiles, but also of voluntary migrants, including some from post-colonial countries, who have joined the metropolitan elites. In terms of post-colonial theory, many of the obituaries tellingly portray economic or professional migrants who subsequently returned to their homelands, acting there as the voice for otherwise silent or dispossessed people (see Smith, 2004).

The Genres of Obituary

To understand the modern obituary properly, it is essential to clarify its subgenres as a narrative form. The obituaries might be seen, as Hume argues, as the collective memory of modern heroes or as the contemporary mythologies which nurture a nation (2000). Yet this is too broad-brushed a view. Even within this restricted literary space, various modes of characterising individual fates emerge. Four subgenres break with the normative, appreciative obituary.

This *traditional positive* obituary needs to be outlined first of all, characterized as it is by an unambiguous celebration of its protagonist and a delineation of a continuous upwards ascent. The normative obituary can be conceptualized even in the case of an artistic modernist such as Sir William Glock, former Controller of Music at the BBC (*The Times*, January 29, 2000). As a student, Glock had broken with academic music, living in Berlin to pursue the work of the new serial composers. His subjective world totally realigned, he returned as the bearer of a guiding 'conviction that this was the music that matters'. Thus when appointed as Director, it was as though 'Luther had just been elected Pope'. Glock had achieved a cultural 'revolution at the BBC'.

Yet it was also one conducted from a particular quarter. Bourdieu invites us also to 'objectify the game of culture'—that is, to situate individuals' artistic choices in terms of their positions both within the cultural fields and within the wider field of power (Bourdieu, 1984:12, 86, 100-101). Such an 'objectification' of Glock shows his highly conventional suitability: his father was a headmaster, he had been to public school (Christ's Hospital) and later to Cambridge. He appears as a man at home in the British elite and the educational sites of modernism. It should be added, however, that even this traditional positive obituary is not entirely devoid of a subtext signifying cultural contradictions. The author hints at the high costs of Glock's innovative experimentalism, not least the greater rift under his leadership between the Third Programme and the wider audience for music.

Usually acts of commemorative homage, obituaries may occasionally be startlingly critical: acts of commemorative retribution. Such *negative* obituaries have the full force of the collective consciousness behind them. They remind us of the dangers of forgetting (Connerton,1989). Amongst them are obituaries of the perpetrators of great abuses of power (cf. Osiel, 1997). The obituaries for Saddam Hussein's sons are of this sort (*Financial Times*, 23 July 2003): Brief and pithy, shorn of all nuance or ambiguity, their attributes are constituted by adjectives devoid of positive connotation: 'ruthless', 'violent', 'unstable', 'hedonistic'. Dropping the usual tone of neutrality, subtlety or balance, these obituaries are singularly defamatory.

Theirs is a polar case. Other negative obituaries operate in a less one-dimensional manner, acknowledging some tragic elements but also serving to distance the reader from the subject, as though from an enemy of the people. In this period, it is their subjects' complicity with Nazism or Stalinism that drives the great majority of negative obituaries, from that for Lila Kedrova, a Czech actress who became Goebbels' mistress (*The Times*, May 4, 2000), to that of Ruth Werner, who helped the Soviet spy, Fuchs, gain access to British nuclear secrets (*The Times*, 10 July 2000). Like others, Werner's negative obituary is not devoid of mitigating complexity.

She had witnessed signs of social breakdown in the interwar years—mass unemployment in the poor working-class districts of Berlin; living babies abandoned in the gutters of Shanghai—and these became the seeds of the resolute anti-capitalism that shaped her life.

There are postcolonial leaders who are revealed as corrupt and unrestrained in their use of force (see, for example, the negative obituaries for Laurent Kabila (*The Independent,* 19 Jan. 2001), Abdul Nasution, (*Le Monde,* 8 Sept. 2000) Joe Modise (*The Times,* 28 Nov. 2001; *The Guardian*, 29 Nov. 2001)). More unusually, there are figures of power whose obituaries initially adopt the heroic mould only to gradually accumulate discreditable features, like a poison masked by sweetness. One such rare case is an obituary for Giovanni Agnelli (the director of Fiat). In many newspapers, Agnelli was openly acknowledged as unilaterally setting the agenda of power for Italian politicians, whilst pursuing a cult of luxury. The harshest judgement on Agnelli's systematic use of corruption appeared in *The Guardian.* But open admission of his senior managers' conviction for corruption in 1997 was included in the newspaper alone, not in the abridged Internet obituary (*The Guardian*, 25 Jan. 2003).

If such negative obituaries are rare, *tragic obituaries* are even rarer. In this case, the great subject is seen as a figure of misfortune and pathos: the object of sympathy rather than admiration. One such was that of the boxer, Bubi Scholtz (*The Independent*, 23 Aug 2000), who has a place within popular memory as a fallen hero. Bubi had risen out of a workers' district of Berlin as a fighter: a boxer who had only ever lost two fights. Indeed, the obituary writer makes his rapid ascent analogous with that of West Germany itself: Bubi was a figure with whom others could identify in a period when hunger was rife. Later, he became a successful businessman, although one wrapped in hubris: 'the dangerous aura of a hero who knows no tomorrow'. He became the embodiment of the new, phoenix-like Germany: "'I am in business, now, the archetype of the successful man' he boasted. 'There are hundreds of thousands like me in the Federal Republic. If I had the courage of megalomania I would say: we are the republic!'" (*The Independent*, 23 Aug. 2000). His nemesis was his drunken shooting of his wife, followed by prison, Alzheimer's, and an obscure death.

More common is the *ironic obituary*, in which a modicum of praise creates a critical effect, without censuring the deceased as the 'other'. It is a device not uncommonly linked to politicians, although its effect can only be grasped by understanding the position within the media field of the newspaper in which it appears. One such obituary is for Viscount Whitelaw. This starts by recounting his distinction—his service as Deputy PM to Margaret Thatcher, the charm that converted those who had never met him into supporters, his razor-sharp shrewdness—and, more concretely, his prison-building programme. It recalls earlier jokes—Mrs Thatcher's 'Every prime minister needs a Willie' and Whitelaw's nonsensical body-swerve on Irish history ('I always think that it is entirely wrong to prejudge the past'). It outlines Whitelaw's privileged background: his education within an elite institution (Winchester), his service in the most patrician military corps, the Guards, and his landownership. It culminates with the judgement that his 'thousands of acres in Lanarkshire' conferred on him an economic freedom that might have freed him for a more autonomous statesmanlike role. The ultimate irony is that Whitelaw's loyalty as a subordinate was to mutate, in the gaze of posterity, as his shame (*The Guardian*, 2 July 1999).

Finally, we might briefly mention the *untraditional yet positive obituary*. One such was that for the economist Nora Kahn Piore (*The New York Times* 15 June 2000). She chose to dedicate all her working life to union research, only becoming a professor—and presidential advisor—very late. What characterizes such an atypical obituary is its break with the continual 'mountain-top ascent' implicit in the bureaucratic or traditional academic career.

The obituary genre as a whole is well known for its tone of objective neutrality. Nevertheless, the profound, yet little-recognized, differences just outlined shape the readers' understanding of the obituaries' factual content. Although their writers can never prevent readings that interpret them 'against the grain', such narrative modes are key structuring devices. Yet they only set the scene. Crucially, we need also to distinguish various types within the obituaries which correspond to the categories of collective memory outlined above.

The Categories of Collective Memory—Dominant, Popular and Counter-Memory

Once virtually universal in *The Times* 1900, the largest number of obituaries now is still those of the dominants. On occasion, personal appraisals strain to the limits the rules of decorous neutrality, so that negative and positive qualities jostle for predominance (see the commodities broker, William Simon, *Daily Telegraph*, 5 June 2000). A judiciously celebratory commemoration is much more common, both for those who spring from deep roots within the dominant class, like the late governor of Hong Kong, Lord Maclehose (*Daily Telegraph* 1 June 2002) or those like Roy Jenkins ('Nature's Old Etonian'), whose distinction was heightened by his origins in a Welsh mining community (*The Independent*, 6 Jan. 2003).[12]

Within the postwar period, the obituary pages have expanded to include popular memory. A small cluster of trade unionists now appears, alongside a much greater numbers of footballers and other sports stars, gospel-singers, jazz players and Hollywood actors. A typical figure of popular memory is Doris Hare, an actress in a long-running TV series (*Daily Telegraph*, 1 June 2000). Another is the footballer Stanley Matthews (*The Independent*, 25 Feb. 2000). Their presence is part of a more general move, encapsulated initially by the Frankfurt theorist Lowenthal as a cultural Continental shift from heroes of production to heroes of consumption (Lowenthal, 1961). Yet popular memory, like popular culture, is also kaleidoscopic: dynamic, not static, heterogeneous, not homogeneous (Schwarz, 1982). Some of its representatives may have been worked on by dominant memory rather than being exponents of an oppositional counter-memory (Misztal, 2003:61-64). Indeed, woven into the memories of the subordinate class or ethnic groups is an important phenomenon that Stuart Hall has entitled the "ventriloquism of the popular" (Hall, 1981). The potential for such memory-images to simply echo ('ventriloquize') a memory current which has greater authoritative force should never be ignored (Schwarz, 1982:74-81).

Much more recently, the obituary has extended to collective representations of counter-memory, as in the articles written in honour of Howard Finster, the iconoclastic Baptist minister who made sculpture from waste (*The Independent*, 29 Oct. 2001), Tony Cliff, the political leader (*The Independent*, 15 April 2000), or Paul Foot, the investigative journalist (e.g., *The Guardian*, 20 July 2004). At their most powerful, these are written by members of the social movements for which they spoke, thus more clearly making the obituary the work of outsiders. On occasion, such obituaries simply recall decisive historical moments. One such was made by the response of Emily Reed, a librarian in the eye of the storm of American civil rights. She had been ordered to dispose of the children's book she stocked: *The Rabbits' Wedding*, depicting the marriage of a black and a white rabbit. She steadfastly refused, thus raising the morale of the protesters (*The New York Times*, 29 May 2000).

Counter-memory may be mingled with honorific institutional recollections. The very long obituary for Christopher Hill (a historian himself of oppositional memory) was no doubt partly explicable by his achievement of hierarchical pre-eminence as the Master of Balliol. Official institutional recognition, in other words, eradicates the tensions around figures of counter-memory, who might otherwise be excluded or reduced to the status of insignificant obituary figures (*The Guardian*, 26 Feb. 2003).

More commonly, however, counter-memory is recognized, but in *other* countries. It is in these terms that we might characterize the ideal type of counter-memory via the figure of Jacek Kuron, a critic of the Polish state socialist regime originating from an ordinary Polish socialist family, who was imprisoned three times and tortured. Later, with the return to capitalism, it was Kuron who tried to soften the economic shock therapy, with welfare measures. These even came to be christened with his own name '*kuroniowkas*'. The obituary defines him as unique within collective memory, having been a politician able to speak both for workers and intellectuals (*The Independent*, 21 June 2004).

Yet important as it is, the classification into dominants' memory, popular memory and counter-memory does not quite do justice to the complexity of the obituaries. These concepts spring from the Gramscian framework of organic, hegemonic and counter-hegemonic intellectuals (Popular Memory Group, 1982:211-215). But we need to address also the more Halbwachian angle, that of the obituary of the occupational public sphere. This is not to deny the continued significance of social groups, especially generation and class, within the field of power, where they set the limits for the occupational resources. But it is to argue that we should not short-circuit the independent effects exerted by the field itself with its history of its own producers. Such a concern also returns us to Benjamin's fertile explorations of cultural production, museumization and the debates about the collective inheritance these opened up.

Today's obituaries frequently commemorate those who, in the arts and sciences, have been engaged with the production of use-values, irrespective of their monetary or exchange-values. Unlike the contemporary making of celebrities, which focus intensely on the private sphere, the obituaries stress only their disinterested public concerns. I might mention the apparently harmonious careers of numerous scientists, such as the exemplary figure of Professor Keith Scott, who dedicated himself to improving crop yields (*Daily Telegraph*, 5 June 2000). Alternatively, there is the more conflict-wracked career of the flamboyant cosmologist Fred Hoyle, who eventually took flight from Cambridge due to committees hindering his work (*The Guardian*, 23 August 2001). Like many other obituaries, these two examples reveal their subjects' favoured positions in the classification of prestigious universities and well-stocked labs. Indeed, their obituaries help to shed light sociologically on the context of their discoveries.

More than any other category, we find artists, musicians, architects and writers, richer in cultural than economic capital, all grappling with the heritage of high modernism and—in the cases of the architects—struggling to find niches for their visions of urban improvement. In terms of Benjamin's analysis of 'cultural inheritance' the obituary columns represent an important stage of cultural canonization, winnowing out those with greater recognition from their competitors. Since the 1960s, however, they have increasingly incorporated producers in best-selling genres, that is, they more easily encompass popular artistic memory. Intriguingly, the obituary columnists' understanding of consecration is now often sharply divergent from those critics defending a minority culture tradition. For example, in a reversal of the Kantian aesthetic, the obituary for Winston Graham, author of the Poldark saga, assumes his entry into the literary canon precisely *because* of the pleasure he has given his readers as a mass (*The Guardian*, 14 June 2003).

Yet the obituaries also illuminate the great divergences globally within the social conditions of cultural production. Outside the West, the writers and artists remembered in the obituaries are usually figures who combined a cultural reputation amongst the educated and a popular public. I call these emblems of popular and counter-memory 'prophetic' figures, not least because they have run the risks of exile and death to use their voice (Bourdieu, 1993; see also Winter, 1995:184, 227). Amongst the many, I would choose here three writers to exemplify this point: Hoshang Golchiri (Iran, *The Independent*, 7 June 2000); *Le Monde*, 8 June 2000, Fadwa Tuqan (Palestinian, *The Times*, 3 Jan. 2004) and Ahmadou Karouma (Ivory Coast, *The Independent*, 16 Dec. 2003).

Conclusion

I have discussed obituaries that open windows onto fields of scientific and artistic production normally closed except to their occupational peer-groups. One of the attractions of the contemporary obituary is its potential reconnection of these separated or fragmented spheres of modernity, even given the clash of testimonies or evaluations of their subjects.

This set of national broadsheet portraits, however, is still remote from the world of workers and white-collar assistants. Intrinsically, the biographical document of life appeals to everyone. Adorno wrote famously of the two torn halves of Western culture, thus inviting hopes of their reunification. In terms of such cultural politics, could we not also hope that the transformation of the obituary will develop much further? By means of a greater democratization and a relegation of the old equivalence between masculinity and 'universalism', the older elite and patriarchal world might be superseded.

This would involve a wider set of ethical judgements than the restricted codes of the Establishment or the haute bourgeoisie defining the people who have shaped our world. It would involve a fresh set of calculations about what an exemplary or memorable life is, in a context sharply different from the relative freedom from material urgencies which obituary subjects up to now have generally possessed.[13] Such new models of exemplary prophetic action might appear unlikely, possibly even at odds with the inherent nature of distinction. Yet it is worth remembering that it was initially thought that the middle-class novel could never equal literature with aristocratic protagonists, and this manifestly proved to be false. Placing the lives of both the elite and other significant citizens under the scrutiny of the whole community was once the objective of Greek drama. It could become the extended function of the obituary.

Notes

1. The author is greatly indebted to the anonymous reviewers of an earlier draft, whose criticism helped her to clarify the argument.
2. "Memory is like a great field or spacious palace, a storehouse for countless images of all kinds … It is a vast, immeasurable sanctuary. Who can plumb its depths?" (Augustine, quoted Casey, 1987:205).
3. It is this notion of relative autonomy that Bourdieu (1993) will elaborate, in the context of secular literary or scientific fields.
4. Ricoeur's application of Halbwachs' subtext, aimed at avoiding the dangers of transcendental idealism, can be combined usefully with Bourdieu's deployment of Halbwachs in his theory of habitus.
5. Such amnesia is at stake, for example, in post-1945 East Germany's highlighting of their country's Communist and socialist resistance—to the exclusion of Jewish wartime suffering in the Second World War (Misztal, 2003:59).
6. I use this phrase to mean his increasing focus on texts alone.
7. Modern obituaries increasingly adopt the pattern of being written by fellow-specialists for the general public: this is an unusually illuminating form of communication.
8. The systematic study consists of a discourse analysis of approximately 100 obituaries from 2000 to 1, from the four British London-based broadsheets (*Daily Telegraph, The Times, The Guardian and The Independent*) and, for comparison, from *The New York Times and Le Monde.* A historical study is included, with two further *Times* samples, from 1900 and 1948. Since the systematic sample did not yield sufficient figures in each occupational group (scientists, architects, etc.) a qualitative study supplements this, drawn on a wider reading of obituaries from 1999 to 2004. Note that where percentages are used, the basis is the systematic sample only.
9. This goes up to 7 percent of the contemporary British newspaper sample.
10. My use of this term is the equivalent of the 'dominant' occupational groups classified by Bourdieu (1984) or, in Britain, by the Registrar-General's categories I and II.
11. Bytheway and Johnson's study found a similar 16 percent women in *The Guardian,* in 1995.
12. The memory of the dominants includes a declining number who have obituaries entirely because of their position, for example Sir W. Verco, the Herald of the College of Arms (*The Independent,* 15 March 2001).

13. Tam Dalyell has provided us with one model for this in his obituary for the railway toolmaker and politician, Richard Buchanan (*The Independent*, 24 Jan. 2003). Such obituaries are much more likely to appear in regional newspapers. See, for example, the obituary of Agnes Davies a primary head and local councillor (*The* [Glasgow] *Herald*, 21 Aug. 2003).

References

Benjamin, W. (1999) *The Arcades Project*. Cambridge, MA: Belknap Press of Harvard University Press.

Bergson, H. (1991 [1896]) *Matter and Memory*. New York: Zone.

Bloch, E. (1986) *The Principle of Hope*, vols I-III. Oxford: Blackwell.

Bourdieu, P. (1984) *Distinction*. London: RKP.

Bourdieu, P. (1993) *The Field of Cultural Production*. Cambridge: Polity Press.

Bytheway, B., & Johnson, J. (1996). Valuing lives? Obituaries and the life course. *Mortality*, 1(2):219–234.

Casey, E. (1987) *Remembering: A Phenomenological Study*. Bloomington: Indiana University Press.

Connerton, P. (1989) *How Societies Remember*. Cambridge: Cambridge University Press.

Coser, L. A. (ed.). (1992) *Maurice Halbwachs' On collective memory*. Chicago: University of Chicago Press.

Durkheim, E. (1964) *The Division of Labour*. Glencoe, IL: Free Press.

Durkheim, E. (1965) *Sociology and Philosophy*. London: Cohen & West.

Eiland, H., & Jennings, M.W. (eds) (2002) *Walter Benjamin: Selected Writings*. vol 3. Cambridge, MA: Belknap Press of Harvard University Press.

Ferguson, H. (2004) 'The Sublime and the Subliminal', *Theory, Culture and Society*, 21(3):1–34.

Foucault, M. (1977) *Language, Counter-Memory, Practice*. Ithaca: Cornell University Press.

Frisby, D. (1985) *Fragments of Modernity*. Cambridge: Polity.

Halbwachs, M. (1958) *The Psychology of Social Class*. London: Heinemann.

Halbwachs, M. (1980) *The Collective Memory*. London: Harper & Row.

Hall, S. (1981) 'Notes on Deconstructing the Popular', in R. Samuel (ed.), *People's History and Socialist Theory*, (pp. 227–40). London: Routledge.

Houlbrooke, R. (1998) *Death, Religion and the Family in England, 1480–1750*. Oxford: Clarendon Press.

Hume, J. (2000) *Obituaries in American Culture*. Jackson: University Press of Mississippi.

Hutton, P. (1993) *History as an Art of Memory*. Hanover: University of Vermont Press.

Lawlor, L. (2003). *The challenge of Bergsonism*. New York: Continuum.

Lowenthal, L. (1961) *Literature, Popular Culture and Society*. Palo Alto, CA: Pacific Books.

Marx, K. (1995 [1852]) The Eighteenth Brumaire of Louis Napoleon, in T. Carver (ed.) *Marx: Later Political Writings*. Cambridge: Cambridge University Press.

Matsuda, M. (1996) *The Memory of the Modern.* New York and Oxford: Oxford University Press.
Misztal, B. (2003) *Theories of Social Remembering.* Maidenhead: Open University Press.
Nora, P., et al. (1992) *Lieux de Mémoire.* vol. 3. Paris: Gallimard.
Nora, P., et al. (1996) *Realms of Memory.* vol. 1. New York: Columbia University Press.
Osiel, M. (1997) *Mass Atrocity, Collective Memory and the Law.* New Brunswick, NJ: Transaction.
Popular Memory Group (1982) 'Popular memory', pp. 205–252 in R. Johnson, G. McLennan, B. Schwarz and D. Sutton (eds) *Making Histories.* London: Hutchinson.
Ricoeur, P. (2000) *La Mémoire, l'histoire, l'oubli.* Paris: Seuil.
Schwartz, B. M. (1982) 'The Social Context of Commemoration: A Study in Collective Memory', *Social Forces, 61*(2), 374–397.
Schwarz, B. (1982) 'The "people" in History', pp. 44–95 in R. Johnson, G. McLennan, B. Schwarz and D. Sutton (eds) *Making Histories.* London: Hutchinson.
Smith, A. (2004) 'Migrancy, Hybridity and Postcolonial Studies', pp. 241–261 in N. Lazarus (ed.), *The Cambridge Companion to Postcolonial Literary Studies.* Cambridge: Cambridge University Press.
Stedman-Jones, S. (2001) *Durkheim Reconsidered.* Cambridge: Polity.
Winter, J. (1995) *Sites of Memory, Sites of Mourning.* Cambridge: Cambridge University Press.

CHAPTER 6
Fever*

KATHRYN HUGHES

During my apprentice years as a biographer, I could never quite understand this business of literary haunting. Writers much more experienced than I would appear in the press talking half-mournfully, half-ecstatically about the way in which their subjects regularly took over their lives. To hear them speak you would imagine that Catullus, Byron and Virginia Woolf were mostly to be found lounging round a Highbury kitchen, shoes kicked off, glass of Pinot Grigio in hand, waiting until their biographer emerged from their study ready for an evening of glorious reminiscence and high-quality literary chat.

For me it was never like that. My subjects did not take over my life. Indeed, I made sure that they knew their place, which was not in my head but in my computer, where they were obliged to stay until I commenced work at 8 o'clock sharp the next morning. I did not encourage fraternizing, day dreaming or speculation. 'Footstepping'—the practice of folding your own life into your subject's in order to get closer to him—had never worked for me. I had spent many chilly hours standing in historic houses and churchyards trying to force a fellow-feeling that stubbornly refused to come. This was often because there were nearly always other people present who insisted unwittingly on breaking the spell. One dreamy visit to a reconstructed Victorian schoolroom for a book I was writing on

* Originally published in *Lives for Sale* edited by Mark Bostridge and published by Continuum in 2004. Reprinted with permission.

governesses ended abruptly when one little girl whispered loudly, 'Mummy, what's that lady *for*?'

But halfway though my last book, a biography of George Eliot, something changed. I finally began to understand what all those seasoned biographers had been writing about all along. I'm not talking here simply about the writerly madness that comes from spending too much time on your own, in pyjamas, so that when you finally emerge blinking for a quick dash to the shops you become convinced that the police car on the corner has been staking out your house prior to arresting you for a crime so heinous that you can't even begin to think what it might be. I mean more the growing conviction that comes over biographers that their subjects have chosen them to tell their story (rather than the other way round) and are sending them uncanny messages from beyond the grave.

When I embarked on the George Eliot biography ten years ago I loved her work but knew little of her life. Within the first few months of research I discovered that as a young woman Eliot had been a frequent visitor to the unremarkable East London square where I live: a house I can see from my window happened to be the home of her best friend. A year into the project I was showing my then boyfriend photographs of the building in the Strand where Eliot had boarded and worked for several years when he suddenly announced that for most of the twentieth century the place had actually belonged to his family.

A non-biographer might see nothing strange here — in social and cultural terms Victorian London was a smaller place than it is today, with the same groups of busy, clever people popping up in different contexts all the time. But to me it was a sign that I had been uniquely chosen to write this book. Oh, all right then, to show you how mad I had actually become, I thought that *Eliot herself* had chosen me to write the book and was sending me encouraging little prods from beyond the grave to let me know that she was happy with her choice and the way that my work was going.

It gets madder, though. About four years into the Eliot project my 8-year-old godson asked me why I was 'talking funny'. By this I don't think Joe meant that I had suddenly adopted Eliot's carefully poshed-up Nuneaton accent. It was more that my sentences had become extraordinarily long, full of qualifying phrases, inflected with a knowing resignation about the folly of the human race combined with a tender affection for its basic, silly goodness. Joe, though, just found it tedious to wait while I meandered through a long, thoughtful disquisition on human appetite when all he'd asked for was a glass of Sunny D.

The moment the Eliot book was published, I was free from her haunting. She was no longer there when I woke up in the morning, sitting at the end of my bed nodding and smiling gently with encouragement. She no longer hovered over my shoulder looking at the VDU screen as I typed away. My speech even reverted to its usual jerky, fractured pattern and I found that, to be quite honest, I couldn't care less about suffering humanity and the pickle into which it had got itself. All I wanted to do was have fun—a particularly un-Eliot type concept.

I still feel slightly queasy coming clean about my biographical fever, with its hallucinations and manic grandiosity. It seems so shaming, exactly the kind of sentimental approach that the scrupulous scholar must take care to avoid. The end result, otherwise, is a kind of narcissistic identification with one's subject which can lead to some truly awful blunders. (No one, surely, wants to be accused of writing perennially about themselves — that is what we have Autobiography for.) But I think now that, used properly, this fever must be a good thing. For without that central, pulsing madness, how else could anyone give up five years of their life to living with an imaginary friend whom only they can see?

CHAPTER 7

The Will

Inheritance Distribution and Feuding Families

DEIRDRE DRAKE

> Fred made no answer: he was too utterly depressed. Twenty-four hours ago he had thought that instead of needing to know what he should do, he should by this time know that he needed to do nothing: that he should hunt in pink, have a first-rate hunter, ride to cover on a fine hack, be generally respected for doing so; moreover, that he should at once be able to pay Mr. Garth, and that Mary could no longer have any reason for not marrying him. All this was to have come without study or other inconvenience, purely by the favour of providence in the shape of an old man's caprice. But now, at the end of twenty-four hours, all those firm expectations were upset. (George Eliot, *Middlemarch*)

Inheritances given and received are the mainstay of Victorian novels. Plots hinge on whether someone becomes a beneficiary unexpectedly or—as the above example illustrates—expectations of great wealth fail to eventuate. Life trajectories, as those authors show us, can be irrevocably altered at the whim of a capricious testator. Battles over inheritance still excite attention, as continued interest in the sensationalized reporting of Anna Nicole Smith's story attests: the "scheming women" and "roguish companions" in Mr. Justice Hannen's 1885 judgment in *Wingrove v. Wingrove* routinely reappear in contemporary court cases.

Inheritance giving is the process by which one person's assets are transferred to others after death. The transfer of property under inheritance arrangements is important in the relationship between parents and children because it represents a provision for the next generation and acts as a tangible expression of intergenerational affection and family continuity. For most people, the giving or receiving of an inheritance becomes a normal part of experience at some point in the lifespan. Making decisions about inheritance may also serve as an important developmental task for adults in the latter part of life (Havighurst, 1972), if not before, with expectations that they will make wills and leave their goods to one or more beneficiaries. Conflicts arise when inheritance provisions are judged to be unfair (someone is disadvantaged), and such conflict is likely to sour relations within families, even bringing relatives before the courts. The effects of such conflicts over inheritance may persist in families for generations. Most people have a story to tell.

So who is interested in these stories, with their psychological importance, symbolic meaning, and legal implications? Researchers have taken a variety of approaches to the topic. A majority, mostly lawyers, have investigated inheritance distributions in samples of wills within the context of proposals for law reform, in relation either to intestacy (where there is no valid will) or to freedom of testation where personal dispositions are at stake (Browder, 1969; Dunham, 1963; Friedman, 1966). The focus in legal studies has been on assessing whether legislation accurately embodies people's perceptions of appropriate inheritance arrangements.

Working from another perspective, several sociologists have conceptualized inheritance as one component in a web of reciprocal assistance that binds generations together within families. They have used samples of wills (Rossi & Rossi, 1990) or samples of wills and interviews (Finch et al., 1996; Finch & Mason, 2000; Sussman et al., 1970) to consider the meaning of family relationships, for decisions about inheritance distribution arrangements have profound implications for relationships within families. As the noted anthropologist Jack Goody has argued: "The manner of splitting property is a manner of splitting people; it creates (or in some cases reflects) a particular constellation of ties and cleavages between husband and wife, parents and children, sibling and sibling, as well as wider kin" (1976, p. 3).

Both legal and social approaches recognize that inheritance distributions express (and create) relationships within particular families, between parents and children, and between siblings. These arrangements may consolidate intergenerational continuity, providing a model of parental affection and responsibility, or they may have the reverse effect, sowing discord between siblings and their descendants. The Wentworth case illustrates the potential for testamentary provisions to embroil beneficiaries in expensive legal disputes, exposing their most intimate family relations and financial transactions to the legal spotlight. Ms. Wentworth was the second daughter and second child of a wealthy land-owning family. She and her sister, together with their brother, were educated at boarding schools, and she and her sister then attended university in Sydney. Her brother left school and returned to work on the family properties, and their father made it clear that he intended to leave his estate to his son. Ms. Wentworth had been given sums of money from family assets at various times prior to her father's death in 1989; however, she was excluded from her father's will. Ms. Wentworth successfully appealed to the court for a share in her father's estate, although the judge held that any provision should be a modest one, taking into account "the unmeritorious aspects of her character and conduct." Ms. Wentworth appealed the case, which proceeded to come before the Australian courts, including the High Court of Australia, on various issues on several occasions.

Yet while giving or receiving an inheritance may be psychologically important for both will makers and their heirs, relatively few psychologists have examined contemporary inheritance as an expression of family relationships. The psychological research that does exist is largely confined to clinical forensic assessments of testamentary competence—that is, whether a testator has the cognitive capacity to make a valid will (e.g., Spar & Garb, 1992). Studies that have looked at the interesting aspects of normative expectations surrounding will making—that is, what inheritance means to people, and what constitutes fair or appropriate distribution—have been far rarer.

There are particular features of inheritance that set it apart from other aspects of family relationships as a focus for research. Uniquely, perhaps, in the context of family relationships, inheritance distributions are arrangements to which no further adjustments can be made by the will maker, since they take effect only after the death of one of the parties. In this sense, although inheritance may extend the relationship between relatives, usually parent and child, beyond death, it also represents the final act in that relationship.

Inheritance giving is also an odd domain in that it is both public and private, extremely personal yet formal and legally constrained. Writing a will is a personal and private activity in that the wishes of the testator expressed in the will may be known to very few people while the will maker is still alive, and his or her wishes take effect in the form of a document that becomes public only after death. Even those who will benefit later under the will need not know about the testator's wishes for the distribution of his or her property. However, although wills describe individuals' personal desires for the disposition of their property, these dispositions take place by means of the law. As Finch et al. observe, "the law creates the very concept of a will as the mechanism for the transmission of property" (1996, p. 20). Indeed, a will must meet certain legal criteria to be accepted as legally valid, and, in common law jurisdictions such as the United Kingdom, Australia, and New Zealand, there are legislative provisions for family members to challenge the distribution if they consider that they have not been adequately recognized. This means that inheritance distributions not only involve personal choices but to some extent are dictated by the law.

Notwithstanding the dual nature of inheritance arrangements as both private and public and both personal and legally constrained, such arrangements would appear to warrant explicit consideration as an expression of what Erikson (1997) called the "grand-generativity" of older age, incorporating care for the future of one's family. Decisions about the distribution of one's estate typically involve acknowledging relationships that have been important to the testator and making contributions to future generations, for writing a will that gives effect to one's wishes for the distribution of one's estate is very much a developmental task of later life. Does writing a will have distinctive meaning for older adults? After all, there are many life transitions when it is appropriate to make a will—for example, on the acquisition of assets, marriage (or divorce), or the birth of a child. Yet Finch et al. (1996) found that making a final will was an activity of older people. In Britain, 75% of testators write their wills in the ten years prior to their deaths, at a median age of 77 years. Of course, this does not rule out the possibility that many testators may have made previous wills in their younger years, which they later revised. Certainly a proportion of adults either die young or die leaving an unrevised will written many years previously. Nonetheless, the fact that so many final wills are written in a person's later years points to the importance of characterizing testamentary judgments as a developmental task for older adults.

In both English (Finch et al., 1996) and American (Sussman et al., 1970) samples, older and younger testators made different types of wills, reflecting "two different underlying rationales, or frameworks of meaning related to the act of bequeathing" (Finch et al., p. 84). Older testators, for example, were less egalitarian than their younger counterparts, Sussman et al. found. Wills made by younger testators in Finch et al.'s study were more likely to describe kin "ascriptively," so that what was significant was their genealogical position in relation to the testator, resulting in division of the estate into portions among several beneficiaries of the same type (e.g., children). In older testators' wills, however, particularly those of women, a beneficiary's portion was contingent on other aspects of the testator's relationship with him or her (e.g., a close emotional relationship) and acknowledged the individuality of particular relationships. Widows, in particular, divided estates in ways that were distinctively personal and acknowledged a wide range of relationships. Wills of younger testators may distinguish less between beneficiaries because these parents have not yet experienced differential caregiving provided by their children (Sussman et al.), or because they recognize that by the time such wills take effect, any circumstances of need or desert that prompted original distinctions will most likely have changed (Finch et al.).

Differences between wills of older and younger testators, Finch et al. (1996) claimed, reflect distinct underlying rationales. For younger testators, a will is intended to cater for an unlikely calamity: the unexpected death of the will maker. For older testators, writing a will involves a realistic confrontation with their own mortality and an opportunity for a life review. In later life, these studies reveal, writing a will represents a way of acknowledging the particularity of one's own circumstances—for example, where an older person is in receipt of assistance from children that cannot be reciprocated, or where a parent recognizes an adult child's particular needs. Older adults look back over a lifetime of family relationships to make final judgments about distributions in anticipation of death.

Inheritance not only completes some vital developmental tasks at the end of the lifespan, it is also important for individuals in locating the self within an intergenerational cycle. Erikson, Erikson, and Kivnick (1986) and Kotre (1984) both suggest that people rework familial heritages before passing them on to future generations. In Erikson et al.'s study, children were seen to be a validation of parents' generativity. Grandchildren were the extension of the self into the future. Accordingly, generativity received final confirmation in the way in which older adults hoped to be remembered by their grandchildren after death. Similarly, "dying well" was the last parental imperative identified by Huyk (1989, p. 143): leaving a fair will (fairness was undefined) is one way that parents can show their concern for surviving generations. From this perspective, writing a will to provide for children becomes a final generative act, one that not only demonstrates a concern for children but also describes the summing up of affairs, an acknowledgment of the inevitability of death. Indeed, Whitbourne and Weinstock (1979) characterized failing to write a will as symptomatic of a "foreclosed" older adult who is unable to confront death with integrity.

Responsibility to future generations notwithstanding, contemporary married testators overwhelmingly favor leaving their entire estate to the spouse who survives them, generally to the widow, given the gender differential in longevity (Browder, 1969; Dunham, 1963; Engler-Bowles & Kart, 1983; Finch et al., 1996). This contrasts with nineteenth-century inheritance practices that emphasized lineal over conjugal relationships

(Shammas, Salmon, & Dahlin, 1987). The intergenerational dimension of inheritance is not usurped, however; it is merely postponed. Widowed parents usually pass the estate on to their children (Dunham, 1963).

What, then, are the issues that face parents who may want to recognize children in the will? From the perspective of an older parent of adult children who is aware that time is finite and death approaches (Neugarten, 1976), writing a will raises two fundamental questions: first, whether there is an imperative to include children in inheritance dispositions, and second, if there is such an imperative, how the estate should be divided between them.

The imperative to include children in inheritance dispositions is a complex issue. Testators have the right to dispose of their property as they desire: common law legal systems (United Kingdom, Canada, Australia, New Zealand, much U.S. law) allow testators freedom of testation and hence the power to disinherit children altogether if they so wish. Other legal systems (e.g., France and Italy) do not allow the same degree of testamentary freedom; rather, they dictate that at least a proportion of the estate be given to children and be divided among them in specified ways. It would be a mistake, however, to see testamentary freedom in common law jurisdictions as completely unfettered. Legal mechanisms may be invoked that have the effect of altering the will under various circumstances. Thus, courts are prepared to alter wills where they find that the testator was not competent to make a will, or was subject to "undue influence," or where provisions in the will are considered to be contrary to public interest (for example, conditional gifts in restraint of marriage: "I bequeath my estate to my son, provided that he refrain from marrying"). These jurisdictions also have legislation (usually known as "Testator's Family Maintenance" or "Family Provision") that allows beneficiaries—or family members who feel they ought to be beneficiaries—to apply to the court for a share of the estate if they have not been properly provided for in the will.

Cases where parents have tried to control the estate from beyond the grave have reflected concerns of the time. Older cases often involved religion. The High Court of Australia case of *Church Property Trustees, Diocese of Newcastle v. Ebbeck*, decided in 1960, is typical. The testator, who died in 1957, had in his last will, following a life interest to his widow, left his considerable estate to his three sons in equal shares. The bequests to the sons were subject to a proviso that each son and his wife should "profess the Protestant faith," and that if the trustees were not satisfied that the son and his wife professed the Protestant faith, then that son "should absolutely forfeit his share." In fact, prior to the will being written, two of the sons had married Roman Catholics, and the third was about to do so. More recently, in *Littras and Anor v. Littras and Anor*, decided in the

Victorian Supreme Court in 1995, the father's bequest to his children, who were in their early teens at the time of his death, was subject to their using his surname. The father and the children's mother had divorced when the children were very young, and the children's surname had been the topic of considerable disagreement.

Although common law societies allow testators self-determination in the distribution of their assets, as Delphy and Leonard (1992) point out, bequeathing property outside the family requires the intention to be formally recorded in a will, unlike devolution to spouse or children, which happens automatically under intestacy legislation. This implies that inheritance by children needs no justification. Certainly the legal system describes testation as subject to "a moral responsibility of no ordinary importance" where to disinherit children "violates ... an obligation of the moral law" (*Banks v. Goodfellow*, 1870). Studies by lawyers also suggest that people have strong feelings that children should not be disinherited (Dunham, 1963) and regard disinheritance as unnatural (Friedman, 1966). Accordingly, wills that disinherit children in favor of outsiders are likely to be scrutinized for signs of testamentary incompetence (Friedman). The common usage of the word "disinherit" is a further illustration of societal expectation: a non-family member who does not benefit from a person's will is unlikely to be described as having been disinherited, yet the verb describing a negating action would almost certainly be used in the case of a child or close family member who was not provided for in the will.

In fact, most contemporary testators *do* leave their estates predominantly to their families (Finch et al., 1996). Nearly three-quarters of Finch et al.'s English sample left their entire estates to family, with only 2% bequeathing all of it to non-kin. Clignet's (1992) review of U.S. studies of inheritance patterns revealed similarly low levels of disinheritance. The proportion of individuals bequeathing their estates to family in Finch et al.'s research had not changed over the four decades covered by the study, implying consistent ideas about who ought to be included in inheritance dispositions. Further, the people most commonly included in the will—spouse, children, and, less frequently, grandchildren, nieces and nephews—suggested a narrow and conventional definition of family relationships.

So why not simply mandate that children be included in inheritance distributions to prevent the possibility that testators may ignore their responsibilities? In the words of Mr. Justice Cockburn in the seminal English case of *Banks v. Goodfellow* (1870), upholding the right of testators to divide their estates as they see fit ensures that the distribution will be "accurately adjusted to the requirements of each particular case" because "some may be better provided for than others; some may be more deserving than others; some from age, or sex, or physical infirmity, may stand in greater need of assistance" (p. 563). He later adds that being able to determine who will inherit from them provides older adults with a useful way of ensuring that they are looked after in their old age. Paradoxically—given public disapproval of disinheritance—when asked about testamentary freedom, a majority of Sussman et al.'s (1970) participants rejected the proposition that testators ought to be legally compelled to include children in the estate. Participants with higher levels of formal education were more likely to uphold testamentary freedom, leading Sussman et al. to speculate that they were better able to distinguish between legal and moral responsibility. Similarly, a testator's right to self-determination was rated as being very important by participants in their seventies responding to scenarios based on contested cases involving disinheritance (Drake, 2000). Yet the participants in Drake's study also thought that children should be included in the will.

Does a normative expectation that parents will leave their estate to their children create a corresponding right of the children to receive? Although most people do leave their estates to their children, there is considerable resistance to the idea that it should be compulsory: people oppose any sense of automatic inheritance by children (Finch & Mason, 2000; Sussman et al., 1970; Todd & Jones, 1972). The responsibility is something to be taken up (or not) as the parent wishes. Responsibility in families generally does not give rise to a right to assistance in those to whom responsibility is owed (Finch, 1989). Needy family members should not *expect* to be helped. The expectation takes away from the giver the discretion to help, and hence diminishes the gratitude the giver is owed. Consequently, even though people believe that parents have a responsibility to include children in the will, they also value the right to self-determination expressed by including children if they wish.

The coexistence of concern about disinheritance of children (Dunham, 1963; Friedman, 1966) with rejection of mandatory inclusion of children in the inheritance reveals a great deal about the symbolic meaning of inheritance. Freedom of testation is justified on the basis that it enables testators to distribute their estates so as to cater for their families' particular circumstances, but this explanation is only partial. After all, social welfare services assess individuals' needs regularly when allocating benefits, and the courts take on an assessment role when adjudicating cases under Family Provision legislation. Although a state-run system of inheritance distribution might be more costly to administer, it is hardly impossible to envisage. It would seem, however, that the idea of legally dictating how inheritance is to be distributed undermines the status of inheritance as a gift from one generation to the next. Instead, parents *choose* to leave their possessions to their children. It is precisely the discretionary quality of inheritance giving that renders it powerfully symbolic of parental responsibility and affection.

How Should an Inheritance Be Divided Among Children?

Research on inheritance practices suggests that the majority of parents in the late twentieth century divide their estates equally among their children (Finch et al., 1996). Further, distribution preference studies (e.g., Simon, Fellows, & Rau, 1982) reveal that, when asked in fairly abstract terms, most people endorse equality as their preferred distribution principle. Intestacy legislation also dictates that children should receive equal shares in their parents' estate. The high incidence of equal distribution in recent samples of wills, described with little comment by both Finch et al. (1996) and Sussman et al. (1970), implies that equality is such a dominant assumption as to go unquestioned. Yet not all estates are divided equally among children. For example, Dunham (1963), Finch et al., and Sussman et al. all identify cases where children were given different shares, or where one or more children were excluded altogether. In situations where children differ in their life circumstances, older adults may need to temper their commitment to general principles in light of specific circumstances (Pratt & Norris, 1994).

What, then, are some of the factors that influence the distribution of inheritance? First, no discussion of inheritance giving is complete without considering the role of gender. Historically, gender has been supremely important, and gender-based inheritance distributions prior to the twentieth century were explicit: both testators and beneficiaries were predominantly male. Although gender is not as prominent a factor in contemporary Western inheritance distributions as it was under primogeniture, disposing of assets by will is intimately linked with the traditional masculine role of provider/manager of money. Historical studies of inheritance practices suggest that concern about a "bad spouse"—a widow who might disinherit children against the father's expectation that his wealth be transmitted to his descendants—and lack of faith in women's financial acumen were common before the second half of the twentieth century (Shammas, Salmon, & Dahlin, 1987). Early nineteenth century testators left their widows a life interest or bequeathed the estate directly to sons with explicit instructions to care for the widowed mother, thus bypassing the widow altogether in terms of self-determination (Engler-Bowles & Kart, 1983). Although this testamentary practice has changed such that most widows now inherit their husband's estate in their own right (Finch et al., 1996), this change in practice has not necessarily been accompanied by cultural expectations that widows should do what they wish with the estate. When contemporary widows do inherit the estate, they may be seen as only temporary owners. Rosenfeld (1980) suggests that, although widows gain power within the family from the inheritance, it is also the case that "families often reappraise a widow's financial abilities, not to mention her tastes and spending habits, after she has inherited an estate" (p. 331).

In studies where women as well as men have had money or other assets to bequeath, the gender of the testator also seems to have exerted an influence on the type of distribution preferred. Women who inherit money from their husbands rather than earning it themselves are more likely than those who have earned money to feel that they do not have a say in how the money is distributed and that they ought to follow their deceased husbands' distribution preferences (Clignet, 1992). In Clignet's study, overall, women were more egalitarian with sons but tended to punish daughters for particularistic reasons (e.g., where daughters had disregarded their mother's wishes). Women were also more likely to disinherit children than were men, who confined themselves to disinheriting more distant kin (Rosenfeld, 1982). Rosenfeld attributed women's greater tendency to disinherit children to their higher expectations of filial assistance.

Historically, the gender of inheritors was also crucial, especially under primogeniture practices. The first half of the twentieth century saw a decrease in the unequal treatment of children, especially in terms of inegalitarianism between sons and daughters (Clignet, 1992). Daughters, especially if unmarried, were commonly left the family home (Clignet, 1992; Finch, 1989). Overall, Clignet concluded that in the first half of the twentieth century, parents had very different expectations of their sons and daughters. Sons were to succeed professionally, whereas daughters were to marry well, but also to be prepared to return home to care for their aging parents. Indeed, filial behaviors fulfilled parental expectations. Sons were more mobile and more likely to move away from their parents than were daughters, who generally remained close by, positioned to help when necessary. Children were disinherited if they were perceived as failing to follow the norm of reciprocity by not assisting their parents.

Although egalitarian treatment of sons and daughters seems to be the common practice in English-speaking countries at the start of the twenty-first century (Finch et al., 1996), caution must be exercised before one concludes that gender is no longer a factor in inheritance judgments. Finch et al. found that children were treated equally in a broad sense but were often given different bequests on the basis of gender; for instance, daughters are given jewelry and sons are given watches. Even though distinctions made between beneficiaries on the basis of gender were less significant, or less consistent, than distinctions due to kin type, Finch et al. speculate that there may still be some difference in the value of bequests left to men and women. However, data obtained from analyses of wills do not allow further examination of this point, because most wills do not incorporate a valuation of the bequests included. Even examination of the economic value of assets may not always, in isolation, reveal disadvantage. In a materialist analysis of inheritance, Delphy and Leonard (1992) emphasize that transmission of status often occurs alongside the transmission of property. Thus, a son inherits the status of farmer along with the farm, but where daughters inherit assets of comparable value to what their brothers receive, they are more likely to be given cash than land or business interests.

Gender is not the only factor that may reduce adherence by testators to equal distribution. Contemporary and historical distribution studies provide examples of other arrangements that operate in addition to equality in the domain of inheritance, often reflecting particular family circumstances. In nineteenth-century farming communities in Ireland (Kennedy, 1991) and Europe (Goody, 1976), explicit written agreements were drawn up between generations that promised the farm to one child, who, in return, was required to care for the parents for the rest of their lives. Contested legal cases often involve situations where children feel their contributions, whether instrumental or financial, have been overlooked. Not all exchanges are formal: Schwartz (1993), Engler-Bowles and Kart (1983), and Sussman et al. (1970) identify wills where testators made bequests that acknowledged assistance given to them, whether by family members or others such as friends. In these cases, there was no evidence of any agreement that care would be recognized in the will or that the care was provided on that basis.

Attempts to describe distribution principles are few. Sussman et al.'s (1970) analysis of wills and interviews with family members of testators is an exception. Sussman et al. conclude that inheritance constitutes a reward for services rendered: children "provide parents with physical care, emotional support, affection and the niceties of social interaction in their declining years; in return, they receive financial compensation" (p. 119). Sussman et al. found that, as a minimum requirement to justify being left an inheritance, a child should be in contact with parents. A child who provided care to a parent who needed it, usually to the extent of taking the parent into his or her home, was entitled to be recognized for the care in the will. However, mere closeness or greater contact did not lead to a larger share in cases where the parent was independent. Where unequal distributions generated family conflict, siblings did not dispute the fairness of the reciprocity principle itself, but argued about whether reciprocity was justified in their particular case. In these cases, the dispute was likely to be over how much assistance had actually been given to parents. Other empirical evidence from the study, however, belies Sussman et al.'s conclusions. Whereas some individuals accepted that unequal distribution was an appropriate response to differential caregiving, several relatives who received smaller shares or were disinherited in favor of their more "caring" kin felt that the blood relationship was a more important basis for distribution than was the provision of assistance. A number of disinherited children and other kin spoke disparagingly of relatives who provided care with the expectation of being rewarded in the inheritance. Care, they suggested, should be provided out of affection, not mercenary anticipation. Other unequal distributions documented by Sussman et al. were based on children's special needs, from extreme cases of disability, to youth (young orphans with adult siblings), to divorce. In two studies that asked older adults to respond to hypothetical scenarios where one child was more needy or more deserving (in terms of having assisted an elderly parent) than the other, Drake (2000) found that most respondents were prepared to endorse an unequal distribution under certain circumstances, despite having stated their preference for equal distribution in the abstract. Both principles, need and deservingness, were qualified significantly. Children who were needier than their siblings as a result of circumstances clearly not of their own doing (e.g., ill health) were given more than those whose needs arose more ambiguously (e.g., employment difficulties). These data mirror the legal description of testamentary responsibility: parental obligation toward "lame ducks" does not extend to those who are "morally or otherwise undeserving" (Dickey, 1993, p. 81).

Judgments about reciprocity, too, appear to involve subtle, contextualized discriminations instead of a blanket application of a normative rule. Most strikingly, participants rarely labeled leaving a larger share to a child in terms of repayment. Rather, they referred to, for example, appropriate recognition. By hesitating to see the inheritance as the payment of a debt, these participants were acknowledging the complex role reciprocity plays in close relationships. Reciprocity operates implicitly, and people prefer to see their relationships in terms of affection rather than exchange (Clark & Chrisman, 1994).

Inheritance giving requires older adults to make important decisions that involve determining responsibilities, evaluating contributions, making reciprocal contributions across generations and, primarily, expressing family relationships. There is no question that decisions about inheritance giving are an important developmental task for older adults (Havighurst, 1972). In their effects, both positive and negative, they are important for the well-being of the testator's family. Implicit in people's judgments is the recognition that inheritance distributions are a special activity. They constitute at once a financial provision for children, which can take care of their material needs, and a symbolic acknowledgment of the relationship between parent and child. This parental role-related activity involves interpreting abstract, sometimes conflicting, culturally normative principles in the specific situations that arise in family life.

Making appropriate dispositions requires drawing on complex sets of social expectations about relationships, about roles as parents, sons, and daughters in families, and about responsibilities between generations. Parents provide for children as particular individuals and as members of the generations of their families who will succeed them and through whom they live on into the future. Including children in distributions is a final imperative for older parents, an expression of the parental role that encompasses—as a 73-year-old man interviewed by Drake (2000) describes it—"a duty to provide, to be loyal and not to leave a bitter heritage."

References

Banks v. Goodfellow, L.R. 5 Q.B., 549 (Queen's Bench, 1870).

Browder, O. J. (1969). Recent patterns of testate succession in the United States and England. *Michigan Law Review, 67*, 1303–1360.

Clark, M. S., & Chrisman, K. (1994). Resource allocation in intimate relationships: trying to make sense of a confusing literature. In M. J. Lerner & G. Mikula (Eds.), *Entitlement and the affectional bond: Justice in close relationships* (pp. 65-88). New York: Plenum.

Clignet, R. (1992). *Death, deeds and descendants: Inheritance in modern America.* New York: Aldine de Gruyter.

Delphy, C., & Leonard, D. (1992). *Familiar exploitation: A new analysis of marriage in contemporary western society.* Cambridge: Polity.

Dickey, A. (1992). *Family provision after death.* Sydney: Law Book Company Limited.

Drake, D. G., (2000). *Older adults' views of inheritance-giving: responsibility and distribution.* Unpublished doctoral dissertation, University of Melbourne, Australia.

Dunham, A. (1963). The method, process and frequency of wealth transmission at death. *The University of Chicago Law Review, 30*, 241–285.

Eliot, G., (1871/1985). *Middlemarch.* Middlesex: Penguin.

Engler-Bowles, C. A., & Kart, C. S. (1983). Intergenerational relations and testamentary patterns: An exploration. *The Gerontologist, 23*(2), 167–173.

Erikson, E. H., Erikson, J. M., & Kivnick, H. Q. (1986). *Vital involvement in old age.* New York: W. W. Norton & Company.

Erikson, E. H., & Erikson, J. M. (1997 [1982]). *The life cycle completed.* New York: W. W. Norton & Company.

Finch, J. (1989). *Family obligations and social change.* Cambridge: Polity Press.

Finch, J., Hayes, L., Mason, J., Masson, J., & Wallis, L. (1996). *Wills, inheritance and families.* Oxford: Clarendon.

Finch, J., & Mason, J. (2000). *Passing on: Kinship and inheritance in England.* London: Routledge.

Friedman, L. M. (1966). The law of the living, the law of the dead: Property, succession and society. *Wisconsin Law Review, 1966*(Spring), 340–378.

Goody, J. (1976). Introduction. In J. Goody (Ed.), *Family and Inheritance: Rural society in Western Europe* (pp. 1–10). Cambridge: Cambridge University Press.

Havighurst, R. J. (1972). *Developmental tasks and education.* 3rd ed. New York: Longman.

Huyck, M. H. (1989). Midlife parental imperatives. In R. A. Kalish (Ed.), *Midlife loss: Coping strategies* (pp. 115–148). Newbury Park, CA: Sage.
Kennedy, L. (1991). Farm succession in modern Ireland: Elements of a theory of inheritance. *Economic History Review*, *64*(3), 477–499.
Kotre, J. (1984). *Outliving the self: Generativity and the interpretation of lives*. Baltimore: Johns Hopkins University Press.
Neugarten, B. L. (1976). Adaptation and the life cycle. *Counselling Psychologist*, *6*(1), 16–20.
Pratt, M. W., & Norris, J. E. (1994). *The social psychology of aging: A cognitive perspective*. Oxford: Blackwell.
Rosenfeld, J. P. (1980). Social strain of probate. *Journal of Marriage and Family Therapy*, 6(3), 327–334.
Rosenfeld, J. P. (1982). Disinheritance and will contests. *Marriage and Family Review*, *5*(3), 75–86.
Rossi, A., & Rossi, P. (1990). *Of human bonding: Parent-child relations across the life course*. New York: Aldine de Gruyter.
Schwartz, T. P. (1993). Testamentary behavior: Issues and evidence about individuality, altruism and social influences. *Sociological Quarterly*, *34*(2), 337–355.
Shammas, C., Salmon, M., & Dahlin, M. (1987). *Inheritance in America: From colonial times to the present*. New Brunswick: Rutgers University Press.
Simon, R. J., Fellows, M. L., & Rau, W. (1982). Public opinion about property distribution at death. *Marriage and Family Review*, *5*(3), 25–38.
Sussman, M. B., Cates, J. N., & Smith, D. T. (1970). *The family and inheritance*. New York: Russell Sage Foundation.
Todd, J. E., & Jones, L. M. (1972). *Matrimonial property*. London: Stationery Office.
Whitbourne, S. K., & Weinstock, C. S. (1979). *Adult development: The differentiation of experience*. New York: Holt, Rinehart & Winston.

CHAPTER 8

Complaints About Health Care in the United Kingdom Following a Person's Death

JUDITH ALLSOP

Introduction

The unanticipated death of a loved one combined with a perception of wrongdoing by a health care provider may result in private grief entering the public domain. The action can be taken by an aggrieved individual, or through some form of group or class action if others in a similar position are identified. Matters can also be brought into the political arena, as was the case in the Shipman Inquiry (see Fifth Report 4), following the deaths of at least 15, and probably over 200 mainly elderly patients over a period of years who were treated by Harold Shipman, a general practitioner in Manchester in the United Kingdom.

As Jennings commented in an address to the American Political Science Association in 1999, the process of pursuing a complaint has received little research attention, despite the great deal of interest shown by the media in such cases of what he calls "pain and loss" experiences. This chapter draws on an analysis of written complaints made over two decades in a particular health area in the United Kingdom, and describes the socio-psychological factors drawn from these data that motivate complaint following the death.

When a death occurs in circumstances that trouble those with a close affective relationship, there are strong psychological and social drivers based on the relationship with the dead person to seek an explanation, and perhaps some form of public resolution to the bereavement. This is particularly the case if the death is sudden, unexpected, or untimely and there is also concern about the treatment provided by medical practitioners. Survivors may be bound, as was Hamlet, by the social relationship and obligations they had in life to the dead person, pledging to avenge and to remember the deceased person "while memory holds a seat." Contemporary society offers the opportunity for resolution other than by the sword through the making of a complaint to an appropriate public body.

I will also describe recent cases in the United Kingdom during which groups have formed to take collective action following the death of loved ones where wrongdoing on the part of health providers is alleged. Several of these cases have reached the national political level and are leading to policy change. Whether this is individual or collective action, the socio-psychological motivations to take action appear to be deeply embedded in the human consciousness.

The chapter is structured in the following way. First, I discuss complaint making in general and some of the theoretical approaches to understanding disputes: that is, when a complaint is accepted as legitimate by a third party. Second, I describe the methodology used to analyze data from the study and report some key findings. Third, I present data on the characteristics of complainants, with an emphasis on the subset of cases where a death occurred. Fourth, I look at different types of social relationship between the complainant and the dead person and what complainants said about their moral obligations to the person who had died, and I speculate on what complainants might gain from making a complaint by pursuing it to the level of a tribunal. Finally, I consider under what circumstances collective action is likely to occur based on cases in the United Kingdom, and also how United Kingdom government policy with regard to medical practice has developed in response.

Naming, Blaming, and Complaining

The theoretical literature on dispute over the past 25 years draws on several social science disciplines and provides several different approaches to understanding complaint making (Hirschman, 1970; Felstiner, Abel & Sarat,1981; Trubek, 1981; Gulliver, 1979; Mather & Yngvesson, 1981; Coates & Penrod, 1981). In addition to these, in the United Kingdom there have been a few empirical studies of complaints in health care settings (Owen,

1991; Lloyd-Bostock, 1992; Allsop, 1994; Rosenthal, Mulcahy, & Lloyd-Bostock, 1999).

To complain is to bring a private hurt into the public arena, so requiring a public response. Complaint making has been shown to be shaped by the complainant's perception of the severity of an incident, as well as his or her own social position and other characteristics, such as age. Individualistic motivations and assessment of what will be gained by making a complaint are also implicated. Moreover, the availability of social support networks tends to facilitate the likelihood of a person making a complaint (Mulcahy, Allsop, & Shirley, 1996). These characteristics of the complainant will vary according to cultural assumptions and the particular complaint setting. Furthermore, the options available for complainants, their knowledge of procedures, and the response of complaint handlers will affect the particular course a complaint takes.

Felstiner, Abel, and Sarat (1981) conceptualized the process of complaint making as involving several components: an incident must be "named" as injurious, and someone or something must be "blamed" for the injury in order for a "claim" or "voicing" to occur. Festinger et al. also showed that the propensity to "name, blame and claim" varies with the particular circumstances. This model draws implicitly on attribution theory (Tedeschi & Reiss, 1981; Tennen & Affleck, 1990), an approach that has been extended by Jennings (1999), who argues that the attribution of cause has shifted over time from what could be thought of as impersonal or "supernatural" forces to personalizing blame and responsibility to individuals. In addition, changing social forces, including media amplification, serve to make collective action more likely and, in turn, to gain wider political support for certain causes over others.

Complaint Handling in the General Practice Setting: Context, Data Collection, and Analysis

The chapter draws on an empirical study undertaken by the author using data collected over an eleven-year period, 1976–1986 inclusive, and published later as a PhD thesis (Allsop, 1998). The data were the case files of all complaints in one health area in the United Kingdom (Three Boroughs Health Authority) that reached a local-level tribunal (at the time called a Medical Service Committee), and the notes from the researcher's participant observation as a committee member. Medical Service Committees were statutory committees of health area-based Family Practitioner Committees (FPCs), the bodies then responsible for administering family practitioners' (GPs') contracts.

The remit of the tribunal related to GPs' contractual obligations. GPs were expected to provide first-line medical care of a reasonable standard to their registered patients in the surgery and, if necessary, at the patient's home over the 24-hour period. They were also expected to refer patients to other specialist services where necessary and to provide emergency medical treatment to anyone. Complaints received were screened by the administrative staff within the FPC and passed to the lay chair of the tribunal to decide whether the allegations constituted a *prima facie* breach in the GP's terms of service. Over the study period, 10% of the complaints received each year reached a hearing. Since the time of this study the structures available for complaint making have changed and Medical Service Committees no longer exist. In 1996, this complaint system was replaced with a less formal local process geared to learning from complaints (Department of Health, 1996), and in 2004 the Healthcare Commission took over the responsibility for handling all complainants dissatisfied with the local process.

The Medical Service Committee, in effect at the time of the data collection, consisted of three local GPs and three lay members, with a lay chair, and it followed a formal legal format. Both the complainant and the medical practitioner had the opportunity to put their cases in writing and orally, and each party could be accompanied by a supporter and witnesses, if they so chose. In circumstances where the committee found that the doctor had not met his or her contractual obligations, it had a range of sanctions available. The committee could recommend a reprimand or financial withholding, or could have the matter be referred to another, rarely used employment tribunal with powers to terminate the doctor's contract with the U.K. National Health Service (NHS). Following the hearing, the complainant received a report of the proceedings, which included the recommendation(s) that had been made. If complainants were still dissatisfied, it was then open to them to appeal, or to pursue the issue through the professional body, the General Medical Council and eventually to the civil courts as a claim on the grounds of negligence.

Over the 11 years of the study, 110 cases were adjudicated. The complainant's letters found in the case files provide naturalistic data for study because they give accounts in the complainants' own words of what had happened, and what they wanted to happen. As such, they were *cultural scripts* revealing both the complainants' understanding of the world and their construction of an account (Giddens, 1991; Cohen, 1994). The accounts reflect complainants' notions of responsibility and obligation and their view of the responsibility of health professionals, in this case the GP. Data were also drawn from field notes from most of the hearings (85%). The method of analysis adopted in the main study was inductive and is described here in detail because it underpinned the later analysis of the subset of complaints in cases where a death had occurred.

Initially, descriptive information was taken from the record of each case. From these it was possible to establish who had complained, what aspect of medical care they complained about, and what they wanted to happen as a result of the complaint. An early finding was that (apart from three cases where complaints were made by the FPC itself and related to improper claims for fees and allowances) all cases heard by the tribunal related to the care provided for ill people (107). A large majority of complaints about health care (85%) were made by those with a caring responsibility for them: 80 (73%) were brought by relatives or friends on behalf of a patient, 19 (17%) were brought by the patients themselves, 6 (5%) were brought by the Government Social Services Department, and the remaining two by the local Community Health Council and a charitable body. (Three Boroughs Medical Service Committee Hearings, 1976–1986).

The Structure of Complaint Letters

The complaint letters relating to the care of patients (107) typically contain a complex temporal account of events surrounding an illness episode from the complainant's perspective, understanding, and knowledge. Letters describe interactions with other family members and with health and social service professionals in the surgery, over the telephone, and/or in the patient's home. In the home setting, interactions were shaped by the patient's domestic arrangements where the patient or carer bore some responsibility for deciding on the action to be taken.

Considered as narratives, the letters have a similar dramatic structure. Central to the story is the patient. The complainant and those for whom he or she stood are cast as heroes whose actions were justified in terms of what was necessary for the care of the patient and the carer's moral obligation to do the best for that person. Complainants also seek to justify the action of complaining, and most do so in terms of their altruistic motives—to prevent the same thing happening to others. This could also be interpreted as a means to preserve their moral identity as worthy complainants. In the United Kingdom at the time period under study (1976–1986), a common cultural assumption was that making a complaint required justification (Allsop, 1994).

Conversely, complainants often cast the doctor as the villain who was incompetent and uncaring. Performance is assessed against an implicit ideal of the service a doctor ought to give and how a doctor ought to behave. In other words, a notion of professional competence and morality is invoked against the doctor, who is found wanting. In the study, all complainants criticize the doctor's manner using terms such as "unconcerned," "disinterested," "lethargic," "unprofessional," and "rude," or in general not behaving "as a doctor should." Some are described as being a "threat to the public" or "dangerously incompetent."

Many letters are collective accounts. As Kidder (1981, p. 725) remarks: "Individuals may become involved in disputing as agents of collectives and individual actions may be shaped primarily by the internal dynamics of the groups to which they belong." The complainant stands for others who, typically, are other members of a family group—for example, one letter says explicitly: "We, the family wish you to take action against Dr. Y." Understandings and constructions of family obligations are manifest in both the complaint letters and in the testimony of those who attended the tribunal hearing as friends or supportive witnesses.

A number of studies have shown that women play a larger role as health caregivers within families than do men. Finch (1989) for example, discusses the importance of feelings of obligation and duty in family relationships and suggests that these are honored through the network of kin relationships where gender is a principal filter. Although who does what for whom is often negotiated, gender roles mean that women more frequently play a dominant role in health care. The question to be asked is whether this also applies to who makes complaints in health care settings. The data from the main study show that women made more complaints than men about their own care. This may not be surprising, given that women consult more frequently than do men, principally for the additional care needs associated with gynecological problems and in connection with reproduction. When cases relating to these medical conditions were controlled for, the complaint rates for men and for women were roughly similar. Women were also marginally more likely to complain about the care provided for others.

However, in the tribunal hearings, in matters relating to the care of children and the elderly and frail, although women as witnesses gave the details of what had happened during the course of the illness, men were more likely to take the role of complainant. It was as if acting as a complainant in a public setting was seen as men's work. This was particularly the case with those from ethnic minority backgrounds and those from manual-class working families. The difficulties of attribution or categorizing class and ethnicity are well documented, and in these cases, for the most part, attribution was made by complainants themselves in their letters or at the hearing.

Overall, three major themes were identified that provided a theoretically grounded framework for categorizing and coding the letters of complaint as *cultural scripts* (Giddens 1991). Drawing on attribution theory, it was found that all letters have a similar purpose: to describe and name the troubling course of events in an illness episode. Second, by a variety of means, all those who complained sought to protect their moral identity as competent carers and complainants. Third, all complaint letters attribute a duty to the doctor both to be technically expert and to demonstrate a concern for the patient. Responsibility for what the complainant sees as having "gone wrong" is attributed to the doctors in their role as professionals. They also defend the caring identity of the complainant. Put another way, letters were written to persuade an audience of potential readers of the veracity of the writer's account and to put into question the doctor's expertise.

Summary of Findings From the Main Complaint Study

In the study as a whole, allegations about the poor service provided by the doctor were divided into the following:

problems with access to the doctor;
the refusal of a doctor to visit the patient at home following a telephone request;
the delay between the request being made and the arrival of the doctor;
criticisms about patient examination; and
failure to make a diagnosis; and criticisms of the treatment given and a failure to refer to hospital or other services.

Most letters contain two to three allegations as well as criticism of the doctors' behavior. Thus, doctors are alleged to have not fulfilled their contract of service and also to have breached normative codes of professional behavior.

Cases were also categorized in terms of the outcome of the illness episode, because it was hypothesized that this would likely be related to the motivation to complain. A fourfold classification was made of all 107 cases. Death was the outcome in almost half the cases, some of which were miscarriages, ectopic pregnancies, or stillbirths. Furthermore, some deaths occurred after the complaint was made but before the hearing took place. On the grounds that the complainants were suffering from bereavement that in their minds was associated with poor medical care, I included both these categories. In the only other relevant study identified, Owen (1991), using data on doctors using the services of the Medical Protection Society, found similar results in that a death had occurred in one-third (31%) of the one thousand cases studied.

In my data, the outcome of the illness episode in complaint cases was death (49), patient and/or carer felt they had experienced a "near miss" (39), patients felt they had been treated in a disrespectful way, or their concerns had not been taken seriously (16), and in three cases the patient was left with an ongoing health problem or disability (Three Boroughs Medical Service Committee complaint files, 1976–1986).

Complaints Where a Death Occurred

Whereas the authorization of the patient to act "on their behalf" was usually required under the tribunal rules, for obvious reasons anyone could make a complaint about the medical care provided to a deceased person. The 49 complaints where the patient had died were made by people with a close relationship with the person who had died: by adult children about the care of their parent (18); by a surviving partner (9); by parents whose child had died (8); by women who had lost a pre-term baby (6); by social service agencies in relation to clients (4); or by siblings or other relatives (4); none, however, were made by friends or neighbors (Medical Service Committee files, 1976–1986.) Many complaints were made by families and were collective accounts. For example, one came from a Sikh family where the complainant's son had died of a myocardial infarction. The father of the young man who had died brought as witnesses his wife, accompanied by an interpreter, three sons, a daughter, and his late son's wife. This was unusual only in the number of people who came and could be interpreted as a demonstration of how social support resources may be used to overcome perceived disadvantages of culture and language.

Letters of complaint when a person had died reflect the same characteristics as the main complaint data set. However, perhaps because the patient had died, the language of the complainant expresses strong emotions, with words such as "betrayal," "anger," and "anguish" being commonly used. Complainants are also more likely to say that they want the doctor to be "punished," "prevented from working," or "dismissed." Case files are often voluminous, containing an array of hospital admission reports, clinical records, and post mortem reports. As was clear in the main study, the complainant's sense of grievance was often exacerbated by the doctor's written response, particularly if the family's or complainant's own actions were criticized. If other documents served to confirm the carer's lay diagnosis, this also hardened the complainants' sense of grievance and their determination to pursue the dispute. This was irrespective of the demands on time and emotional resources required by the process to achieve at best an explanation rather than any monetary compensation.

Why Complainants Seek Explanation When the Patient Has Died

The qualitative analysis of the letters where a death had occurred suggested some socio-psychological motivations for pursuing a complaint that were embedded in the social relationships with the dead person. It appeared that the dead person continued to have a living presence in the complainant's social world, to the extent that the people concerned could not rest until they had received an explanation and some form of justice. Central to this was a sense of responsibility for caring, since patients were mostly at home or had been cared for at home, which had resulted in strong emotional and social ties and physical closeness. Additional motivations to complain derived from deaths that had elements of pain and horror for the dying person, and where the carer had experienced distress and anguish as a consequence. Caring identities were also at stake, drawing into question whether the complainant as carer had done all that she or he could. There was a sense in which people were driven to pursue a course of action until they were satisfied that everything that could be done had been done as a final obligation to the dead person.

An analysis of the qualitative data in my research study reiterated these themes of haunting and justice (shown in the excerpts below in my added italic). Examples of the data are presented below.

Complaints and the Death of Older People

Two-thirds of the complaints ensued on a death related to an adult's caring responsibilities for his or her parent. For example, one woman had became extremely concerned about her mother, with whom she lived. She telephoned the surgery out of hours, connecting with an answer-phone giving the telephone number of a deputizing service, from which she requested a visit. Some hours later a doctor visited and, after examination, said that the patient should be admitted to hospital the next day. However, the complainant said her mother's condition continued to deteriorate to the extent that she called for an ambulance, but the crew would not admit the patient without further authorization from a doctor. The deputizing service had been called again. This time a different doctor visited and said that her mother did *not* require hospitalization; when finally admitted to hospital, her mother was subsequently diagnosed as having meningitis. The complainant wrote:

> It took two hours to get my mother into bed, and she could not stand and was in agony with pains in her spine. All night long she was screaming out in agony with pains in her back, she did not know anybody, *I shall never forget it as long as I live.* If she had been in hospital she would have been able to ease the pain she was in. … I realise I cannot bring my mother back but she deserved better treatment from your emergency service.

Another woman wrote: "Only when I had read the death certificate 'cancer', did the shock of realising stir me to take action." She went on to say that her husband had not been visited by his GP for nine months but had received prescriptions for his illness when he had telephoned to ask. He had become very ill, and the deputizing doctor who visited him the day before he died had helped to ease his symptoms and had advised him to contact his own GP. The next day the GP still did not come to examine him but authorized an ambulance to admit the patient to hospital, where he died soon after.

Two other cases illustrate the link between a perceived duty to the dead person and the public interest. In one case, the complainant's father was in a local authority nursing home. His son visited him and found him to be very ill; he died of pneumonia a day later in hospital. The son wrote:

> I asked the two staff on duty if he had received medical attention and they informed me that his doctor (a GP) had prescribed drugs over the phone ... The emergency doctor described the prescribing of drugs over the phone and treating the elderly as expendable human beings as appalling ... *My father paid with his life through neglect ... the only comfort my family can have now is that something can be done to help the remaining inmates.*

In another case a woman in her late forties had died of bowel cancer, and her brother asked for the case to be investigated. Disturbed by what he saw as neglect by the GP, he wrote: "After taking legal advice, I arrived at the conclusion that it is *my duty as a brother and it is also in the public interest to bring these matters to your attention.*"

A similar emphasis was placed on duty by social workers in relation to their clients. One such letter of complaint read:

> The social services department considers that it has a duty towards vulnerable clients and that in exercising this duty it must take steps to help them gain access to all service to which they are entitled. The medical services being one important service ... [however] *the response [from the GP] was not one that we would expect from a registered medical practitioner. [It] was neither adequate nor prompt and therefore we believe we must pursue this complaint.*

A social worker from a charity who checked on a client found him to be very ill and blue with cold. He had been doubly incontinent. She arranged a hospital admission, but the patient soon died. The social worker knew that the GP had visited her client a few hours before she had, as a prescription had been left. She wrote:

> I am most concerned that Dr. Y should have left Mr. B's prescription on the side table as he was obviously unable to do anything for himself. *I am also upset that nothing was done to alleviate the dreadful condition he was in ...* Above all, I feel that an earlier admission to hospital would have led to a different outcome for Mr. B.

In relation to elderly people, the most common criticism of GPs was that they had been difficult to contact, or that they had refused to visit. When they did visit, the main criticism was that they had not examined the patient properly, or did not listen to the carer's concerns about how ill the patient was. In consequence, carers often had to deal with distressing and traumatic events on their own, without support. Typically, complainants believed that the dead person had died prematurely and/or had suffered an unnecessarily painful and undignified death. The responsibility and blame for what happened was attributed to the doctor. Ironically, some of these vulnerable older people generated more medical time and attention in death than they had ever done in life.

Complaints and the Death of Children and Young People

The death of a child or the death of a fetus generated, not surprisingly, particular anguish for parents. Here, a common assumption was that the death or loss could have been prevented had the doctor exercised greater care and attention. In the case of children, the onset of the illness had often been rapid and the death unexpected and sudden. In almost all cases studied, the patient had been seen by a doctor within the previous 24 hours. A common allegation was that the doctor had failed to respond to the parents' concerns and their perception of the seriousness of the child's illness. Parents were bewildered that a death could have occurred so soon after seeing a doctor and from a disease that was, as they perceived, treatable. There was anger and grief that they had accepted the doctor's reassurances.

In many cases, it was only at the hearing itself that the parents were provided with a full explanation of the cause of death and the reasons why particular decisions were made, or gained an understanding of what had gone wrong in the communication process. The anguish of complainants remained intense at the hearing, typically held about a year after the events. Their concern was to hold the doctor accountable, and such complainants were more likely to say they wished to punish the doctors in some way by stopping them from continuing in practice. This was rationalized in terms of preventing the same thing's happening to others rather than as revenge per se. For example, one father wrote:

> In our opinion, L did not get the proper medical attention before we took him to hospital I also know that nothing will bring our son back, but if by writing to you I can prevent another family going through the same ordeal as we are going through now, then this letter will have been worthwhile.

At one hearing, family members argued vehemently that a teenage boy's symptoms of excessive thirst had been ignored (he was subsequently diagnosed with rapid onset diabetes). In this case, the family dynamics were complicated by the boy's mother's absence at the time, leaving other family members in charge. The deputizing doctor had been called the previous evening and had left a distalgesic. He advised the family to call their own GP in the morning, but the boy's condition had by then deteriorated, and he could not be saved. The father wrote:

> Dr. M. in my opinion totally disregarded the signs and symptoms of diabetes my son had. I feel that had she, and the emergency doctor, paid proper care and attention to my son when they saw him that maybe he would have been alive today.

This group of parents was also much more likely to refer in their letters to having consulted their member of Parliament and solicitors, to have support at the hearing from the Community Health Council (an advocacy service), and to bring a number of family members as witnesses to support them.

Complaints and the Death of Pre-Term Babies

A characteristic of complaints relating to the deaths of pre-term babies was that the mother herself always acted as the complainant, usually accompanied by a female friend or husband rather than a wider kin network. The loss could perhaps be seen as a more a private affair. Lovell (1997) has described late miscarriage and stillbirth as "bereavements with a difference" and has noted the difficulties of health service staff in dealing with the ambiguous status of the woman concerned as a "mother." Miscarriages are a relatively common phenomenon, and a late stillbirth may not be recorded or treated as a "death" because the fetus does not have status as a person. "Deaths" in this category may thus carry a different social meaning. However, the data indicate that women in this data set had complained because their experience had been traumatic; they had a strong sense of loss, and there the loss had an impact on their own health and sense of well-being. Again, the case study data suggest that complainants believed that more could have been done. They saw the doctor as at least partly to blame, technically or because of a lack of compassion, or both. For example, one wrote:

> I am absolutely certain that if my doctor had taken swifter action, after the description of my situation, my baby would have been saved. … As I result, I am looking to see if I can change my doctor—apart from suing him.

Another woman whose baby was almost full-term also blamed the doctor for not taking action when she presented with symptoms of toxemia. She referred to her own suffering and that of her unborn child:

I am therefore convinced that *the doctor did not carry out his full duty as my doctor* and therefore put *both myself and my unborn* child through a lot of serious and unnecessary danger and suffering. My child was alive when I went to his surgery and by Saturday my baby had died due to the placenta breaking away and starving my baby of oxygen and all this caused by my toxaemia, and that does not happen overnight I am quite sure … I have tried and longed for a child for many years.

The Outcome of Complaints When the Patient Had Died

The Medical Service Committee's task was to adjudicate the complaints brought before it in order to determine whether the doctor was in breach of his or her terms of service, and specifically whether the doctor had met his or her service obligations and had provided care of a reasonable standard. Whether the patient had died was not necessarily material to their decision. Complainants had the opportunity to access documents, to cross-question the doctor whom they saw as being at fault, and to question medical panel members.

The proportion of doctors found to have been in breach of their terms of service was higher in the subset of complaints where the patient had died (48%), compared to the main study (35%). In the majority of cases where a breach was found, the doctor was reprimanded. In a few cases financial withholding was imposed. This was generally where there had been previous breaches, and further proceedings were taken against one doctor as a consequence of cumulative evidence of poor performance.

Complaints, Collective Action, and Public Policy

The Benefit to Complainants of Making a Complaint

As Seale (1998) has described, a death can disrupt the basic sense of security of being in the world. In the group of complaints under study, the people had died in circumstances that were distressing and unexpected. The memory of the suffering of the dead person appeared to be a significant motivation for the complainant. Underneath the surface of many complaints was also a concern on the part of relatives that they, the carers, had not done enough. There was often misunderstanding, confusion, and muddle. A death could leave some with a sense of unease and an obligation to the dead person to name what had gone wrong, to seek solace by allocating blame away from themselves as carers. One significant consequence of making a complaint and persisting to a hearing was that the dead person continued to play a part in shaping current and future action, sometimes over a considerable time.

Irrespective of the outcome of the hearing, a complaint can be seen as an attempt to reconstruct the moral identity of the complainant in the face of untoward events. Furthermore, in many cases where a death had occurred, a complaint was a family affair in which family relations and lines of authority, obligation, and influence were played out through the process of holding the doctor to account.

Making a complaint can also play a part in the process of mourning and provide a form of ritual closure. However in the United Kingdom, very little research has been carried out on people's satisfaction with either the process or the outcome of Medical Service Committee hearings. May, Allsop, and Coyle (1993) and Mulcahy, Allsop, and Shirley (1996) have conducted two interview-based studies of complainants' views of the complaint process. Both studies found a degree of satisfaction with the process. In the first study there was satisfaction with outcome, but in the second the findings were equivocal. The numbers in both studies were, however, small.

A tribunal may provide information, explanations, and an audience. Sometimes, sympathy and condolences can be offered and the doctor may express regret. Based on the participant observation data from the hearings in the present study, it seemed that the complainants could obtain a fuller and more detailed explanation, and this might help to "lay the ghosts to rest" through constructing a different reality. From the limited evidence, for most complainants this provided an end point, and it is possible that some felt vindicated by the process in which they participated. Even where a breach was not found, complainants often received an explanation of what had occurred or an explanation of the illness that demonstrated that no one was at fault. On occasion there was an acknowledgment of distress, and an apology was offered by the doctor as well as tribunal members. There were inevitably some situations where, owing to a misunderstanding or ignorance of the system, it was clear that family members had not taken appropriate action and were partly responsible for the poor outcome. A small minority of complainants continued to pursue matters. Ruptures were not healed, and new audiences were sought in what could be seen is a contemporary form of haunting. In a recent example in the United Kingdom, a father, Robert Powell, has continued to seek justice for his son, aged twelve, who died when his diagnosis of Addison's disease was missed and the subsequent investigation of the complaint was handled poorly (Davies, 2006; Powell, 1998).

Seeking Justice Through Collective Action

Over the past decade, the propensity of people to make complaints about health care has been rising. This has been found in a range of institutions that deal with consumers' dissatisfaction with health care. This includes health authorities, the General Medical Council, and to a lesser degree the Parliamentary Commissioner, who is the institution of final resource for complaints about the National Health Service in the United Kingdom. The number of settlements and the amount of compensation of claims for medical negligence have also risen (Allsop & Mulcahy, 2001), indicating an increased inclination to name an injurious experience, to blame health and medical professionals, and to make a claim to a public body. Additionally, a relatively new phenomenon has emerged: collective action by people who believe they have suffered from a "pain and loss" experience from an injury or a family death. Little is known about how such groups form, although geographical clustering through the failings of a particular hospital or doctor, the gender and age of the victims, and the role of the media in publicizing events or the actions of advocates have all been shown to be associated with collective action (Allsop, Jones, & Baggott, 2004). When clusters of similar incidents come to light, it has a major impact in the political sphere.

Some of the higher-profile inquiries will be considered briefly. Of these, it is interesting to note that most victims have been children or elderly people, and, typically, a family member or several families will form a group to take action. The Bristol Inquiry (2001; for Final Report see http://www.bristol-inquiry.org.uk/final_report/report/index.htm) was set up to investigate the unusually high rate of deaths of children undergoing heart surgery in a pediatric unit at the Bristol Royal Infirmary in the United Kingdom. Concerns came to light when parents whose children were treated at the hospital came together and discussed their experiences, subsequently forming a group for action. Similarly, in 2001, parents who discovered that their children's organs had been retained by the Royal Liverpool Children's Hospital in Alder Hey formed a group to call for an investigation (http://www.rlcinquiry.org.uk).

The daughter of one of the elderly female victims of the serial killer GP Harold Shipman was the instigator of an action that led to a police investigation. With the assistance of the solicitor acting for some families, a group was also formed to provide support. Other inquiries into the actions of particular doctors have taken place within the Department of Health, at the request of those harmed by the doctors concerned.

The Policy Response to Pain and Loss Experiences

In conclusion, pain and loss experiences, such as a death where the health care received is seen to have been faulty, can act as a powerful driver to individuals to pursue a complaint. When others in a similar position are identified, collective action can ensue. In the UK context, there is evidence of a political response, and the process followed by the inquiries referred to above demonstrates a shift in policy. Those damaged by instances of poor care have participated fully in the inquiries and—unless those affected wish otherwise—the inquiries have taken place taken in a very public and accountable manner. For example, the Bristol Inquiry into child deaths had its own Web site with daily transcripts of proceedings posted (http://www.bristol-inquiry.org.uk/final_report/report/index.htm); the Shipman Inquiry (2002) ran into five volumes, each with hundreds of pages (http://www.the-shipman-inquiry.org.uk/); and the Health Committee in its inquiry into "complaints and adverse events" called on individuals and groups to give evidence (Health Committee, 1999). One outcome of these inquiries is to acknowledge failures in health care. In addition, there is an implicit agenda that participation in a public exposure of the circumstances and a full inquiry might aid the mourning process of individuals and families who had suffered.

Health policy in relation to dealing with bereavement and with people who have suffered other consequences as a result of poor medical care has changed in a number of other respects. For example, many health trusts, particularly those that care for children, now have special arrangements for bereavement counseling. Mediation is encouraged as a way of resolving negligence claims in situations where both parties agree to the process. Changes are also underway to encourage health trusts to settle small claims out of court. Quality assurance and risk management initiatives have also been strengthened. Currently, in the wake of the Shipman Inquiry, measures to tighten the regulation of health professionals are under consideration. While political action is motivated by the UK government's desire to ensure that health professionals, and particularly doctors, maintain consistently high standards of performance, there is also far greater recognition of the consequences of pain and loss for individuals. The cultural and political context has changed significantly for the better, allowing those who want assurance that their loved ones did not die in vain an audience and an opportunity to right wrongs and obtain appropriate recognition and compensation. The developments suggest a shift in both state/medical profession relations and greater opportunities for consumer voicing.

References

Allsop, J. (1994). Two sides to every story: The perspectives of complainants and doctors. *Law and Policy, 16*(2), 148–183.

Allsop, J. (1998). *Complaints and disputes in the Family Practitioner Committee setting: An empirical and theoretical study.* Unpublished doctoral dissertation, University of London.

Allsop J., May A., and Coyle J. (1994) High hopes, charters and complaints: An account of people's experiences in National Health Service complaints systems. London: Social Sciences Research Centre, South Bank University.
Allsop, J., & Mulcahy, L. (2001). Dealing with clinical complaints. In C. Vincent (Ed.), *Clinical risk management: Enhancing patient safety* (2nd ed.) London: BMA Books.
Allsop, J., Jones, K., & Baggott, R. (2004). Health consumer groups: A new social movement? *Sociology of Health and Illness 26*(6), 737–756.
Bristol Inquiry (2001). *Learning from Bristol: Public inquiry into children's heart surgery at the Bristol Royal Infirmary 1984–1995.* Chair, Ian Kennedy. London: Stationery Office.
Coates, D., & Penrod, S. (1981). Social psychology and the emergence of disputes. *Law and Society Review, 15,* 655–680.
Cohen, A. (1994). *Self-consciousness: An alternative anthropology of identity.* London: Routledge.
Davies, N. (2006, January 4). Fatal flaws. *The Guardian*, pp. 1–2.
Department of Health (1996). *Complaints: Listening ... acting ... improving: Guidance on implementation of the NHS complaints procedures.* Leeds: Department of Health.
Felstiner, W., Abel, R., & Sarat, A. (1981). The emergence and transformation of disputes: Naming, blaming, claiming. *Law and Society Review, 15,* 631–654.
Finch, J. (1989). *Family obligations and social change.* Cambridge: Polity Press.
Giddens, A. (1991). *Modernity and self-identity: Self and society in the late modern age.* Cambridge: Polity Press.
Gulliver, P. (1979). *Disputes and negotiations.* New York: Academic Press.
Health Committee, House of Commons (1999). *Procedures related to adverse clinical incidents and outcomes in medical care.* London: Stationery Office.
Hirschman, A. (1970). *Exit, voice and loyalty.* Cambridge, MA: Harvard University Press.
Jennings, M. K. (1999). Political responses to pain and loss: Presidential address at the 1998 American Political Science Association. *American Political Science Review, 93,* 1–15.
Kidder, R. (1981). The end of the road?: Problems in the analysis of disputes. *Law and Society Review, 15,* 717–725.
Lloyd-Bostock, S. (1992). Attributions and apologies in letters of complaint to hospitals and letters of response (pp. 209–220). In J. Harvey, T. Orbuc, & A. Weber (Eds.), *Attributions, accounts and close relationships.* New York: Springer.
Lloyd-Bostock, S., & Mulcahy, L. (1994). The social psychology of making and responding to hospital complaints: An account model of complaint processes. *Law and Policy, 16,* 185–208.
Lovell, A. (1997). Death at the beginning of life. In D. Field, J. Hockey, & N. Small (Eds.), *Death, gender and ethnicity*(pp. 29–51). London: Routledge.
Mulcahy, L., Allsop, J., & Shirley, C. (1996). *Different voices: A study of complaints to Family Health Service authorities.* Social Science Research Papers Series. London: School of Education, Politics and Social Sciences, South Bank University.
Mather, L., & Yngvesson, B. (1981). Language, audience, and the transformation of disputes. *Law and Society Review, 15,* 775–821.
Owen, C. (1991). Formal complaints against general practitioners: A study of 1000 cases. *British Journal of General Practice, 41,* 113–115.

Powell, R. (1998). A father's experience of the complaints procedure. *Bulletin of Medical Ethics*, September, 16–19.

Rosenthal, M.M., Mulcahy, L., Lloyd-Bostock, S. (Eds). (1999). Medical mishaps. Pieces of the puzzle. Buckingham, UK: Open University Press.

Royal Liverpool Children's Inquiry (2001). *Royal Liverpool Children's Inquiry report*. Chair, Michael Redfern. London: Stationery Office.

Seale, C. (1998). Theories and studying the care of dying people. *British Medical Journal, 317*, 1518–1520.

Shipman Inquiry (2002-4). *Independent public inquiry into the issues arising from the case of Harold Frederick Shipman*. Chair, Dame Janet Smith. London: Stationery Office. http://www.the-shipman-inquiry.org.U.K.

Tedeschi, J., & Reiss, M. (1981). Verbal strategies in impression management. In C. Antaki (Ed.), *The psychology of ordinary explanations in social behaviour*. London: Academic Press.

Tennen, H., & Affleck, G. (1990). Blaming others for threatening events. *Psychological Bulletin, 108*, 209–232.

Trubek, D. (1981). The construction and deconstruction of a disputes-focussed approach: An afterword. *Law and Society Review 15*, 727–747.

CHAPTER 9

Knowing by Heart

Remembering Victims of Intrafamilial Homicide

CAROLYN HARRIS JOHNSON

The majority of homicides are committed by persons known to their victims and family members (Daly & Wilson, 1988, p. 19; Mouzos, 2005, p. 15), and, as Gelles and Straus have pointed out, "a person is more likely to be hit or killed in his or her home, by another family member, than anywhere else or by anyone else" (1985, p. 88). Losing a loved one to intrafamilial or spousal homicide is an experience vastly different from loss through natural causes or by accident. The grief response by family members to this form of death is compounded and complicated; survivors report imagining their loved ones' final moments of fear and terror as they faced their attackers. To know that a loved one was terrorized, restrained, beaten, or humiliated prior to death places an extra burden on survivors, who suffer vicarious trauma. With homicide, as with accidental and other sudden death, there is no opportunity to say goodbye. Intrafamilial homicide, which may be followed by the suicide of the perpetrator, causes ongoing trauma in survivors because of the way the victim was killed, or through profound erosion of feelings of personal safety.

The perpetrator is usually well known to the victim's family and, if the relationship is of long standing, is considered part of the family. The death generates confusion, discord, and torn loyalties among family members as they try to provide support, mediate the conflict, or obtain the best outcome for children. In addition, they need to try to make sense of what happened and to reconstruct their lives. The discord can develop into what has been called "tribal warfare" (Johnston & Campbell, 1988, p. 47), in which each family aligns behind the spousal partner "belonging" to them, escalating the conflict throughout the extended families. This manner of death has a lifelong impact, which necessarily creates an enduring relationship with the deceased victim, the perpetrator, and extended family members.

The experience of intrafamilial homicide has also been described as a "double death"—the death of the individual killed, and the "death" of the family as it was before. Families interviewed in two studies of spousal and intrafamilial homicide described the homicide as a profoundly life-changing event, with long-term consequences for all family members (Johnson, 2005). One participant, Danni, had been a member of a close and loving family. Following the death of her two small children, killed by their father, she said:

> It killed us, it killed our family, but it's not just us who were affected. It's like a pebble in a pond. The ripples are still pulsating.

Vivienne, whose home was the scene of her sister's murder, said:

> It's life-changing, it's massive, its totally life-changing. It changes everything, the way you think and the way you feel. You wrap your kids in cotton wool. I still get scared at night. I have to leave the light on.

Because intrafamilial homicide most often occurs in the home (Mouzos, 2000, p. 19), it is likely to be witnessed by a family member, or the body will be discovered by a family member or be identified by one at the request of police. In some cases, children may have witnessed the homicide or have been present in the home when the offense occurred. Survivors typically remember the day it happened with great clarity and are able to describe it in detail. Danni recalled that her family were together as they celebrated a family birthday when they received news:

> We were at the party, having a great time. Halfway through the party, the police came. We were waving at them! They said they wanted to speak to the head of the family. My brother went. When he came back, we knew by the look on his face that it was the end of our lives.

The Studies

I have conducted two qualitative studies into intrafamilial homicide, looking at the experiences of survivors of the offenses (Johnson, 2005). I was motivated to conduct this study because, while I was working in prisons, no one had ever been able to explain satisfactorily to me why people who are not psychotic, kill themselves following homicide, often with the suicide planned to occur as part of the homicide event. There are major difficulties in researching homicide because access to the data is necessarily restricted for a range of ethical reasons, and also as a consequence of current or anticipated privacy legislation. Quantitative studies of homicide are available through the Australian Institute of Criminology, which has responsibility for the National Homicide Monitoring Program (Mouzos, 2000, 2005), but qualitative data are much harder to find. Any qualitative studies that are available often use a single or limited case study approach, but these are most often based on secondary data obtained by document searches.

Studies that involve interviews with survivors or perpetrators are rare, and are most often undertaken by those already working with a client group comprised of either perpetrators or survivors. If not already engaged with such a client group, the researcher faces many ethical and practical problems in both accessing and engaging with respondents. Because the data are not held in one place. it is necessary to gain ethical approval from each of the agencies involved, in addition to the Human Research Ethics Committee at the university. In the present studies, this meant gaining approval from the Justice Department, the Family Court, the Victim Support Service (VSS), the coroner, and the Western Australia Police service—a total of six ethics approvals, even though the VSS and the Family Court are part of the Justice Department. No application can be submitted until a university committee has approved it, so the time frame for access becomes a huge challenge. Most ethics committees wish to see copies of all the other ethics applications and approvals, so there can be problems with agencies dealing with applications and seeking to have input to them concurrently, when none is finalized. In addition, links need to be forged with each agency, and relationships built to facilitate the data access. I called this building relationships on eggshells in a minefield of sensitivities. Each agency will usually have several sections with which the researcher must interact, and it is necessary for the researcher to build relationships and engage with staff at each level. In the case of prisons, relationships had to be built separately with key people in each of five maximum security prisons in Western Australia, to gain access to respondents. Security and trust were major issues to be dealt with in these environments. My own knowledge of, and sensitivity to, prison culture proved very helpful in this study. Having been allowed access to potential individual respondents, I had to reestablish trust to enable the interview. The results presented in this chapter and published in my book *Come with Daddy* (Johnson, 2005) represent many months of work. As such, I hope that the effort will achieve one of my aims: to develop predictors of this behavior in order to design preventive strategies where possible.

The first study was an exploratory investigation of familicide—intrafamilial homicide followed by suicide of the perpetrator—following marital separation. It was undertaken to determine whether there were commonalities among these offenses that might help with identification of risk factors. In order to investigate this, I studied in depth seven cases of familicide in Western Australia and spoke to survivors about their experiences. The accounts showed common themes in what had led up to the offense. In particular, there were common characteristics among perpetrators (in this study all were male). These were a history of domestic violence, threats of self-harm, threats to harm others, egocentricity, obsessiveness, lack of individuation, pathological jealousy, and before the offense, behavioral indicators that the man's mental health had deteriorated. I propose three possible motivations for familicide: *retaliatory*, where the perpetrator killed the children to pay his wife back for leaving him; a suicidal depression in the perpetrator that appeared to have been extended through a *lack of psychological individuation* to include the children; and possessiveness and the *man's proprietary attitude* that, in his mind, gave him permission to kill.

A second study is underway looking at the possibility of a link between childhood trauma and intimate homicide and familicide. In this investigation, perpetrators, their family members, and members of the victims' families are being interviewed to determine their experience of the homicide event and its aftermath. Perpetrators are also asked to complete the Child Trauma Questionnaire (Bernstein & Fink, 1998), which is a retrospective measure of childhood trauma. As with the earlier study, it is hoped that the information gained will contribute to knowledge of this type of homicide and ultimately to prevention. Eleven perpetrators and six family members have been interviewed at this point. It appears that childhood trauma in the perpetrator and a history of domestic violence in the couple relationship are linked to subsequent homicide, but the strength of the relationship is not yet possible to determine.

Two examples from the second study demonstrate the extremity of the domestic violence preceding the homicide. Bryony had left her husband only to return as his rage extended to members of her family—threatening to kill her and her mother and sister, and to commit suicide. His sadistic abuse, including his killing of her pet animals, extended to his taking her to his workshop to show her a chair set in the middle of a huge sheet of plastic, where he said he had planned to "blow his brains out." The plastic sheet, he explained, would make it easier for those who found him to "clean up the mess." He had always owned firearms, and Bryony had no doubt about his threat. She said of her return: "By coming back I gave up any hope of being me. That's when the really sadistic, violent stuff started." She described her emotional state in the marriage as being "in a constant state of watching and waiting." She had had six miscarriages and had become pregnant again, and upon her telling her husband of the pregnancy, "He beat me really badly and kicked me in the stomach. He told me I wasn't fit to be a mother." Following the beating, he forced her to simulate sex with the barrel of a rifle. This was the final straw. Finally, after twelve years of abuse, she shot him as he slept. She miscarried again four days after being arrested for his murder.

Josephine had been beaten and threatened by her violent husband over several years. Finally, her family moved her and her children from the marital home to a place where they thought they would be safe—their parents' home. The husband, Martin, was enraged. He stalked her, broke into her parents' house, and seriously assaulted his wife and her father. In spite of having a current restraining order, Josephine continued to be stalked by her husband up until the evening when he followed her to her brother's house and while the rest of the family was at the back of the house, he entered and stabbed her to death. After the homicide and during the trial, the husband's extended family continued to threaten and harass the wife's family, threatening that Martin would kill them too when he was released from prison.

Fractured Families: Feelings Toward Perpetrators and Their Families

Many victims and victims' families in the studies reported extreme anger toward perpetrators and their families, expressed in fantasies of revenge—especially by male members of the family. The following quotes from the interviews underline the strength of ongoing emotion:

> I want revenge, I have fantasies of doing the same thing to him.

> I hate him so much, I can't get the anger out! For five years I've been so angry!

> Know what I hate? No one had to swear on oath. No one had to be responsible. His family were not made to go to court for failing to provide supervision. If someone on supervised contact goes out of sight they should be followed. Those bastards in his family knew he was gone for seven hours. They didn't even look. My overwhelming feeling is anger. It's eating me away. I know he planned it. I feel frustrated. He made the mess, now I've got to clean it up.

> I fantasise about waiting for him to walk out of jail and killing him there and then, before he has a chance to kill any more of us. Because

> that's what he will do he'll kill us all. He's threatened to do it and when he gets out he will.

> I don't understand people who can forgive after homicide. Maybe they see it as a way to get closure. They might want to kill but they cover it up so they can just get on with life.

The children of spousal homicide lose both parents—one is murdered and the other imprisoned, or the children are orphaned in cases of suicide after spousal homicide. The needs of the children for care and protection from their extended family serve as a constant reminder to family members of the loss of the parent, and of the homicide itself. The animosity between the maternal and paternal families further damages children and alienates them from the perpetrator's family, with much conflict regarding whether the children should have contact with them, their extended biological family. The children, by their very existence, their genetic makeup, and their shared experience, provide an ongoing reminder to both maternal and paternal families of the deceased parent, of the offending parent, and of the relationship that once joined them as a family.

Vivienne described how one of her murdered sister's children was the image of his father (the perpetrator):

> We had problems with him at first because he is his father's double. When we looked at him it was like looking at his father. He knows he looks like his Dad but wouldn't want to grow up like him. He's a lovely kid now, but I wonder if it will be a problem for him as he grows up.

There also appeared to be little awareness in the victims' families of the parallel traumatic grief experienced by the perpetrators' families. When asked how paternal families coped with the children's deaths, typical responses were:

> I wouldn't know. I never see them. They didn't come to her funeral. I didn't want them there.

> I've never heard from them. They try to cover it up. It's an emotional issue. I have never spoken to his family since the offense.

Indeed, only one of the maternal families interviewed in the study had any contact with the paternal family—always initiated by the perpetrator, who had survived his suicide attempt. The contact would always follow publicity about a similar offense and consisted in his asking forgiveness of his wife's family, who resolutely refused.

Each respondent reported reliving the trauma of the offense each time they heard of a similar offense: "When there is another one [familicide] my brother says, 'Another selfish prick'." There was just one note of forgiveness: "Jesus and Buddha were like psychologists, they realized the path to happiness is forgiveness. I have forgiven, but I cannot forget."

Family Discourses

Survivors described how family discourse changed. New and unspoken rules developed about how certain subjects were raised, or how deceased children were spoken about. One family never described the children's death as "murder" but referred to the murders as "when the children passed," and the anniversary of their death was always referred as "That Day" or "The Day." In another family, the perpetrator's name was not mentioned: "My family call him 'the animal', they can't even say his name." Another respondent said: "My mother can't talk about her [murdered daughter]. If she hears her name she cries." When asked how her family made sense of it, another said: "They don't. They shake their heads. The men can't see how … can't get over how he could do it … They can't get over it."

Ongoing Guilt and Ongoing Questions: Could We Have Prevented It?

The intrafamilial homicide is usually preceded by serious family conflict. Questions then arise in the immediate and extended family: What could cause an intimate family relationship to deteriorate to homicidal violence? Why were family members unable to detect the impending tragedy? Whether or not there were warning signs, Why could no one have prevented it? The answers to these and other questions can be intensely distressing to surviving family members as they grapple with the reality of the offense and try to assimilate it into their lives. All respondents reported feeling some level of guilt for failing to have seen the risk to the children, or for failing to protect them. One said:

> I'll never forgive myself. I told him to bring her back. He said he'd never hurt them! She told me he had put a pillow over her face. He said she choked on a biscuit! She was three years old, she knew the difference between a pillow and a biscuit.

They also expressed extreme anger toward others who, they thought, should have protected the children. Clare, whose husband appeared to have rehearsed the killing of their daughter, asked, "Why didn't they listen at the Family Court? Nobody cared."

Family survivors expressed frustration and feelings of powerlessness at the impotence they experienced in the face of homicidal threats to their loved ones. In particular, there was frustration at the lack of help available for suicidal people, some of whom committed homicide, with or without a suicidal component. There was also an apparent naïveté about the possible link between homicide and suicide, in an individual exhibiting characteristics consistent with a lack of individuation. Here are some examples of what survivors say:

> Two days before he murdered her he attended the mental health clinic. He told them he wanted to kill her and to harm other people too. They assessed him as no risk. They let him go. I'm so bitter with the mental health system! Anyone who says they want to kill someone should be followed up.
>
> I was scared to tell too many people of my fears. My credibility was being challenged in court, the Family Court.
>
> You have to be basically dead before the health service will help. You have to attempt suicide or be assessed as an extreme risk before the counsellor can help you.
>
> He told police he was going to suicide. The day he killed her he was going to run in front of a bus … he told the cops.
>
> She had a violence restraining order. He broke it three times. The last time he killed her. He bashed her once with their child in the house. He was arrested and taken away. On his second breach he got released and fined $200. The third breach was homicide.

It was not surprising to hear survivors express the belief that they would never fully recover from the event. One severely traumatized woman suffered acute guilt over her children's deaths, believing she did not deserve to recover. As can be seen from the above narratives, warning signs—unheeded by families and friends or uncommunicated before the event—seem to become obvious only afterward (Johnson, 2005, p. 104).

Somatic Effects on Survivors

Many surviving family members also had somatic effects, including severe sleep difficulties, with sufferers becoming reliant on alcohol or prescribed or illicit drugs to help alleviate the problem. Julie said:

> I had a heart attack after finding my daughter's body, but I was so stressed I wouldn't go to hospital. My daughter's best friend died of a brain hemorrhage twelve months to the day after she was murdered.

> Everyone says it was the stress of the murder. She was only 28 years old. Now her husband is depressed and suicidal, he can't see the point of going on.

The seven intrafamilial homicides studied had resulted in 21 deaths. Family members also reported other related deaths, not limited to the victims' families. In one maternal family, the murdered children's great-grandfather had a heart attack the day after he was told the news of the children's murder and subsequently died. Similarly, in a paternal family a relative who found the children's bodies had a fatal heart attack two weeks later. One respondent had heard that the perpetrator's father had become very ill after the offense, and she believed the shock and trauma of it had caused the illness.

Fertility was a big issue for women who had experienced their children's murder. Narelle explained that even though she had three children, born after the offense, and did not wish to have any more, she was incapable of undergoing tubal ligation. Twice she had made appointments to have the procedure and twice had not been able to stay long enough to keep the appointment. She interpreted her own behavior as a response to a biological safety valve, to ensure that she was not left childless "just in case" of future illness, accident, or further violence.

Memories, Dreams, and Reflections

Clare described how, five years after the offense, she still felt she had a long way to go in order to resolve her anger and grief:

> I'm all emotional and I feel I'm not halfway through it. … Sometimes you feel guilty 'cos you go a couple of days without thinking of them. … I tend to cry at night when there's no one here, when my husband is on night shift. The sad thing is, sometimes I want to cry and I can't. I look at the photos and it hurts so much, but I can't cry. Then I feel guilty, because I think I should be able to. Time evolves, you learn to continue daily duties. I still have numb days. The wound is still there. The knife is still in it. I'm on an emotional roller coaster.

One respondent described a frightening, apparently paranormal experience during which she felt that the perpetrator had visited her after his death. She reported feeling that she and he had become merged, as one "spirit," so he had been forced to experience her pain, while simultaneously becoming aware for the first time of the enormity of his crime and its ramifications. She wondered if it had been a ghost:

> Once, I felt something cold behind me. It was him. He was looking in my eyes, in my hair. I couldn't move. I felt locked. It was like I was feeling his emotion. I couldn't believe what I [as him] had done. The pain was so deep. I [as him] looked over at the photos of our daughter. I was so frightened! How quickly your mind can get absorbed, you can quickly go from being normal to being in a breakdown. I was so scared! What scared me was I couldn't move.

Diminished Social Participation

Respondents also reported a lack of understanding from others about their experience and their emotional response to such an extreme event. After initial support from friends, survivors' ongoing emotionality and an inability to "get on" with day-to-day life had a negative effect on relationships. Gina reported that her friends found it impossible to deal with the reality of violent death or to relate to her strong emotional reaction. She stated that she had lost friends, who had stopped visiting. Respondents felt that they were allowed an acceptable grieving period during which they were expected to recover, and when they did not, support was withdrawn. They reported diminished social contact and losing friends.

Narelle spoke of her experience:

> I still get upset. I'm supposed to be a different person. It was many years ago now, but they want me to be who I was before it happened. Some people acknowledge it, some people don't. Maybe the trauma is too much. We're suffering more because they can't express it, I get angry when people say "You should get over it" I can't get over it. It's like having a life that should be pushed under the carpet. I get upset people want me to be who I was before it happened. I have had my children murdered and I'm not the same. People need to understand that."

The mother of two children who were murdered became very emotionally withdrawn, saying, "You don't want to live, you really just want to die. You should have someone come every day, just to put a vase of flowers on the table, to make you look at life."

There were also clear structural reasons why families could not resolve their feelings. The formal processes resulting from a homicide can stall or prolong the mourning process and reactivate trauma for family members—in particular when the offender appeals the conviction and/or sentence. It is common for murder trials to run for over a year, and these extended criminal court processes, respondents found, denied closure. As Spungen

(1998, p. 9) has indicated, the victims carry on in the family members who represent them at trial: "[They deal] with the medical examiner, the criminal justice system, and the media. These interactions may go on for several years, some for a lifetime."

Julie's daughter's personal effects were held by police for many months after the offense because they were required for evidence in an appeal mounted by the offender. She said:

> What makes me really angry about all this is I can't have her things, her belongings because he is appealing. The police can't release them, they might be needed by the court case. I haven't grieved yet. If I could hold her jewelry in my hands I could grieve.

Some family members appeared to have coped using denial. An aunt of two of the children kept exceptionally busy, while their grandmother had become religious and had gone overseas to work with disadvantaged children. The children's mother, who was very open to talking about the impact on her family, said: "My mum and sister don't want to talk about it. My sister hides a lot. She keeps going, keeps busy, doesn't deal with it." A mother whose daughter was the victim of intimate partner homicide explained:

> Her brother isn't coping. He can't put it into words, he's gone into his shell. He doesn't see people any more, doesn't go out with his friends. I couldn't mention her name for 18 months or he would shed tears and go into his room. He said he wanted to be with her. He was suicidal.

It is clear from both of my studies that the victims "lived on" in some ways within the family, continuing to affect the behavior of those who loved them. Clare's house was full of photographs and mementos of her murdered child, killed at the age of three by her husband following a highly conflicted separation. She commented that her youngest daughter, born after the death, was two years of age before she bought a camera to take her photograph, so preoccupied had she been with mourning the loss of her firstborn child. Clare's attempts to come to terms with the trauma had consumed her energy over many years. Her other children, including those who had not known their deceased sibling, believed she was in heaven and had a poignant ritual in which they would go outside, look up at the stars, and wave goodnight.

Survivors in mourning may continue to seek the victim. One little boy was reported to have run after a man with a small daughter who resembled his murdered sister. He called out his sister's name, but when the man and child turned round, he realized his mistake and became very distressed.

Narelle, whose children were killed by their father's poisoning them with carbon monoxide, found that the smell of exhaust fumes still caused her to react strongly, even though the offense happened many years ago: "I pull up at the traffic lights and smell the fumes of the car in front. I get distressed. I think to myself, I hope no one can see."

Survivors reported being unable to take care of mundane household tasks after the killing. They found the need to cook, clean the house, shop, and pay bills simply escaped their notice, their thoughts being totally consumed with their loss. Ruth wished there had been someone who could have come each day to remind her to cook, shop, and pay bills. One couple reported that their children were severely traumatized after witnessing the homicide of a relative in their home, and had to arrange private counseling for the children to deal with this, resulting in severe financial problems:

> If we'd had the counseling provided by the government the children would have had to wait six months, but they needed help then. It was a priority for us, we couldn't work and were paying $470 a week for their therapy and everything else got left and the bills piled up.

Life Enhancement and "Ensuring They Did Not Die in Vain"

Although families are co-victimized and fractured when a loved one is killed in this way, experiencing severe and often enduring trauma, there is also evidence of some positive outcomes. Some grew and changed in positive ways through their experience and were even able to help others. One bereaved mother was surprised to discover that there were no services for bereaved parents in her area, so she set up a support group for parents who had lost children through accident or illness. She was unable to speak herself in the meetings, but she found listening to others helpful. Another was instrumental in setting up a support group for the families of homicide victims and also undertook university study to try to increase her knowledge of homicide and its effect on survivors. After experiencing a particularly intense and traumatic grieving process that lasted for years, the mother of one murdered child joined a political party and ran for pre-selection as a candidate for Parliament. She was unsuccessful but now campaigns at both state and federal levels for the safety for women and children going through marital separation and the Family Court.

One described a positive experience:

> My brother-in-law sits me down. He says, "I try to comprehend what you've been through. You're the strongest person I know—to get up every morning and smile at the kids [her nephews and nieces]. That makes me feel better!"

Other comments about positive outcomes were:

> It makes you a better person. A gift is given back, wisdom, strength, compassion.
>
> You treat your children better, treat all children better, even food tastes better.
>
> We were a close family before, now we are even closer.

I have to be involved (with homicide prevention) so my sister didn't die in vain.

Conclusion

The inner representations of intrafamilial homicide victims held by those who loved them ensure that they live on within the family, and with significant others, interacting with them daily. Their presence is manifest in changes in the way family members relate to one another, in the individual's physiological and behavioral responses, in survivors' feelings toward the perpetrators, in their discourse, memories, dreams, and reflections, and in the way in which victims are remembered in survivors' commitment to other family and friends. Their presence is manifest, too, in the determination many have not to allow the death of their loved one under these terrible circumstances to have been in vain.

Acknowledgments

Some of the material in this chapter in relation to my study on familicide is reproduced with the permission of University of Western Australia Press, Crawley, Western Australia, and was originally published in *Come with Daddy* (2005) by Carolyn Harris Johnson. I would like to thank Margaret Mitchell for her editorial work, which greatly enhanced the readability of this chapter, and Glenn Ross, for his constructive advice on the final draft.

References

Bernstein, D. P., & Fink, L. (1998). Child trauma questionnaire: A retrospective self-report manual. San Antonio, TX: The Psychological Corporation.

Daly, M., & Wilson, M. (1988). *Homicide.* New York: Aldine de Gruyter.

Gelles, R. J., & Straus, M. A. (1985). Violence in the American family. In A. J. Lincoln & M. A. Straus (Eds.), *Crime and the family* (pp. 88–110). Springfield, IL: Charles C. Thomas Publisher, Ltd.

Johnson, C. H. (2005). *Come with Daddy: Child homicide-suicide after family breakdown.* Crawley: University of Western Australia Press.

Johnston, J. R., & Campbell, L. E. G. (1988). *Impasses of Divorce.* New York: Free Press.

Mouzos, J. (2000). *Homicidal encounters: A study of homicide in Australia 1989–1999.* Canberra: Australian Institute of Criminology.

Mouzos, J. (2005). *Homicide in Australia 2003–2004: National Homicide Monitoring Program (NHMP) Annual Report.* Canberra: Australian Institute of Criminology.

Spungen, D. (1998). *Homicide: The hidden victims.* Thousand Oaks, CA: Sage.

CHAPTER 10
Psychosocial Death Following Traumatic Brain Injury

CAMILLA HERBERT

> The spouse cannot mourn decently. Although he has lost his mate as surely and permanently as if by death, since the familiar body remains, society neither recognises the spouse's grief nor provides support and comfort that surrounds the bereaved by death. (Lezak, 1987)

A Brief Epidemiology of Traumatic Brain Injury

Traumatic brain injury occurs as a result of an external event such as an assault, fall, or traffic accident, as distinct from an internal event such as a stroke or brain infection. It is difficult to obtain precise data regarding the incidence of traumatic brain injury, owing to variations in definition and methods of data collection. Jennett and MacMillan (1981) cited estimates of the incidence of hospitalization following head injury in Britain and the United States as between 200 and 300 per 100,000 of the population. Within the United Kingdom, the Department of Health Web site briefing paper on National Service Frameworks stated that head injury accounts for 10% of all accident and emergency attendances, and hospital admission occurs for 300 per 100,000 population. Although most head injuries are minor, 4 persons per 100,000 population have handicap or disability six months after a head injury, and 0.37 per 100,000 require long-stay care as a result of traumatic brain injury. Thornhill et al. (2000) reported high rates of moderate or severe disability at one year post injury in a study of mild, moderate, and severe head injuries (disability rates of 47%, 45%, and 48%, respectively) in Glasgow.

More than two-thirds of those who sustain traumatic brain injury are under 30 years of age. The majority of traumatic brain injuries occur among those 15 to 24 years of age (Jennett & MacMillan, 1981). The ratio of male to female is between two and three to one. It occurs more commonly in the lower socio-economic classes and among those who are unemployed (Rimel & Jane, 1983). Improvements in acute care have resulted in reduced mortality rates in recent years. This, together with the relative youth of those who sustain traumatic brain injury, has led to a rapid growth in the number of survivors of traumatic brain injury living in the community. The vast majority of these survivors return to live with family members, who are often ill equipped to respond to the changes in lifestyle and caregiver burden imposed by the injury and its cognitive, emotional, and behavioral sequelae.

Psychosocial Burden on Carers

In a series of longitudinal studies of carers in the 1980s, Livingston and Brooks (1988) described a pattern of rapidly developing high levels of distress over three months post injury, which persists for one, five, and seven years post injury. Other authors have found similar raised levels of distress (Kreutzer et al., 1992; Wallace, 1998), and there have also been a number of studies reviewing family functioning and marital adjustment following traumatic brain injury that provide indirect evidence of stress and distress (Gosling & Oddy, 1999; Douglas & Spellacy, 1996; Kreutzer et al., 1994; Moore et al., 1991). Attempts to explain the likely burden on carers have focused on a number of explanatory models involving injury-related factors, psychopathology of both the injured person and the relatives, life stress, and models of loss and grief. Injury-related and socio-demographic variables have consistently been found to be poor predictors of psychological adjustment of both the injured person and relatives (Oddy et al., 1978; Gervasio & Kreutzer, 1997; Gillen et al., 1998). Consistent relationships have been found both between the relatives' perception of the extent of the brain-injured person's deficits and in relation to particular changes in the brain-injured person. Cognitive and personality changes appear to be more related to family distress than to other consequences such as physical deficits or difficulties with activities of daily living.

Mourning and Loss After Traumatic Brain Injury

In some cases, the family members report that the fundamental aspects of the injured person's personality have changed such that the person they knew and loved is "dead." The fact that the injured person is still in the family, yet so changed, can lead to a refusal on the part of family members to acknowledge the impact. The "old" person, as he was before the injury, remains as a continual reminder, yet is fundamentally changed. The description of the individual as "a stranger" or as "no longer the same person" is a common experience in clinical practice and in the literature (Oddy, 1995; Gosling & Oddy, 1999).

Case Vignette 1

John, a 29-year-old married man, was knocked from his motorcycle and sustained a closed head injury and a broken pelvis. He made a rapid physical recovery and initially denied any significant cognitive or personality changes. He and his wife, Susan, were keen for him to be discharged quickly from hospital so that they could get back to their normal life. Susan became pregnant, and John returned to work in the family firm. However, over the next twelve months John's memory problems and subtle changes in his personality became more apparent to his family. Most noticeable was his poor temper control, which became more obvious after the birth of their son, Liam, with the additional stress that this produced. With support from rehabilitation staff, John and Susan attempted to adapt to these problems, with periods of considerable success. Although initially keen to deny any significant changes, gradually Susan began to seek more support from family and therapists, describing John as "looking the same but not being the same." The changes were recognized by close members of his family, including his mother, who said, "He's not like my son any more." Eventually, after a number of separations and attempts to resolve the problems, the marriage broke down and Susan and Liam moved on.

Models of normal grief are not particularly helpful in understanding the sense of loss after traumatic brain injury because they focus on bereavement. In particular, the depression models, with their primary focus on intrapersonal analysis, are inadequate to account for the complex set of demands and expectations placed on families after traumatic brain injury. The continued presence of the individual makes it difficult to go through the process of severing existing ties, as required by both psychoanalytic theory and attachment theory. The life-stress models provide a framework for analyzing the resources available to family members, and potentially for identifying who will need additional support. Kreutzer et al. (1994) compared the adaptation of families after traumatic brain injury with more general psychological models of stress and models of coping with chronic illness such as Alzheimer's disease (Vitaliano et al., 1991). Moore et al. (1989, 1991, 1993) published a series of studies examining the relationship between individual coping and system coping in individuals and families with traumatic brain injury. They found that family coping and marital resources were overwhelmed by the brain injury, and that coping skills had only a minor role in eventual outcome, suggesting that the emotional impact of the injury for the family is crucial. If relatives are able to recognize what they are experiencing as a grieving process, they may then be able to reappraise their approach to the situation, even if they are unable to change the reality of the day-to-day experience.

Pathological or Abnormal Grief Responses

Many of the defining characteristics of traumatic brain injury are also consistent with the risk factors for pathological or abnormal grief responses. It is by definition a sudden, traumatic, and unanticipated event. There is usually an element of liability to be established, which may result in blame being attached to the injured person, a relative directly (e.g., if the relative was driving the car but was unhurt), or indirectly (e.g., where relatives blame themselves for not preventing the accident), or to a third person who may or may not be criminally liable. In addition, traumatic brain injury affects a young, predominantly male population, and the grievers are predominantly parents and partners. The nature of the loss is sudden and unpredicted, and the cause of the injury may give rise to conflicting emotions of guilt, anger, and denial.

It has been recognized at a descriptive level that carers of traumatically brain-injured patients often use denial. Romano (1974) observed the responses of families and found relatively little progress beyond the initial stage of denial. Families had a strong tendency to maintain the fantasy that the patient would "wake up" and return to his or her previous level of functioning. Relatives would often deny or minimize the patient's disabilities and hold unreasonable expectations about ultimate level of functioning. This denial could extend over many years. Thomsen (1984) reported mothers of brain-damaged patients who continued to deny the impact of the injury for as much as ten or fifteen years. The recovery process is such an uncertain one, with many reasons for hope and despair, that feelings about the changes may continue to be in turmoil for months and years.

Mobile Mourning

The prolonged uncertainty and the concomitant disorganization of the grieving process have resulted in the development of the term "mobile mourning" (Muir et al., 1990). The experience of grieving can be put off, sometimes indefinitely, a strategy that has been termed "grieving in abeyance" (Perlesz & McLachlan, 1986). Perlesz and her colleagues have argued that until the emotional task of grieving has commenced, the family cannot take steps to reorganize itself from the crisis state brought about as a response to the initial trauma of the injury to a more adaptive organization (Perlesz et al., 1992) that can cope with the burden of long-term care. This process can be made more difficult when the roles and relationships were not already clarified before the injury. Traumatic brain injury occurs particularly within the 18–30 age group, when relationships are often in a state of flux or change. Young people may have only recently achieved independence from their parents and be seeking to create a new identity for themselves. When young children are involved, they may have only a vague memory of their parent pre-injury and be accepting of the person as they now are. Older children, however, often have a clear sense of the changes and may grieve for what they no longer have. In extreme cases, the injured may not recall their children and have difficulty relating to them as a result.

Case Vignette 2

Karen, a 30-year-old woman, suffered a severe head injury in a road traffic accident. She made a good physical recovery with no obvious weakness or disability. She had some difficulty learning new information, but her major disability was her complete loss of memory for events preceding her injury. While it is common for people to lose a few hours, weeks, or months prior to the injury, it is unusual for people to forget where they grew up, their family holidays, and so on. Karen had no recollection of these events, or of the birth of her son seven years before. She had no knowledge of the world nor any ability to judge situations. She found it difficult to make a new relationship with her son, as she did not know how to play or to consider life through the eyes of a child. Her mother became the carer for the child and provided continual support and guidance for Karen. Karen's world was very much day-to-day. She looked forward to very little and had few memories. Although she was capable of learning some new skills, each was acquired in isolation and without a framework.

Within a family the sense of loss can be highlighted when siblings develop new skills, achieve personal milestones, and gain independence. Explicitly or implicitly, comparisons may be made with the injured person's more limited potential and lost opportunities.

Case Vignette 3

Cindy, a 23-year-old woman severely physically and cognitively disabled in a road traffic accident, four years post injury requires 24-hour care and assistance to wash, dress, toilet, and feed herself. She is able to speak in short sentences and expresses a desire to be normal. She can contemplate throwing away her old self, but she does not want her new self to be as it is now. Her family love her and care for her but continue to grieve for what might have been. As her sister moves on with her life, there are constant opportunities for painful comparisons and reawakening of the sense of loss.

Disenfranchised Grief

Where a person experiences a sense of loss but does not have a socially recognized right, role, or capacity to grieve, his or her grief is disenfranchised. The person suffers a loss but has little or no opportunity to mourn publicly (Doka, 1989, 2002). This concept has been used to describe problems in grieving in a range of populations, such as parents experiencing perinatal or prenatal death of children (Raphael, 1983), ex-spouses (Doka, 1986), and older people in nursing home care (Moss et al., 2003). Other groups include families of Alzheimer's patients (Doka, 1985) and adults with learning disabilities (Lipe-Goodson & Goebel, 1983; Edgerton, Bollinger, & Herr, 1984). The case vignettes above and the concepts of mobile mourning and grief in abeyance suggest that the concept can be extended to include the relatives of those who have sustained a traumatic brain injury.

The concept of disenfranchised grief recognizes that societies have sets of norms or grieving rules that attempt to specify who, when, where, how, and how long people should grieve, and for whom. These rules may be implicit or explicit—for example, codified in personnel policies (e.g., a week off for the death of a spouse or child, three days for the loss of a parent or sibling). In any given society these grieving rules may not correspond to the nature of attachments, the sense of loss, or the feelings of survivors. Doka (1989) argued that there are three main reasons, discussed below, why people may be excluded from the normal grieving process.

The Relationship Itself Is Not Recognized.

In general, society recognizes kin-based relationships. The underlying assumption is made that closeness of relationship exists only among spouses and/or immediate kin (Polka & Deck, 1976). Although relationships with stepchildren, caregivers, colleagues, or roommates (e.g., in nursing homes) may be long-lasting and are recognized, mourners may be expected to support and assist family members rather than to grieve publicly themselves. Other nontraditional relationships such as extramarital affairs or homosexual partnerships have tenuous public acceptance and limited legal standing, and grief at the death of a partner may not be acknowledged or socially supported. Ex-spouses or former friends may have limited contact, but the death of the significant other can still cause a grief reaction because it brings finality to the earlier loss, ending any remaining contact or fantasy of reconciliation or reinvolvement. These feelings may also be shared by others in their world, such as parents or children mourning the loss of "what might have been" or "what once was" (Doka, 1989).

The Griever Is Not Recognized.

Here the person is not socially defined as capable of grief; therefore, there is little or no social recognition of his or her sense of loss or need to mourn. It is the personal characteristics of the bereaved that in effect disenfranchise their grief. The very old and the very young are typically perceived by others as having little comprehension of or reaction to the death of a significant other. Similarly, mentally disabled persons may also be disenfranchised in grief (Lipe-Goodson & Goebel, 1983; Edgerton, Bollinger, & Herr 1984).

The Loss Is Not Recognized.

Some losses are not socially defined as significant. Perinatal death, for example, is still regarded by many as a relatively minor loss in spite of a rapidly growing literature detailing the strength of the grief reaction experienced by many women (Raphael, 1983). Abortion too can create a sense of loss that is hidden and confounded by the additional conflicts surrounding personal beliefs about the sanctity of life. Another loss that is often not perceived as significant is the loss of a pet; nevertheless, research does show strong ties between pets and humans and profound reactions to loss (Kay, Nieberg, & Kutscher, 1984).

Mental illness, chronic brain disorders such as Alzheimer's disease, substance abuse, and, of course, traumatic brain injury can have a significant impact on the personality of an individual and can radically affect the lives of others around him or her. All relationships change over time as people grow and develop. Not all changes create problems, the differentiation being between sudden and dramatic changes in a relationship and the normal incremental changes over time. In some situations the changes in one party or dissimilar changes in both may lead to the dissolution of the relationship—"We've grown apart." However when change is dramatic, and particularly when it is not perceived as intentional or as under the control of the person, options like divorce or separation may be effectively precluded.

It has long been recognized that relatives of people with Alzheimer's often experience deep feelings of loss. Cole, Griffin, and Ruiz (1986) reviewed the issues that arise for families as they cope with caring for someone with a chronic degenerative condition. They note that "family members may also feel a profound sense of loss, as a loved one who was once a vital person gradually loses mental, physical and social abilities." The qualities of the person to whom one was attached are no longer present. As one spouse of an Alzheimer's victim said, "All you have is a shell mocking what once was." The person is psychologically dead.

Work exploring the effects of psychosocial death in relation to Alzheimer's disease has been carried out (Wasow, 1986; Liptzin et al., 1988; Quayhagen & Quayhagen, 1988). One of the most pervasive reactions is guilt, either because of a belief that the relative could or should have responded to symptoms earlier that might have delayed or prevented subsequent difficulties, or because relatives feel that it was their own inability to be an effective parent or good spouse that contributed to the problem. In addition to guilt about causation, there is often guilt about the ways in which the relatives are coping: where the condition is perceived as beyond the control of the victim, relatives may feel it is inappropriate to respond angrily or to get irritated. Relatives may also feel guilty about their own negative feelings toward the victim.

Themes in Grief and Adjustment

Little work has been done investigating the role of grief in the adjustment of families following traumatic brain injury, but similar themes seem to emerge. In a study by Herbert (1998), the level of grief in relatives on average 43 months post injury was measured using a modified version of the Inventory of Complicated Grief (Prigerson et al., 1994) to see if this could explain successful family adaptation. The sample included relatives of people who had been admitted to hospital originally for three days or more and included those who had sustained mild, moderate, or severe head injuries. From an original sample of 104, approximately 50% of the injured people could not be traced, illustrating the transient lifestyle of this predominantly younger and socio-economically deprived population. Of those with whom contact was made, only half were prepared to consent to follow-up. The sample, although small, was not significantly different from those not interviewed, not contacted, or from whom was no response. A total of 34 relatives were interviewed at times ranging from 14 months to 56 months post injury. Approximately one-third of the relatives scored significantly high on standardized assessments of mood, compared with an estimate of only 12% for the general population. This reinforced the findings described earlier of high levels of distress and burden among family members. The study attempted to identify a factor of complicated grief over and above the effects of anxiety and depression that might account for successful family adaptation, but the items were highly intercorrelated and specific effects could not be identified. However, a number of questions were particularly highly correlated both with total grief rating and with measures of family functioning and mood. These identified loneliness, emptiness, and envy of those who have not lost someone. These are difficult emotions to elicit from relatives, particularly when the loved one is still alive, because respondents often perceive them as evidence of disloyalty or selfishness. Relatives described feeling guilty for talking in this way about their loved one.

Although the intensity and nature of grief reactions to psychosocial losses are affected by all the same variables that affect any response to loss (such as the nature of the relationship, family and social support, and circumstances surrounding loss), Doka (1989) argues that two variables are unique to this form of loss: first, the extent to which knowledge of the level of disability or change in the person is shared and/or perceived by others, and second, the extent to which the underlying condition causing psychosocial death can be viewed along a continuum from reversibility to irreversibility. In the case vignette of John and Susan, it was the support of John's mother that allowed Susan eventually to leave. Recognition of the changes by another close family member can be crucial. For Karen's mother also, it was important that she was able to provide a buffer between Karen and her son, a place where the son could try to understand why his mother was so different.

With irreversible conditions, the loss is certain, and although that knowledge may be resisted by defense mechanisms such as denial, there will often be a sense of hopelessness. For the family of Cindy, in case vignette 3, the severity of her physical and cognitive deficits was such that hopes of a full or substantial recovery were unrealistic. The irreversibility of the loss may create high levels of ambivalence and subsequent guilt as one copes with the daily tasks of life. There may be deep, guilt-provoking desires for the victim's institutionalization or even death.

In situations that are perceived as reversible, which is usually the case during the first few months or years of rehabilitation, there may be increased impatience with the slow pace of recovery and intensified feelings of anger toward a victim who is perceived to have some sense of control. Liptzin, Grob, and Eisen (1988) found that over time relatives of depressed patients felt more burden than did relatives of dementia patients, since the latter often grew to accept the fact that the relative's decline was inevitable, irreversible, and thus beyond their control. Bennett and Bennett (1984) noted that hopelessness can help families experience less blame and measure accomplishments in terms of endurance and adaptation rather than cure.

The problem of disenfranchised grief lies in the paradox that the very nature of this type of grief exacerbates the problems of grief, while at the same time removing or minimizing the usual sources of support. Disenfranchising grief can intensify the feelings of anger, guilt, or powerlessness that can form part of the normal grief experience. In addition, both ambivalent relationships and concurrent crises have been identified in the literature as conditions that complicate grief (Worden, 1982; Raphael, 1983; Rando, 1984).

Resolution of Grief

Resolution of grief associated with psychosocial death may be difficult to achieve. Worden (1982) suggested that four tasks are necessary before grief can be resolved: accepting the reality of death, experiencing the pain of grief, adjusting to a life without the deceased person, and withdrawing emotional energy from the deceased person and reinvesting it in others. Following traumatic brain injury, this may involve the prolonged process of recognizing the nature and extent of the personality change and experiencing fully the sense of loss, and here there is a parallel with the difference between anticipatory grief and forewarning of loss. Many family members may describe changes without acknowledging the losses these changes entail. The injured person's physical appearance and many of the mannerisms may stay the same, giving the illusion that nothing has changed and contributing to a situation in which the bereaved may continue to deny the reality of the loss. The emotional catharsis first described by Freud (1957 [1917]), which forms the core of most grief work, involves a review of the relationship and a resolution of the feelings inherent in such a review. Although theoretically possible, social expectations and practical constraints mean that such a process is rarely observed in clinical practice following psychosocial loss.

The literature on anticipatory grief also suggests that the burden of caring may prevent or inhibit this process of review. Apart from the practical problem of lack of time when the griever is also a carer, there is no space for emotional detachment. The demands of time spent caring, supervising the individual, or taking on roles that the injured person can no longer fulfill is likely to increase. Instead of becoming more detached, the relationship often will also develop in less positive ways, involving as it may the growing demands of care and the changed and often bizarre behavior of the injured person, which causes new stress, shame, guilt, anger, and helplessness. At a time when they need support from family or society, the changed behavior of the person may result in increasing isolation. Societal and family pressures can make it difficult to withdraw from the situation either practically or emotionally, let alone invest in a new relationship. There may be conflicting pressures on a partner who has to consider the needs of the injured adult against the needs of dependent children. The spouse may become what Grossman and Grossman (1983) called a "pseudowidow" or a "cryptowidow"; he or she remains legally, but not behaviorally, married. As Lezak (1987) said in the quotation at the beginning of this chapter: "The spouse cannot mourn decently. Although he has lost his mate as surely and permanently as if by death, since the familiar body remains, society neither recognizes the spouse's grief nor provides support and comfort that surrounds the bereaved by death."

There is an extensive literature on how burdensome the process is, and how stressed many families become and remain. It is also clearly true that many families do adjust, and we do not yet know how or why (Perlesz et al., 1999). Very little is known about the effects on carers who decide to leave the situation. The divorce rate after traumatic brain injury is high (Stillwell et al., 1997; Wood & Yurdakul, 1997), and there is some evidence to suggest that parents provide care longer than spouses do. In spite of the parallels with elderly carers and their relatives with dementia, the main difference with the traumatic brain-injured patients may lie in the relative youth of the population. Most people who sustain traumatic brain injury are between 18 and 30 years old and have a near-normal life expectancy. For the carers and relatives who remain, it is unclear if they need or have achieved some resolution of feelings that allows them to maintain emotional equilibrium, recognizing the losses experienced while continuing to care for the injured person in spite of the changes, and whether this is what constitutes "adaptation" after brain injury. If some form of adaptation or resolution is achieved, is this a stable state, or does it represent some state of partial suspension of a grieving process? Herbert (1998), in the study described earlier, found that some of the cognitions associated with complicated grief were meaningful for the relatives of people who had been changed by their traumatic brain injury. The study concluded that there are grief-related features in the experience of carers in the years after injury, but that we do not yet have a sufficient understanding of how these features influence the levels of stress experienced or the extent to which family members have adapted to the situation. There is a need for more research into family coping, and Perlesz et al. (1999) in particular have argued eloquently for more family outcome research to develop a theoretically coherent framework to understand relatives' psychosocial outcome following traumatic brain injury, with an emphasis on family resilience.

Conclusion

Traumatic brain injury has profound psychological consequences for relatives. Long-term distress among carers cannot be explained in terms of the increasing tasks associated with caring. Thinking of the carer's experience as one of disenfranchised grief following the psychological and social death of a partner forms a theoretical framework that can explain the findings and provide a basis for clinical practice.

Acknowledgment

I would like to thank Professor Sheina Orbell, who supervised my doctoral thesis at the University of Sheffield (Herbert, 1998).

References

Bennett, M. I., & Bennett, M. B. (1984). The uses of hopelessness. *American Journal of Psychiatry, 141,* 559–562.

Cole, L., Griffin, K., & Ruiz, B. (1986). A comprehensive approach to working with families of Alzheimer's patients. *Journal of Gerontological Social Work, 9,* 27–39.

Doka, K. J. (1985). Crypto death and real grief. Paper presented to a symposium of the Foundation of Thanatology, New York, March.

Doka, K. J. (1986). Loss upon loss: Death after divorce. *Death Studies, 10,* 441–449.

Doka, K. J. (1989). Disenfranchised grief. In K. J. Doka (Ed.), *Disenfranchised grief: Recognizing hidden sorrow* (pp. 3–11). Lexington, MA: D. C. Heath.

Doka, K. J. (2002). *Disenfranchised grief: New directions, challenges and strategies for practice.* Champaign, IL: Research Press.

Douglas, J. M., & Spellacy, F. J. (1996). Indicators of long term family functioning following severe traumatic brain injury in adults. *Brain Injury, 10,* 819–839.

Edgerton, R. B., Bollinger, M., & Herr, B. (1984). The cloak of competence: After two decades. *American Journal of Mental Deficiency, 88,* 345–351.

Freud, S. (1957 [1917]). Mourning and melancholia. In J. Strachey (Ed. and Trans.), *Standard edition of the complete psychological works of Sigmund Freud,* Vol. 14 (pp. 239–258). London: Hogarth.

Gervasio, A. H., & Kreutzer, J. S. (1997). Kinship and family members' psychological distress after traumatic brain injury: A large sample study. *Journal of Head Trauma Rehabilitation 12*(3), 14–26.

Gillen, R., Tennen, H., et al. (1998). Distress, depressive symptoms and depressive disorder among caregivers of patients with brain injury. *Journal of Head Trauma Rehabilitation 13*(3), 31–43.

Gosling, J., & Oddy, M. (1999). Rearranged marriages: Marital relationships after head injury. *Brain Injury 13,* 785–796.

Grossman, S., & Grossman, C. A. (1983). And then there was one. Paper presented to the Northeastern Gerontological Society, Newport, RI, May 6.

Herbert, C. M. (1998). *Grief and loss following traumatic brain injury.* Unpublished doctoral dissertation, University of Sheffield.

Imel, R.W. & Jane, J. A (1983) Patient characteristics. In N. M. Rosenthal, E.R. Griffith, M. R. Bond, & J. D. Miller (Eds.) *Rehabilitation of the head injured adult* (pp. 9–20). Philadelphia: David.

Jennett, B., & MacMillan, R. (1981). Epidemiology of head injury. *British Medical Journal, 282,* 101–104.

Kay, W. J., Nieburg, H. A. & Kutscher, A. H, 1984 Pet Loss and Human Bereavement. New York: Arno Press.

Kreutzer, J. S., Gervasio, A. H., & Camplair, P. S. (1994). Primary caregivers' psychological status and family functioning after traumatic brain injury. *Brain Injury, 8,* 197–210.

Kreutzer, J. S., Maritz, J. H., & Kepler, K. (1992). Traumatic brain injury: Family response and outcome. *Archives of Physical Medicine and Rehabilitation, 73,* 771–778.

Lezak, M. D. (1987). Living with the characteriologically altered brain injured patient. *Journal of Clinical Psychiatry, 34,* 592–598.

Lipe-Goodson, P. S., & Goebel, B. I. (1983). Perception of age and death in mentally retarded adults. *Mental Retardation, 21,* 68–75.

Liptzin, B., Grob, M. C., & Eisen, S. V. (1988). Family burden of demented and depressed elderly psychiatric in-patients. *Gerontologist, 28,* 397–410.

Livingston, M. G. (1987). Head injury: The relatives' response. *Brain Injury, 1,* 33–39.

Moore, A. D., Stambrook, M., et al. (1991). Family coping and marital adjustment after traumatic brain injury. *Journal of Head Trauma Rehabilitation,* 6, 83–89.

Moore, A. D., Stambrook, M., et al. (1993). Centripetal and centrifugal family life cycle factors in long term outcome following traumatic brain injury. *Brain Injury 7,* 247–255.

Moore, A. D., Stambrook, M. & Peters, L. C. (1989) Coping strategies and adjustment after closed head injury: A cluster analytical approach. *Brain Injury 3,* 171–176.

Moss, M. S., Moss, S. Z., Rubinstein, R. L., & Black, H. K (2003). The metaphor of "family" in staff communication about dying and death. *Journals of Gerontology, Series B: Psychological Sciences and Social Sciences, 58B*(5), S290.

Muir, C. A., Rosenthal, M., & Diehl, L. N. (1990). Methods of family intervention. In M. Rosenthal et al. (Eds.), *Rehabilitation of the head injured adult,* 1st ed. (pp. 407–419). Philadelphia: F. A. Davis.

Oddy, M. (1995). He's no longer the same person: How families adjust to personality change after head injury. In N. V. T. Chamberlain (Ed.), *Traumatic brain injury rehabilitation*. London: Chapman & Hall.

Oddy, M., Humphrey, M., et al. (1978). Stresses upon the relatives of head-injured patients. *British Journal of Psychiatry, 133,* 507–513.
Perlesz, A., Furlong, M., & McLachlan, D. (1992). Family centred rehabilitation: Family therapy for the head injured and their relatives. *Australian and New Zealand Journal of Family Therapy, 13,* 145–153.
Perlesz, A., Kinsella, G., & Crowe, S. (1999). Impact of traumatic brain injury on the family: A critical review. *Rehabilitation Psychology, 44,* 6–35.
Perlesz, A., & McLachlan, D. I. (1986). *Grieving in abeyance: Head injury and family beliefs.* Paper presented at the Parkville Centre, Melbourne, Victoria, Australia.
Polka, J., & Deck, G. (1986). Grief, the funeral and the friend. In V. Pine et al. (Eds.), *Acute grief and the funeral.* Springfield, IL: Charles C. Thomas Publisher, Ltd.
Prigerson, H. G., Maciejewski, P. K., Reynolds, C. F., Bierhals, A. J., Newsom, J. T., Fasiczka, A., Frank, E., Doman, F., & Miller, M. (1995). Inventory of complicated grief: A scale to measure maladaptive symptoms of loss. *Psychiatry Review, 59,* 65–79.
Quayhagen, M. P., & Quayhagen, M. (1988). Alzheimer's stress: Coping with the caregiving role. *Gerontologist, 28,* 391–396.
Rando, T. (1984). *Grief, dying and death: Clinical interventions for caregivers.* Champaign, IL: Research Press.
Raphael, B. (1983). *The anatomy of bereavement.* New York: Basic Books.
Romano, M. D. (1974). Family response to traumatic brain injury. *Scandinavian Journal of Rehabilitation Medicine, 6,* 1–4.
Thornhill, S., Teasdale, G. M., Murray, G. D., McEwen, J., Roy, C. W., & Penny, K. I. (2000). Disability in young people and adults one year after head injury: Prospective cohort study. *British Medical Journal, 320,* 631–635.
Vitaliano, P. P., Russo, J., Young, H. M., et al. (1991). Predictors of burden in spouse caregivers of individuals with Alzheimer's disease. *Psychology and Aging, 6,* 392–492.
Wood, R. L., & Yurdakul, L. K. (1997). Change in relationship status following traumatic brain injury. *Brain Injury, 11,* 491–502.
Wallace, C. A., Bognor, J., Corrigan, J. D., Cinchot, D., Mysiw, W. J., & Fugate, L. P. (1998). Primary caregivers of persons with brain injury: Life changes 1 year after injury. *Brain Injury 112,* 483–493.
Wasow, M. (1986). Support groups for family caregivers and patients with Alzheimer's disease. *Social Work, 31,* 93–97.
Worden, J. W. (1982). *Grief counselling and grief therapy.* New York: Springer.

CHAPTER 11

Should Suicide Be Reported in the Media?

A Critique of Research

GERARD SULLIVAN

Particularly in cases where there is publicity about a death, a person's "reach from the grave" can have unexpected and wide impact beyond immediate family and friends. A body of literature has been accumulating over many years, concluding that publicity about suicide leads to imitation. This has led health authorities in several countries to issue guidelines for media organizations that warn of this danger and to recommend curtailment of such reports (e.g., Australia, 2004; Sonneck et al., 1994; Michel et al., 2000).

Most studies that have been undertaken to examine the relationship are relatively unsophisticated, either in media analysis; explaining the details of how such an effect might operate, investigating the forms of media reports most likely to provoke imitation; or in examining whether certain groups are more susceptible than others to this type of influence.

A number of studies have concluded that imitation is more likely to occur following publicity about the suicide of a celebrity (Wasserman, 1984; Stack, 1987, 1990). These results have been explained using social learning theory, as proposed by Albert Bandura and others, according to which the more sympathetic publicity an issue receives, the more likely it is to encourage imitation. Furthermore, imitation is more likely when celebrities are involved because people are more likely to identify with them (Blood & Pirkis, 2001).

If there is a connection between publicity about celebrity suicides and imitation, however, the effect is not consistent. In 1994 Kurt Cobain, lead singer of the rock music group Nirvana, died by suicide, an event that received extensive media attention throughout the English-speaking world. The effect of media reports of Cobain's death on the suicide rate was investigated by Martin and Koo (1997). They described Cobain's music in this way:

> [It] speaks of his feelings of apathy, hopelessnes [sic] and anger toward a society from which he was an outcast. He was hailed as an unwilling spokesman for a "generation that was equally tired of being lied to by their parents, by government, and by the music on the radio" (Gaines, 1994, p. 128). He was "the outcast kid's proof that in the end truth would be revealed and justice would prevail… ." (Martin & Koo, 1997, p. 188)

Martin and Koo noted that Cobain's death received extensive media coverage, especially in Seattle where he lived, but also throughout Australia, where it was first reported on April 8, 1994, "subsequently reaching every television channel in both news and music programs, and every newspaper, with extensive detail given" (p.188). They also reported that

> the day after the announcement of Cobain's death, the Seattle Crisis Clinic received more than three hundred calls, nearly 100 more than usual (Toltz & O'Donnell, 1994) … . [A]t least two well-publicized sets of suicide in young Australians are reputed to have been linked, with Cobain's name mentioned in suicide notes (pp.188–189).

In accordance with the literature on the effect of celebrity suicide, Martin and Koo expected that the publicity of Cobain's death would lead to an increase in suicide, particularly among young people:

> On the basis of these reports, the death of Kurt Cobain, the lead singer-guitarist-lyricist of the popular 'grunge' group Nirvana, should have had an impact on the rate of suicide in young people (1997, p. 188).

They compared the suicide rate in Australia in the period following the media coverage of Cobain's suicide with that in the same period in the previous five years, controlling for uneven variability in weekends, Mondays, and holidays. Contrary to their expectation, Martin and Koo found no evidence of an increase in deaths by gunshot, the method Cobain used. Further, they found that while the suicide rate for young people (15–24 years) had been increasing slightly in the April–May period under investigation each year from 1989 to 1993, it dropped (from 39 to 30 cases) in the same period in 1994, which led them to the conclusion that "celebrity suicide had little impact on suicide in young persons in Australia" (1997, p. 187).

Given the results of their study, it is interesting that Martin and Koo's opening sentence summarizing previous research in the field is so uncritical:

> The research evidence that newspaper stories about suicide may lead to imitation is convincing ... despite equivocal finding [sic] .... Hassan (1995) has reinforced both the concerns about imitation or 'copycat' suicide and contagion and the conventional wisdom that a very cautious approach should be taken to media reporting of such events (1997, p. 187).

Martin and Koo referred to an unpublished study by Martin in which he examined the impact of a suicide portrayed in a popular Australian television drama, broadcast in 1993. Although he found "no measurable effect" (1997, p. 189), they explain this as

> not the problem of the design, but rather that the audience penetration of the program was limited to 17% of the Australian viewing public ... arguably the series may not have appealed to, nor been seen by, young people (1997, p. 189).

Once again, given the results, Martin and Koo's conclusions seem extraordinary and indicate slavish loyalty to the media imitation thesis despite a lack of evidence. Martin and Koo restated the thesis and uncritically cite studies that support it:

> The work of Phillips ... stands out as showing that both newspaper reports and television stories may influence particularly young people to suicide. This evidence supports the general public view that if suicide is talked about, particularly if it is glorified, then vulnerable young people will consider it as an alternative when they are struggling with ... problems which at the time appear to be insurmountable (1997, pp. 193–194).

Although they acknowledged dissenting data obtained in previous studies, consistent with their own, they dismissed or ignored these studies:

> Apart from researchers who have had technical difficulties in discerning a clear effect of influence, the one dissenting voice comes from Kessler et al. (1988) who showed that during 1981–1984, teenage suicides decreased after newscasts about suicide. As previously noted, this work has been attacked... (1997, p. 194).

Martin and Koo proceeded to consider a number of reasons why they might not have been able to demonstrate a media imitation effect, and to dismiss each one as implausible. First, they speculated on whether the 1994 data they used might be incomplete owing to a late return of coroners' (medical examiners') reports. Next, they questioned if coroners might have been reluctant to give a verdict of suicide. Surprisingly, Martin and Koo referred to a fundamental design flaw in many studies about the effect of media reporting on imitative suicide, the ecological fallacy, as a way of dismissing their own findings, but again, they found this explanation implausible given the amount of media coverage of Cobain's death. They considered whether the effect might have been undermined by a conspiracy theory published on the Internet that Cobain's death was not suicide, but they also dismissed this explanation because it "was raised too late to have influenced events in the first month" (1997, p. 195).

In the penultimate paragraph of the article, Martin and Koo raised the possibility that their results were "simply part of natural variability from year to year" (1997, p. 196), though they were reluctant to accept this explanation. They also referred to Kessler et al.'s (1989) study, which they had earlier dismissed, citing the suggestion that "increased public sensitivity to teenage suicide may have created a context in which teenagers have become more resistant to the effects of TV" (1997, p. 196), and to Simkin et al. (1995), whom they credit with the idea of "deterrent effects of media reporting in reducing the number of suicides" (1997, p. 196). In the final paragraph, while conceding that "the expected copycat effect did not occur" (1997, p. 196), they also suggested that "[g]iven previous work it is possible that any increase in suicide was disguised by a marked increase in the MVA [motor vehicle accident] rate or other deaths" and recommended "further exploration ... [of] what was special about the reporting in this case that may conceivably have reduced the likelihood of influence" (1997, p. 196).

The Internet

In recent years, concern has also been expressed about the role of the Internet in provoking suicide. The on-demand, unregulated, and interactive nature of this communication medium distinguish it from print and television communications. At any time of the day or night, people can call up sites and "talk" with other users, who may express whatever views and post whatever information they like about suicide. While the Internet has been used as a tool for suicide prevention, it is easy to locate stories on the Internet of people who are thinking about suicide, or about people who have suicided.

Baume, Cantor and Rolfe (1997) were the first to examine suicide-related sites on the Internet and to raise the alarm about the danger of what was then a relatively new communication medium[1]. The question arises as to whether Baume and colleagues raised a false alarm, or whether their concerns were legitimate.

Baume et al. briefly reviewed the literature on the media–suicide imitation thesis and rather injudiciously summarized:

> Many studies have supported a significant relationship between the reporting of suicide and subsequent suicides. ... Both newspaper and television reports have been shown to influence disproportionately young people to engage in suicidal behavior... (1997, p. 73).

In a second and almost identical article on the subject published in 1998, Baume, Rolfe and Clinton's summary of the literature would likely leave little doubt in the mind of readers:

> The social modelling hypothesis is plausible as studies have found a significant relationship between the reporting of a completed suicide and subsequent suicides ... . [S]tudies have demonstrated that press and television reports significantly influence young people to complete suicide ... . This evidence suggests that explicit discussion of completed suicide in the media encourages young people to consider it a viable option. Therefore, young people struggling with seemingly insurmountable problems may be at their most vulnerable when confronted by news of the death by suicide of a celebrity or close friend... (1998, pp. 134–135).

Baume et al. identify the Internet as "a medium of communication which allows access to seemingly limitless amounts of information by anyone, at anytime..." (1997, p. 74). They continued:

> [T]he amount of material relating to suicide available on the internet is enormous. This information ranges from news reports on electronic newspapers, information on suicide methods, self-help information, academic research and interactive discussion, as well as sites dedicated to the memorial of "pop" culture identities who have completed suicide and music groups who embrace a message of suicide. (1997, p. 74).

Baume et al. (1997) were particularly concerned about the Heaven's Gate mass suicide Internet site. They next cited figures showing that Internet use was increasing rapidly, particularly among males and younger people. They used five search engines using the word "suicide" and came up with between under 12,000 to 124,000 hits[2], and then grouped the information into three categories, discussed below.

Entertainment and Alternative Culture Sites

> Over 300 Internet sites chronicle and pay tribute to the life, death, and music of the punk rock musician [Kurt Cobain] from the band Nirvana. Many of the sites include copies of the suicide note and death certificate. Other sites in this category include joke sites ..., computer game sites ..., and music sites... [which] are of particular interest because of the significant associations that appear to exist between a preference for rock or metal music and suicidal thought and self-harm acts, particularly in adolescent girls (Martin, Clarke, & Pearce, 1993; Martin & Koo, 1996 [sic]). (Baume et al., 1997, pp. 74–75)[3]

Crisis, education, and Research Resources

In this category, Baume et al. (1997, 1998) include sites run by the American Association of Suicidology, the Canadian Association for Suicide Prevention, the Suicide Information Centre, the Samaritans, the Australian Institute for Suicide Research and Prevention, Suicide Prevention Australia, and Kids Helpline.

Newsgroups and Mailing Lists

This category included sites for suicide survivors and suicide support. In particular, Baume et al. discussed a popular newsgroup that began to discuss why suicides increased during holiday periods, but developed to discuss suicide more broadly. They reported that the etiquette of the site was:

> ... messages of discouragement, disparagement, or religious disapproval are not welcome. This site is for those who want to discuss options for suicide ... [and includes] a list of [40] suicide methods with comments about the[ir] speed and efficacy ... About half the methods are frivolous (1997, p. 75). They discussed two other sites, including IRC (Internet Relay Chat) channels and concluded: "Whether written or verbal we must acknowledge that these sites are interactive and that essentially they are the open declaration of suicide notes" (p. 75).

Having briefly surveyed Internet content related to suicide, Baume et al. discussed three cases of suicide notes published on the Internet. The age of one author was given as 26 years, but no information was provided on the age of the other two authors. One case describes the lead-up to a suicide attempt following which the author "urged others to reconsider thoughts of suicide" (1997, p. 77; 1998, p. 137). Baume et al. explained:

> In this medium, the authors of suicide notes conduct an interactive communication, often more like a journal or diary than a traditional suicide note ... Nonetheless, the elements ... are similar (1997, p. 76; 1998, pp. 136–137).

The three cases are sometimes heart-rending stories that unfold over a period of days or weeks and include references to depression, indecision and/or resolve to commit suicide, descriptions of unsuccessful attempts, and discussion of the method, followed by silence.

Baume et al. (1997) were concerned about this because of their (cursory) reading of Sonneck et al.'s (1994) work. They write: "Recent work has confirmed that reduced reporting results in a reduction of suicides by imitation" (p. 77). They argued:

> The plea of Nick W ("I'm gonna do it any day now really I promise") suggests that he may have felt compelled by his internet participation to follow through with suicide. If it were not for his public commitments he might have been able to adopt a more constructive approach to problem-solving without losing face. (p. 77; 1998, p. 139)

The problem with statements like this, and the summary of Martin et al.'s and Sonneck et al.'s work, is that Baume and his colleagues do not appear to have assessed the evidence presented to justify the authors' conclusions, which they overstate and appear to accept uncritically.

The field is characterized by superficial scholarship of this type, leading to general acceptance of what is certainly unproven and very well may be an incorrect conclusion that portrayals of suicide in the media stimulate imitation to a significant extent. As in the quote immediately above, authors in this field often appropriately qualify their arguments or summaries of others' work, but by presenting one scenario and excluding others, they imply that it is the case. There is no evidence whatsoever, other than supposition, that Nick W may have felt compelled to suicide because of his declarations. It is even possible that Nick W is not a real person, or that he is alive. Martin et al.'s work is far from supporting the music–suicide imitation thesis, and Sonneck et al. most certainly did not convincingly demonstrate that reduced reporting leads to reduced imitative suicide. Undeterred by these doubts, Baume et al. continued:

> It is all too easy for self-destructive individuals to incite others to kill themselves. Hence, the internet has considerable potential for a powerful collective destructive force to develop, impacting on ambivalence in a way that may make suicide more likely. (1997, p. 77)[4]

That may be so, but it is also the case that the Internet could be a powerful agent in suicide prevention by providing support to people reaching out for help. The weight of argument in Baume et al.'s work, however, is on the negative side. Second, even if the two cases of suicide Baume et al. presented were real, that some people chose to describe their anguish and prospective death on the Internet does not provide evidence that these postings contributed to their deaths, let alone encouraged anyone else to follow suit. The innuendo and speculation continued:

> What is also worth noting in this context is that the individuals who access the internet in general may differ from those who watch more television or videos. These young people seem to be already more vulnerable, with high risk taking behavior, substance abuse, and depression scores than controls (Martin, 1996). As previously mentioned, the bulk of those who access the internet are 18-24 years of age … and this happened to be a group with a high suicide rate, at least in industrialized nations. (Baume et al., 1997, p. 78)

This statement indicates a very low standard of scholarship. Internet users may or may not differ in a host of ways from consumers of other media. Baume et al. presented no evidence whatsoever to indicate any difference, other than a misleading summary of Martin's work on a cohort of teenaged television viewers. Baume et al.'s reference to "controls" implies that Martin et al.'s research used an experimental design. Baume et al.'s comment implying a connection between youth suicide and Internet use displays no understanding whatsoever of the ecological fallacy.

Baume et al. (1997) concluded by stating, "Cybersuicide is now a reality," and calling for an "appreciation of technologically initiated suicides"[5] as well as the effect of the Internet "on vulnerable populations" (p. 78). In 1998, they suggested that something might need to be done, though they were vague about what action needed to be taken:

> There is a need … to consider carefully the special challenges posed by the Internet and, if necessary, to lobby appropriate agencies and government departments for action. In addition, the various State and national bodies concerned with mental health, media regulation and suicide prevention strategies may need to formulate policies to counter the negative influences of the Internet. (Baume et al., 1998, p. 140)

It is both easy and common for academics to suggest that governments should act, but much less common for such action to occur. Despite this, Martin and Baume were influential in the formulation of media guidelines distributed by the Australian government that recommend a curtailment of suicide reporting for fear of imitation (Penrose-Wall, Baume, & Martin, 1999a, 1999b).

Conclusion

Undoubtedly, there are many effects of suicide on the living, particularly for the family, friends, and associates of those who die by suicide. This chapter has examined an aspect of the effect of suicide on the broader community and concludes that based on careful assessment of the presented evidence, skepticism about the link between publicity about suicides and imitation is warranted — contrary to the conclusions of many studies and the common belief that there is a connection between suicide publicity and imitation. As mentioned earlier, owing to the conclusions reached in studies such as those discussed above, the energy and influence of their authors, and popular concern about the issue, health authorities in several countries have issued guidelines recommending curtailment of suicide reports in the media. The extent to which these guidelines alter reporting practices is a separate issue, but at least in some communities, they appear to have an effect. Therefore, this contribution to the understanding how the dead might influence the living concludes that there is an effect on the community. The effect simply is that of self-censorship on the part of journalists and editors at the behest of public health authorities. That there is imitative suicide due to media publicity is yet to be established.

Notes

1. Pierre Baume was founding director of the Australian Institute for Suicide Research and Prevention at Griffith University in Brisbane. Together with Graham Martin and Jonine Penrose-Wall, Baume is credited as an author of the suicide reporting guidelines distributed under the auspices of the Australian government (Penrose-Wall et al., 1999).
2. A Google search conducted in September 2006 produced 140 million hits for "suicide". It also produced 448 million using the word "drugs", 207 million hits for "murder" plus 28.2 million for "homicide", 104 million hits for "divorce", and 91.1 million hits for "rape". Few people seriously suggest that the Internet is responsible for these behaviors. This branch of suicidology would benefit enormously by considering the literature on the impact of media on audiences, and particularly in relation to other behaviors regarded as socially undesirable; and by the development of an adequate theoretical explanation for the imitation thesis.

3. In the second article, Baume et al. are more emphatic about the findings of Martin's research and cite themselves (in what is essentially the same article) as a source to indicate "These sites are important (Baume *et al.*, 1997) because of the significant associations between some kinds of rock music, suicidal thoughts and suicidal behaviour in young people (Martin, Clarke, & Pierce, 1993)" (Baume et al., 1998, p. 136).
4. This quote became stronger in its second iteration. Together with an implication that the first article provides some supporting evidence, by 1998 it had become: "However, the Internet has considerable potential to be a powerful destructive force that turns ambivalence into declarations of suicide from which it might be impossible to retreat (Baume *et al.*, 1997)" (p. 139).
5. In the second article, Baume et al. (1998) cite themselves, in what is essentially the same article, implying that there is evidence of this phenomenon: "The only Australian study published on this topic so far concluded that the Internet may play a major role in influencing the suicide rates of young vulnerable people who look for confirmation of their feelings and problem-solving approaches in sites that provide encouragement for the act of suicide (Baume *et al.*, 1997)" (p. 139).

References

Australia. (2004). Reporting suicide and mental illness: A resource for media professionals. Canberra: Health Priorities and Suicide Prevention Branch, Department of Health and Ageing, Commonwealth of Australia.

Baume, P., Cantor, C. H., & Rolfe, A. (1997). Cybersuicide: The role of interactive suicide notes on the Internet. Crisis, 18(2), 73–79.

Baume, P., Rolfe, A., & Clinton, M. (1998). Suicide on the Internet: A focus for nursing intervention? Australian and New Zealand Journal of Mental Health Nursing, 7, 134–141.

Blood, R. W., & Pirkis, J. E. (2001). Suicide and the media: Part III: Theoretical issues Crisis, 22, 163–169.

Martin, G., & Koo, L. (1997). Celebrity suicide: Did the death of Kurt Cobain influence young suicides in Australia? Archives of Suicide Research, 3, 187–198.

Michel, K., Frey, C., Wyss, K., & Valach, L. (2000). An exercise in improving suicide reporting in print media. Crisis, 21(2), 71–79.

Penrose-Wall, J., Baume, P., & Martin, G. (1999a). Media resource for the reporting of suicide. Canberra: Commonwealth Department of Health and Aged Care.

Penrose-Wall, J., Baume, P., & Martin, G. (1999b). Achieving a balance: A resource kit for Australian media professionals for the reporting and portrayal of suicide and mental illness. Canberra: Commonwealth of Australia.

Stack, S. (1987). Celebrities and suicide: A taxonomy and analysis, 1948–1983 American Sociological Review 52, 401–412.

Stack, S. (1990). A reanalysis of the impact of non-celebrity suicides: A research note. Social Psychiatry and Psychiatric Epidemiology, 25, 269–273.

Sonneck, G., Etzersdorfer, E., & Nagel-Kuess, S. (1994). Imitative suicide on the Viennese subway. Social Science and Medicine, 38, 453–457.

Wasserman, I. M. (1984). Imitation and suicide: A reexamination of the Werther effect. *American Sociological Review, 49,* 427–436.

CHAPTER 12

Family Disputes, Dysfunction, and Division

Case Studies of Road Traffic Deaths

LAUREN BREEN AND MOIRA O'CONNOR

Families are generally considered to be extremely important sources of psychosocial support in times of stress and crisis. However, such a belief implies a number of assumptions concerning family support following a crisis, such as the death of a family member in a road traffic crash. These assumptions are that families are inherently functional, that families remain functional following the significant and completely unexpected crisis that is a crash fatality, and that support from within the family is the "best" kind of support.

Because the majority of deaths that are significant to us are of family members, it is perhaps unsurprising that these losses have the potential to upset the existing balance within a family. As such, a closer examination of the assumptions about family support is warranted in order to determine the nature of family interactions and family support in times of crisis. In this chapter, we discuss these assumptions in light of research on the psychosocial experiences of grief following the death of a family member in a crash and demonstrate that deceased people continue significantly to affect the daily lives of bereaved families. We begin with a summary of the research methodology and then, using case studies, describe and discuss the family dynamics, dysfunction, and division that result following a crash fatality.

The Research

The broad aims of the research were to explore experiences of grief resulting from losing a family member in a crash. The road deaths all occurred in Western Australia. Data were collected through interviews with bereaved informants and many other relevant informants (e.g., coroner's office, justice department, health department, insurance commission, police, and public documents).

In this chapter, we focus on the interview data from bereaved informants. Twenty-one adults aged 24 to 71 years ($M = 47.95$, $SD = 10.83$) from 16 families bereaved through road crashes in Western Australia, were interviewed. Sixteen were women and five were men. The time that had passed since the deaths of their loved ones ranged from 13 months to 23 years ($M = 6.84$ years, $SD = 6.64$). The age of the deceased at the time of their death ranged from 6 to 73 years ($M = 30.17$, $SD = 20.64$). Who had died in the crashes were predominantly children, followed by siblings, parents, a spouse, and a grandparent. Six of the informants' family members had died as a result of being hit as pedestrians by a vehicle; five were involved in two-vehicle crashes; and five died as a result of single-car crashes.

Family Dynamics, Dysfunction, and Division

The data from the interviews indicated that the families experienced significant discord, ranging from minor disputes between individuals to complete disintegration following the death of a family member in a crash. Although most of the bereaved informants obtained at least some support from their families, they were more likely to discuss instances in which they perceived that their family members failed to provide support. The bereaved informants described their families as irrevocably changed following the death of a loved one in a crash. Some described their families using terms such as "disintegrated" (Brooke), "shattered" (Sharon), and "changed forever" (Karen).

Excerpts from the interview data presented below underline these points and emphasize the degree to which the deceased continue to be a very active and highly complex part of the functioning of the family. All names have been changed.

Case Study 1: George, Debra, and Nick

Some of the bereaved informants attempted to support the different ways people within the same family dealt with their grief. They did this by trying to recognize, anticipate, and respond to their needs, because of their realization that grief is an individual experience that differs from person to person. This made it difficult for the informants to find support from within their families, as they too were grieving. As Nick, whose sister was killed, described it, "My family couldn't really help [me] because they were all affected by it in a similar way that I am." His mother, Debra, reflected on the difficulty she and her husband (Nick's father) had supporting Nick while grieving themselves for their daughter:

> George and I have asked each other did we help Nick enough? 'Cause you're trying to keep everyone together, yourself together and then different personalities and with children, and what they're feeling, and they're just sort of in the background … suffering in their own way or [they'll] switch off and just will leave when people are talking about it, just go into another room and … just blank off take themselves away from it. And they have different reactions, for one, because they're the brother or the sister and we're the parents. (Debra)

Case Study 2: Sylvia and Patrick

Instead of bringing families together, the deaths of loved ones, and the different ways of coping with the deaths, tended to exacerbate tensions within the family unit. In many situations, the different ways of dealing with grief continued to be issues of contention, especially in terms of emotional expression, remembering and talking about the deceased person, and seeking help from professionals. For example, Patrick, whose father and brother died in the same crash, exclaimed, "Mum used to say 'men don't cry.' Rubbish! A real man will show his emotions. Have a cry, you'll feel better for it." Sylvia described how her sons (including Patrick) grieved differently than her, and how they had expressed their expectations of her ability to handle the deaths of her husband and youngest son. This family's situation highlights the potential for crashes to involve multiple fatalities, often within the one family:

> I could imagine the two boys (her adult sons) talking behind my back … [One son] used to say, "You've got to let go Mum, you've got to let go" … I would say to him, "I'm managing the best as I know how" … I felt they had expectations of me that were beyond my control. (Sylvia)

Patrick was critical of his mother for her lack of emotional expression over the deaths as well as her inability to "get over" her grief:

> Things that, not so much upset me but make me a little bit angry, is probably Mum (nervous laugh). I hate to say it but really, she does

> get my ire up … She never cried at the funeral, she never cried at all … and she was upset, you could tell she was upset, but she couldn't shed a tear. And that's funny, 'cause even now there are moments where she doesn't shed any tears. Sometimes I just feel she's bottling it up inside her. She needs to get angry and take it out on something or someone, or break down and have a good cry … Even now, it's two years this month, since the incident, and she still has her ups and downs … I kept putting myself in Mum's shoes [thinking] "how must Mum be feeling?" but after a while I think, well I've dealt with this, I think it's time she should've dealt with it. (Patrick)

The reality is that, following the death of a family member in a crash, each surviving family member will likely have vastly different needs. It is well recognized in the literature that although there are commonalities among grief experiences, each grief experience is unique. The bereaved informants in the present study described their emotions as vacillating rather than following linear stages of grief. Such vacillation in feelings often meant that family members were asynchronous in their grief. Despite the earnest attempts to empathize with one another, the bereaved informants reported that it was difficult to anticipate and meet one another's experiences and needs.

Case Study 3: Kelly

Some of the informants (in this case, all women) reported that they had taken on the role of supporting other members of the family emotionally, while trying to maintain their usual role(s) to preserve a semblance of normality in the family. Some took on the support role voluntarily, while others had it forced upon them by others in the family. For example, Kelly felt she was forced to replace the nurturing role of her deceased mother:

> I'd have [my grandmother] crying on my shoulder one minute, and the next she'd be saying to me "Get it together and sort out the family, look after the boys (her older brothers). The boys are the worry, you're alright," so that was not helpful at all … I remember the first Christmas, which was pretty tough 'cause … Mum died in November and we had this Christmas in December, so you can imagine it was pretty emotional for everybody. I was just sitting on the lawn and my grandfather just looked up at me … and said "If you had sunglasses on you could be my daughter," and I just couldn't cope. I thought "But I'm not, I'm me" … and that was so hard, *so* hard, 'cause I was forever trying to fight for them to see that I was who I was and that I

> wasn't Mum, even though the messages were very clearly that I now had to do the Mum kind of things. It was a huge burden. (Kelly)

Photographs usually provide a link to the deceased person, but for Kelly's family, she *herself* was the link to their deceased daughter and mother, primarily because of her physical similarity to her mother.

Case Study 4: Jelena

Many recalled being so focused on their deceased loved one and maintaining a connection with them that they paid no attention to the other important people in their lives, including surviving children and partners, for a significant period of time. Instead of feeling closer, some informants reported feeling isolated and detached from their family. For example, Jelena felt isolated in her family after her brother's death because other family members, particular her mother, were so enveloped in their own grief:

> For a long time, my Mum actually forgot that she had four other kids and a grandson … I would get frustrated with Mum … like she had forgotten that we were there, it was like you know Sasha this, Sasha that, and eventually it was like, Mum, you've forgotten about the four of us that are living. (Jelena)

Case Study 5: Karen

In addition to talking about how they grieved within their family unit, many informants described the impact that the deaths of their loved ones had on their marriages and spousal relationships, including their sexual relationships. For some informants, the death of a loved one was the catalyst for marital or spousal troubles, whereas for others, it exacerbated existing relationship issues and problems. The informants candidly described instances in which they fought with their spouses because they felt they were not supported or understood. For example, Karen stated,

> I have been accused [by my husband] of maybe even having grown closer to God, at one stage or another since Mikey's death. Well you've got to find comfort somewhere.

Sometimes informants reported verbal and physical fights with their spouses. Karen also spoke of quarrels with her husband in which they blamed each other for the death of their six-year-old son:

> I've been through all of that, the guilt feelings, there's naturally guilt feelings yeah and then there's the blame and I've been there too … I know that I have had to forgive myself for any role [in

> Mikey's death] … You have to reach a point to go over it and over it [and] believe me, [I] did that millions of times, to see what, what if, what could have happened if this or what if that how could it have been that, how could the outcome have been different you know if we had changed this that or something else. And we fought about it, my husband and I, it's like oh yes well maybe *you* should have been looking after him. (Karen)

Case Study 6: Iris

At the time of their children's deaths, three women informants were all in long-term relationships with men who were not the fathers of their deceased children. This added an extra dimension to their grief, as their partners could not fully understand and empathize with them, and consequently the men would not want to talk about the deceased person or the bereaved person's experiences of grief. Iris described instances in which she perceived that her second husband had used her grief over her daughter "against her":

> We went to a barbeque before Christmas it was, the beginning of December and she died at the end of September, and I was talking to somebody and [my husband] was talking to somebody. We finished our conversation and I heard what they were saying, and he said "Iris forgets that other people get embarrassed" and I could hear all this *and* we had to walk past that spot where she was killed [to get to the barbeque], and I remember getting very angry with him. Most of the time I wouldn't let on that I was angry, we'd only just been married, but I did tell him then that I resented him talking over my "case history" with other people, and oh to *only* feel embarrassment. So you want me to take my grief, my hurt, and to make sure that nobody else even feels embarrassed? So I'm supposed to carry their embarrassment as well? … Any time [my husband] and I had an argument of any sort which came many years after [Mary-Anne's death], … he'd always bring her death into it … which was like hitting below the belt as far as I was concerned. (Iris)

Discussion

Often, the bereaved informants' relationships with their family members were not characterized by strong connections and open lines of communication before the deaths of their loved ones, and the loss and subsequent grief served to compound existing tensions. Although in some instances the death of a loved one brought the family closer, it was more common that relationship issues within the family were magnified for a number of reasons: the difficulty in empathizing with and supporting others when bereaved, different ways of grieving and remembering deceased people, role changes, experiences of isolation, having unrealistic expectations of others, and estrangement. As a consequence, most familial relationships were irrevocably changed, and some did not survive the death of a loved one in a crash.

In all instances, the family relationships of the bereaved were tested. These effects are "hidden" behind the closed doors of the family system and are then "silent" effects of bereavement. The interviews with these bereaved families contribute to the literature that questions the assumption that following the death of a family member, families are supportive, harmonious, and synchronized. It was also evident that the impact of the death continued for a long time afterward. The different reactions to the death ensure that the deceased are gone but not forgotten, and continue to live on and be the catalyst for changes in the family structure and inter-relationships.

Acknowledgments

The second author was the primary supervisor. We would also like to acknowledge the project's associate supervisor, Associate Professor Margaret Mitchell (Edith Cowan University), and the adjunct supervisor, Dr. Christopher C. Sonn (Victoria University).

CHAPTER 13

Dark Tourism

The Role of Sites of Death in Tourism

J. JOHN LENNON AND MARGARET MITCHELL

Understanding Tourist Demand

This chapter explores the phenomenon of "dark tourism," a term coined by Foley and Lennon (1996) to describe travel and tourism to places of death, disaster, and atrocity. Consideration of ways in which the dead continue to have an impact on everyday life must include the increasing commodification of places of death as tourist destinations. "Ground Zero," the site of the September 11 attacks on the World Trade Center in New York in 2001, has been visited continuously since the area was reopened after the recovery teams had completed their work. A few weeks after the outrage, the demand by people to pay homage to the site, or simply to see it, forced city authorities to build a viewing platform. Ground Zero and the New York State Museum's installation *WTC, 9/11 First 24 hours* timeline (www.nysm.nysed.gov/wtc_timeline/) are now part of most walking and bus tours of New York. At any time of the day one can find visitors posing for photographs against this tragic backdrop, trying to remember to not smile. The NYSM Web site states that more than 25,000 visitors from across the world visit the site and the installation each day.

In other examples, a specialist tour operator, Holts Battlefield Tours (http://www.holts.co.uk), has offered educational holiday packages built around the sites of famous battles for over 30 years. Since 2002, the travel guide series “Lonely Planet” has provided a Web site of “Fatal Attractions” (www.lonelyplanet.com/theme/fatal_attractions/fatal_index.htm). Their Web site states: “It may seem a tad perverse but there’s really no harm watching how other folk go about knocking on heaven’s door ... Death is inexorably linked to history and culture, and there’s often no better way of understanding a strange place than to see how the locals confront the passage from life to the afterworld.”

Interest in death and horror has long roots. As Seaton and Lennon note, Madame Tussaud “started her career in the late 18th century making death masks of political celebrities guillotined during the French Revolution. The history of her wax modelling was thus infected from the start with an emphasis representing the dead and victims of violence, rather than celebrating the living” (2004, p. 23). Tussaud moved from France to London in 1802 and by 1835 had settled in the famous Baker Street premises. Her “product range” expanded to include notorious criminals and reconstructions of crimes and punishment tableaux in what became known as the “Chamber of Horrors.” In the twenty-first century, this is now an interactive site on the World Wide Web (http://www.madame-tussauds.co.uk/experince_chamber.asp) and is an example of Madame Tussaud’s own long reach from the grave! The popularity of Tussaud’s Chamber of Horrors stimulated the development of the London Dungeon visitor attraction by the Merlin Group, and its replication in other busy tourist centers such as York and Edinburgh. These exhibits are dramatic and focus on torture, murder, and incarceration with only a loose historical link. Dark tourism is clearly popular by any measure of consumer demand, developed supply, information about the places, and the catering for visitors’ requirements.

The many museums and visitor centers dedicated to death and the sheer number of visitors to these places attest to their obvious attraction. Dark tourism now merits inclusion in an encyclopedia of tourism (Jafari, 2000) and has become a popular area for undergraduate and postgraduate research. Before Foley and Lennon’s publication in 1996 there was little academic work in this area. Since then, dark tourism has been accepted as a phenomenon, further explored in Lennon and Foley’s definitive text *Dark Tourism: The Attraction of Death and Disaster* (2002).

Perhaps the most famous site associated with the death of a single person is the Texas School Book Depository, from which Lee Harvey Oswald assassinated US President John F. Kennedy in 1963, and the “grassy knoll” where conspiracy theorists think a second assassin lay in wait. Using a close examination of the treatment of this site for visitors and tourists as a foundation, Foley and Lennon (1996) consider a range of other places of death, including the First World War graves in France and Belgium, the extant sites of the Second World War concentration camps in Europe, and incarceration sites in Southeast Asia. Iles (2005) has described the significance of the battle sites of the First World War in Europe:

> As one of the most catastrophic and traumatic wars in European history passes out of living memory, the "war to end all wars" continues to hold our fascination. The appalling and evocative images of the First World War, with its slaughter of soldiers by the millions, its total devastation of the landscape, its brutality and its widely perceived mismanagement have remained firmly etched in the collective memory of the western world. Although much of the battled-scarred landscape of the Western Front has long since disappeared under crop cultivation and urban development, today thousands of tourists are drawn to visit its sites every year. (Iles, 2005)

Several other studies of tourism to battle sites underline the importance of these places to people attempting to understand the past (Foley & Lennon, 1996; Henderson, 1997, 2000; Smith, 1996, 1998; Seaton, 1996; Iles, 2003). Visits to sites of death, battle sites, and places of extermination such as Auschwitz and Belsen, and the related visitor centers and heritage sites, are common holiday activities for many tourists, providing "entertainment" as well as education in the politics and history of the event. Urry (1990) uses the Berlin Gestapo museum to illustrate Foucault's "gaze" in the context of the tourist. Seaton (1996) has also provided a typology of the major forms of dark tourism, and an account of its development. Rojek (1993) and Seaton and Lennon (2004) have described travel to death sites as modern pilgrimage. Visitation to the Second World War Holocaust sites has been studied by Tunbridge and Ashworth (1996), Lennon and Foley (2000), and Lennon and Smith (2004). Other useful reviews of this tourist sector include the work of Dann (1998), who proposes that visiting places of death is a foil to everyday life, offering people the possibility of celebrating retribution and justice and also of encountering deviance and crime.

Cemeteries or internment sites (Seaton, 1996), slavery heritage sites (Dann & Seaton, 2001), celebrity death sites (Palmer, 1993) and prison and penal colonies (Strange & Kempa, 2003; Ashworth, 2004) are also of great interest to tourists. Lennon and Foley (2000) have also looked at site representation in the context of divided nations such as Cyprus, where exhibitions of atrocities perpetrated by Greek and Turkish Cypriots against each other were mirrored on either side of the demilitarized zone that divided the island. Timothy, Prideaux, and Bruce (2004) have further advanced understanding the attraction of borders of conflict and the fascination in "forbidden zones."

Figure 13.1 Tourists at Auschwitz, Poland. (photo J. John Lennon).

Interpretation

Ethical questions and concern about motivation abound in this subject, and it is important to consider the ideologies underpinning the *interpretation* of these sites. Interpretation of death sites, heritage sites, and the content of museums associated with the darkest excesses of human behavior is an effective way of inculcating a dominant ideology. Visitors may see such places as little more than entertainment rather than selective or partial interpretation or, at worst, a form of social engineering. The crucial element in dark tourism, and the degree to which the sites are educational or propagandist, is in the interpretation of the events that took place. Interpretation can be revisionist in terms of the causes and effects of the event represented at these locations and is often constructed from a judgmental position in which the people involved are seen as victims or perpetrators, heroes or oppressors. For example, Lennon and Foley (2000) have examined the interpretation of sites of mass extermination, considering locations such as the Killing Fields of Cambodia as commodified elements of the tourist experience. That these sites of mass killing have enduring fascination is now accepted: it is known that visits are less likely by those with a direct family connection to the historical event than by tourists who are in the area. Both the imagery and the text used at such sites are important to the ideological construction of history underpinning interpretation. This central issue of interpretation and the role and function of death tourism in history and remembrance are themes that will be discussed throughout this chapter.

Sensitivities abound in this area, and the media have done much to create our fascination with visiting death sites, and coverage is often cloaked in the language of sensationalism (Seaton & Lennon, 2004). In the United Kingdom, examples are the media coverage of the 1996 massacre by Thomas Hamilton of 15 children and their teacher in the gymnasium at Dunblane Primary School, in Scotland. At the time, a tabloid newspaper "uncovered" a tour operator interested in providing tours of death sites such as those of the Dunblane and Hungerford (United Kingdom) massacres, or Cromwell Street in Gloucester (home of serial murderers Fred and Rosemary West), and Cranley Gardens (home of serial murderer Dennis Nilson). This was considered exploitive, and the tour operator was described as "Britain's vilest man" (*Daily Star*, August 4, 2002, p. 1). More recently, the house in Soham, England where the children Holly Wells and Jessica Chapman were murdered in 2002 was deemed totally unacceptable as a visitor destination. One week after the arrest of the perpetrator several weeks after the incident, a UK newspaper reported:

> Soham has … become a day trip destination for some visitors attracted by its association with a heinous crime. The streets have been jammed with traffic over the Bank Holiday weekend. Coaches taking tourists to visit nearby Ely cathedral or the sights of Cambridge have made detours to the fenland town. (O'Neill, *Daily Telegraph*, August 26, 2002, p. 4)

It appears to be acceptable to visit a place where a tragic incident took place in the days immediately following in order to show respect and observe in reverence, laying flowers, or leaving letters and gifts. Memorials in the form of an officially sanctioned plaque or marker may be placed, and later, interpretation of the site can take place. Distance in time appears to make tours of older sites where death and tragedy took place more acceptable and less exploitive than those of more recent events. Tours to recent murder sites can be contrasted with the enduring fascination for tourists to London of Jack the Ripper murder tours (http://www.jack-the-ripper-walk.co.uk/) and gangland tours, for example, the Untouchables Gangster Tour of Chicago (http://www.gangstertour.com), each featuring key death sites.

The contemporary and future interpretations at the site of the 9/11 attack in New York will almost certainly be contentious. Museums were keen to respond following the attack on the World Trade Center. Within weeks, a meeting of 30 New York area museums was held (Pearson, 2005). A view taken early on was that the story could not be told only through pictures and film, and that real artifacts from the site were needed. Obtaining artifacts, however, was far from simple. The task of searching for human remains and personal belongings could not be conducted at Ground Zero, and debris was moved to a landfill site on Staten Island. There, more than 4,000 separate human remains and 54,000 personal items were identified. The New York State Museum (NYSM) in Albany was keen to proceed with the development of a curated display, and, from November 2001, museum staff were granted access to some items and later were able to obtain a crushed fire engine and a range of wreckage and other artifacts from the building. In addition, many relatives of victims donated personal items. The exhibition was developed around the themes of rescue, recovery, and response, matched with a touring photographic exhibition with smaller artifacts. An installation at Ground Zero was developed by the NYSM, comprising a 36-foot timeline depicting events that took place from 6:30 am to 11:29 pm on September 11, 2001 (http://www.nysm.nysed.gov/wtc_timeline). The NYSM notes that the timeline was "designed by the museum and developed with the assistance of family members who lost loved ones that day."

The museum's exhibition is patriotic, with the U.S. flag displayed as a symbol of "freedom for the world." There is no mention of the terrorists' names, their motives, or their narratives. Nor in the collection of condolences and artifacts sent from around the world is material from Islamic groups displayed, although such material was collected. Thus, the story of 9/11 and its emerging history remains partial. Yet thinking in terms of potential interpretation of the site, it can be said that it fails to answer or even pose the question "Why?" Much has changed since September 2001, and by 2006 the exhibits are set against a context of growing opposition in the United States to the war in Iraq.

Tourist promotion of Hungary and its recent tragic past shows how memory can be usurped by entrepreneurs to create a commodified experience (Whitington, 2004). The House of Horror Museum at 60 Andrassey Boulevard (www.visithungary.ie) is where much of the torture and killing of the fascist Arrow Cross Party in the 1940s and the subsequent excesses of the Communist regime of the 1950s and 1960s took place. Hungary formed a majority collaborationist government complicit in the Holocaust and the extermination of the Hungarian Jewish population. The first dark use of this nineteenth-century building was by Ferenc Szalasi's extreme fascist party, who were complicit with the Gestapo and SS during the war. Following liberation after the Second World War, the Political Police of the Hungarian Communist Party, led by Peter Gabor, were located in this building. As a site of torture and death for as many as 100,000 people, it is an important site through which to try to understand the complexities of Hungary's recent past, yet the dramatic interpretation of the House and its marketing are intended to attract visitors and invoke a reaction. One travel Web site (http://www.concierge.com) describes the Horror House: "Creepiness has been amplified to the max with recreations of torture chambers, screening of propaganda films, survivor interviews … luxuries belonging to the Orban-era thugs, and walls of coerced 'confessions.' It's part chamber of horrors and part memorial." An example is the video at the exit of the museum, in which a hangman calmly recounts the techniques of strangulation and hanging. The Horror House does not reflect clearly the idea of a nation attempting to understand and take seriously its recent tragic past.

The contemporary Communist Party in China appears not to have objectively reflected on the dark past of the Cultural Revolution (1966–1976) under Mao Zedong, which led to hundreds of thousands of deaths. There has been no objective assessment of what happened during this period, and schoolchildren are taught little about the Cultural Revolution. This period is, however, being reflected in museums that are not officially sanctioned. China's first Museum of the Cultural Revolution has opened near the industrial port city of Shantou in the Guandong district and explores the worst excesses of the Cultural Revolution (Coonan, 2006), and is visited by approximately a thousand people a day. The museum in Shantou provides a radical counterpoint to official history of this period. A driving force behind the museum is the Chinese author Ba Jin, who has commented, "Every town in China should establish a museum about the Cultural Revolution" (Coonan, 2006, p. 28). It is noteworthy also that a significant Hong Kong businessperson, Li Kwa Shing, is a major donor to the project.

Argentina is also facing its dark history with the development of a museum at the site of the former naval medical school where torture and murder occurred during the period of Argentina's "dirty war" (1976–1983). The museum is an authentic heritage site and potentially a location to honor and interpret this period in Argentinean history, but many Argentineans dislike the term dirty war. At the time some supported the coup, seeing it as a means to reduce the violence of the guerrillas and death squads of both left and right and to end strikes and hyperinflation, and there remains much controversy about this period. Human rights groups have recorded the deaths of more than 30,000 *desaparecidos* ("the disappeared") over these years, and the grief of parents, family, and partners of the *desaparecidos* remains. The museum has stimulated huge interest in museum development in Argentina, but it is unlikely to provide closure for the families of the *desaparecidos*. As one woman said of the death of her daughter and husband: "My husband is dead. All this is too painful to become history. First it has to become memory" (quoted in Coonan, 2006, p. 23).

It is evident that ideology and politics can drive the development of such sites both to commemorate victims and to support existing regimes. As Tunbridge and Ashworth (1996) have commented, the power to perpetuate the memory of the dead has always been unequally distributed. There is no relationship between memorials and associated interpretive centers and the extent, for example, of human extermination that took place at the site. This inequality was a major impetus for Lennon and Foley (1996, 2000) in their attempt to understand the contemporary interpretation of sites and the political and social underpinnings of why certain sites were not interpreted and supported financially (and the events and victims' tragic past that the sites represented largely ignored), while at others there is considerable investment.

A clear example of this is found in comparing the interpretation and memorializing of the incarceration and extermination of Roma and Sinti (Gypsies) in the Czech Republic with that of Jews in the same country (Lennon & Smith, 2004). The extent of the Gypsy Holocaust is unknown because there were no Nazi records of Gypsy extermination, although estimates are that fewer than 10% of the 6,000 to 8,000 Roma living in Czech lands in 1942 survived the war. Selective interpretation driven by clear ideological agendas is obvious in the Czech Republic in comparing Lety, in Northern Bohemia, which was a Czech-run camp during the Second World War where hundreds of Roma died through disease, hunger or abuse, and Terezin, a work camp located one hour from Prague where very

Figure 13.2 Roma and Sinti Holocaust interpretation, Lety, Czech Republic (photo, J. John Lennon).

many of the 150,000 Jews incarcerated there perished under Nazi occupation (see www.holocaust.cz and www.pamatnik-terezin.cz). Terezin is well preserved and been repaired following the significant damage by flooding in 2002, with significant investment in interpretation and facilities, but Lety has been almost totally ignored. The reason seems clear: Roma and Sinti annihilation involved the contributions of Czech nationals and so could not be blamed on an oppressive invader.

Remains of the camp at Lety were lost in the communist period, and in the post-communist era, only one sign and an interpretation panel had been placed there (Figure 13.2). Lennon and Smith see this as evidence of a nation as yet unable to deal with this period of its history. The violence against and oppression of the Roma and Sinti peoples remains controversial in the Czech Republic today. The physical sites of death are of enormous social, psychological, and political importance, and in the Czech Republic the site "has long been a polarising issue for the nation's politicians" (Kenety, 2005). The remains of the camp and its mass graves were lost because of a huge pig farm built over the site in the 1970s, which was seen as an affront to the memory of the victims. The Czech Republic has been singled out in a European Parliament resolution for failing to remove the pig farm and create a "graceful memorial to honour victims of the Romani Holocaust" (Kenety, 2005).

The theme of the ideologically selective interpretation of significant death sites has also been explored by Lennon and Wight (2005, 2006) in their examination of Lithuania as an emerging tourism destination. Lithuania has invested significantly in interpretation of its period of Soviet occupation and the partisan struggle between 1944 and 1953 (for tourist sites associated with this and other aspects of Lithuania's history, see www.scantours.com/lithuania_history.htm), which can be contrasted with the selective interpretation given to the incarceration and extermination of Jews in Lithuania perpetrated during the Second World War. Before 1939 Lithuania was a center of Jewish arts, literature, and culture, with a population of 220,000 Jews, comprising almost 25% of Lithuania's population. After the Second World War there were fewer than 20,000. Lithuanians at all levels were involved in the incarceration and extermination process in what was, proportionate to population, the largest per capita annihilation of Jews in Europe. The reasons for this difference in memorializing in Lithuania is obvious, and monuments and memorials to the Jews of this period are decaying owing to lack of investment; maintenance of the Vilnius Jewish Museum is largely based on overseas donations (http://www.muziejai.lt/Vilnius/genocido_auku_muziejus.en.htm).

Dark tourism can be thought of as both a product of the circumstances of the late modern world and a significant influence on it. The ideologies, politics, economics, sociology, and technology of the contemporary world are as important as causal factors in the events on which such tourism is focused as they are now central to the selection and interpretation of sites that become tourist destinations. In developing a theory of dark tourism to understand visitation and interpretation of sites, it is evident that there are elements of the premodern, modern, and postmodern (Foley & Lennon, 1996; Lennon & Foley, 2000). Pilgrimage to sites for mourning, prayer, and reverence reflects the premodern. The many package holidays and structured tours offered by contemporary commercial tourist agents, have their origins in the so called Grand Tour of Europe made by the rich of the late seventeenth and eighteenth centuries. These tours had the aim of enlightening Europe's young elite and have their origins in modernist notions of learning and education. Similarly, Lennon and Foley (2000) have found that contemporary commercial development of many sites of death and tragedy is defended on the grounds of their educational value. To fail to develop the sites, it is argued, would result in the lessons of the past being forgotten; ironically, though, this is the rationale provided where there is blatant exploitation and highly selective interpretation. Beyond its value for educational purposes, each site is evaluated for its cost recovery and revenue generation potential, resulting in commodification, theatricality, and packaging of history. Analysis of interpretation and the content of such sites provides clear evidence that tragedy is being abridged to fit a tourist itinerary.

Postmodernity provides a perspective from which to understand the degree of anxiety and doubt that such events and their extant physical locations create. The emotional valence of such sites and their palpable political and social meanings result in planners and governments often being confused about what to do with them. There was equivocation, for example, about what should be done with the Texas School Book Depository building in Dallas, which visitors to the city wanted to see. It remained undeveloped and practically unused for 26 years as debate continued, until the Sixth Floor Museum at Dealey Plaza was opened in February 1989 to house a museum dealing with President Kennedy's assassination (www.jfk.org).

Often, buildings where a death has occurred under horrific or tragic circumstances will be demolished to stem an unacceptable level of public interest, and replaced with a neutral park or other place of remembrance. The house at 25 Cromwell Street, Gloucester, where Fred and Rosemary West carried out their rape and murder of at least nine young women, was demolished in 1996. To prevent souvenir hunters, the debris was buried some 20 meters underground and the infamous wrought-iron house number sign was removed by the RAF to be destroyed. Similarly, the Dunblane

Primary School Gymnasium, the site of the tragic massacre of school children in Scotland in 1996, has been demolished and replaced with a Garden of Remembrance.

The modern interest in celebrity and in famous places will continue to increase peoples' desire to visit death sites. Similarly, communication—whether by television, radio, pod-cast, mobile telephone, or computer screen—will continue to produce images of violence, war, and tragedy that will attract and stimulate visitation. Crucial is the role of technology, most specifically global communications technology, which will not only stimulate visitation but also reduce the time between an event and tourist visits (Seaton & Lennon, 2004). The nature of such technologies is that remote events can be made local; they can collapse time so that war, atrocities, and disasters can be watched in real time—for example, the clear and compelling images of the attack on the Twin Towers in September 2001.

The certainty is that interest in dark tourism will continue. The importance psychologically of *place* in confronting and memorializing death, whether of an individual or of thousands of disenfranchised people, is a main driver of dark tourism. People want to see where it happened. The selection of sites of death for maintenance and memorial has been driven by contemporary politics and social values, and because of that, their educative function needs to be tempered in the context of their contemporary interpretation.

That the dead continue to influence our lives is obvious from the draw of the sites of their deaths. The importance and meaning of such places is captured by Bruce Scates, who says of the First World War site of Gallipoli in Turkey, where many contemporary Australians and New Zealanders make pilgrimage: "This place is full of souls, some resting and others not" (Scates, 2006).

References

Ashworth, G. (2004). Tourism and the heritage of atrocity: Managing the heritage of South African apartheid for entertainment. In T. V. Singh (Ed.), *New horizons in tourism* (pp. 38–76). Oxfordshire, UK: CABI.

Britain's vilest man. (27 May 1996). *Daily Star*, p. 1.

Coonan, C. (2006). China's first Cultural Revolution museum exposes Mao's war on 'bourgeois culture.' *The Independent*, February 21, 2006, p. 28.

Dann, G. (1998). The dark side of tourism. *Etudes et Rapports/Studies and Reports, Serie Sociology/Psychology/Philosophy/Anthropology*, *14*, 232–254.

Dann, G., & Seaton, A. V. (Eds.). (2001). Slavery contested heritage and thanatourism (pp. 1–30). *Haworth Hospitality Press* (New York).

Foley, M., & Lennon, J. J. (1996). JFK and a fascination with assassination. *International Journal of Heritage Studies*, *2*, 210–226.

Henderson, J. C. (1997). Singapore's wartime heritage attraction. *Journal of Tourism Research*, *8*(2), 39–49.

Henderson, J. C. (2000). War as a tourist attraction: The case of Vietnam. *International Journal of Tourism Research, 2,* 269–280.
Iles, J. (2003). Death, leisure and landscape: British tourism to the Western Front. In M. Dorrian & G. Rose (Eds.), *Deterritorialisations: Revisioning landscapes and politics* (pp. 234–243). London: Black Dog.
Iles, J. (2005). War, death, politics and remembrance: the commemorative landscape of the Western Front. Paper presented at the 7th International Conference on Death, Dying and Disposal, Bath, England, September 15–17, 2005.
Jafari, J. (Ed.). (2000). *Encyclopaedia of tourism.* London: Routledge.
Kenety, B. (2005). Stench of Czech pig farm reaches Brussels. www.radio.cz/en/article/66565. Retrieved April 30, 2006.
Lennon, J. J., & Foley, M. (2000). *Dark tourism: The attraction of death and disaster.* London: Cassell.
Lennon, J. J., & Smith, H. (2004). A tale of two camps: Contrasting approaches to interpretation and commemoration in the sites at Lety and Terezin. *Journal of Tourism Recreation Research, 3*(2), 15–25.
O'Neill, S. (2002, August 26). Soham murder site visitors increase. *Daily Telegraph*, p. 4.
Palmer, G. (1993). *Death: The trip of a lifetime.* New York: Harper Collins.
Pearson, D. (2005). New York stories. *Museums Journal, 105*(9), 30–33.
Rojek, C. (1993). *Ways of escape.* Basingstoke, UK: Macmillan.
Scates, B. (2006). Gallipoli pilgrimage. *Compass*, Australian Broadcasting Corporation, Sunday, 23 April 2006. http://www.abc.net.au/tv/guide/netw/200604/programs/RN0511H018D23042006T221000.htm.
Seaton, A. V. (1996). Guided by the dark: From Thanatopsis to thanatourism. *International Journal of Heritage Studies, 2,* 234–244.
Seaton, A. V., & Lennon, J. J. (2004). Thanatourism in the early 21st century: Moral panics, ulterior motives and alterior desires. In T. V. Singh (Ed.), *New horizons in tourism.* Oxfordshire, UK: CABI.
Smith, V. (1996). War and tourism: An American ethnography. *Annals of Tourism Research, 25,* 202–207.
Strange, C., & Kempa, M. (2003). Shades of dark tourism: Alcatraz and Robben Island. *Annals of Tourism Research, 20,* 386–405.
Timothy, D. J., Prideaux, B., & Kim, S. S. (2004) Tourism at borders of conflict and (de)militarized zones. In T. V. Singh (Ed.), *New horizons in tourism.* Oxfordshire, UK: CABI.
Tunbridge, J. E., & Ashworth, G. (1996). *Dissonant heritage: The management of the past as a resource on conflict.* Chichester, UK: John Wiley.
Whitington, P. (2004). City on the Danube in Cara. *Smurfit Communications* (Ireland), June, pp. 28–34.
Wight, C., & Lennon, J. J. (2005). Towards an understanding of visitor perceptions of 'dark' sites: The case of the Imperial War Museum of the North, Manchester. *Journal of Hospitality and Tourism, 2*(2), 105–122.
Wight, C., & Lennon, J. J. (2007). Selective interpretation and eclectic human heritage. *Tourism Management.*
Uty, J. (1990). The tourist gaze. London: Sage.

CHAPTER 14

Immortality Work

Photographs as Memento Mori

HALLA BELOFF

> Perhaps photography is best understood as the return of the departed. It is a powerful medium haunted by a pre-modern spectral world that lives on in a post-modern electronic universe. (McGrath, 2005, p. 56)

In the age of mechanical reproduction, an absence can be replaced by a visual image. Photographs then become particularly precious residues because they can carry a freight of actuality. This gives all portrait photographs from the past a sharp poignancy for anyone who pays them serious attention, even if they are strangers. All photographs must become *memento mori* (Barthes, 1981).

Existence is a biological imperative. We want to exist and not to vanish at our death. We use our ingenuity to maintain life and, while we live, to create for ourselves a useful, interesting, moral, and loving identity. This is our ambition. We may not succeed, we may not have many tools or props, but that is what we would like. As conscious beings we cease at death, but some traces remain. This is the simplest working hypothesis of a rationalist.

The paradox, then, is that we do not take the absolute imperative of our mortality at all seriously. After all, if we did, we could hardly continue to go about our daily lives. The fact of mortality would have to subsume everything else. It contradicts all our worldly concerns. So we put it to one side. However, here today, we in the condition of postmodernity can take it up in serious style. As intellectuals, it is our function to take on the task of trying to unravel the texture of everyday life and so to understand our condition.

It is identity, the successor of the concept of personality, that psychologists conjure with now: the self as known to the self. Or more specifically, we refer to the subjective experience of our selves in and among the many roles that we play. Personal life then becomes a narrative that we tell ourselves about ourselves. (The plural will be noted.) And in the narrative, the characters of our dear relations and friends play a crucial part.

We hope to be ontologically secure. We need to find evidence that we have not just an existence, but a steady and worthy one. Again, our families and friends support and indeed justify that existence. Then we must recognize that for us in the Western world, the old technology of still photography, invented in 1839, has been and remains one of the powerful ways in which we create, present, consume, and keep ourselves and those we love. After death, that part of our and their presented identity is maintained. For how long is another question. The interaction of such a simple historical technology and the human spirit presents a serious intellectual nexus of modernity, first proposed by Walter Benjamin (1973a, 1973b).

Traces in the Age of Mechanical Reproduction

We all know that in a painting of a person, the skill of the artist and the artist's own identity as a creative character work to separate the result on the canvas from the actual appearance-in-nature of the sitter. Although painting and photography share the framing of the image outcome, traditionally a photograph must consist of the reflection of light from the subject. The print contains information about someone who was there like that. Photography is the child of chemistry, not painting. Beyond the camera obscura and the grid illustrated for us by Dürer, we retain the reflection of the image of light.

The argument for survival through photography cannot be considered either trivial or cynically materialistic. In our hand we can have proof of our existence. And when we are dead, our friends and relations continue to "have" us near them.

A hundred years later, I can see my maternal grandparents in their studio photograph, then called a *carte de visite*—an ironic name. They were poor people who did not "visit" in the sense of paying calls and would never have had any usual kind of visiting card. I am glad to have the image, but my mother got much more pleasure looking at it.

Although I work in the field of photographs, I have surprisingly few photographs of my family. None are on display. But we know this is not the norm. Many people who have had to experience the dreadful death of a child find significant comfort in creating a set of finely framed photographs of the dead one around them.

Immortality Work

The creation of human images is old indeed, as old as magic. Even the rationalist Romans had small sculptured heads commissioned by the parents of a son as he went away as a prefect with the legions. We now see it is a very generalized head with short curly hair, but at the time this was surely a substitute son.

Even more obviously, the character of many of the great people of the past has come to us through sculpture and painting. We believe that we know what Julius Caesar looked like, and indeed what he was like, because we know his portrait head. Madame de Pompadour reclined like this, and David Hume looks at us with a worldly stance to this day in the Scottish National Gallery in Edinburgh. But we also know that the job lot of Scottish kings in the Palace of Holyrood House were painted after their deaths, and we doubt that Napoleon Bonaparte looked quite as beautifully romantic as Gérard David shows him to us, windswept on a white horse.

In a photograph there seems to be a "fact" presented to us; there are few uncertainty tokens. The peculiar power of photography is to produce what seems to us an exact reproduction of a specific individual. Our sepia, two-dimensional copy of our grandmother is an image that brings the subject marvelously near. In its own way, it is solemn and permanent. The technological developments of more recent times promise a wealth of more informal likenesses, produced with little effort or cost; however, their quality of permanence is more ambiguous. Photography has moved from the grave studio occasion, through the box Brownie and Instamatic, and the Polaroid for the impatient, now to digital images that appear on one's computer screen. The pleasure of informality and natural settings is paid for by impermanence. We must consider that in the future people may not have pictures of themselves as children and none of their parents, when their computer has been traded in for a cleverer one. The life of traces is in danger.

I am nominating for immortality here photographs of people as their remains, even though I cannot deny that lighting, retouching, and even the famous smidgen of Vaseline on the lens may interfere with brute naturalism. However, I claim that there has been, up to now, the reality of the event of photographing. More than that, there is Walter Benjamin's quotation from A. J. Wiertz: "In photography images become intellectually reflective and therefore agitational" (Buck-Morss, 1995, p. 132).

What is meant by "intellectually reflective" and "agitational"? It is not a complicated idea. When we pay serious attention to a photograph, which we rather rarely do, it not only makes us think, but we have to think about some aspects of ourselves in association. This may be part of the pleasure or the poignancy. Benjamin and, more recently, Roland Barthes have both argued for the special status of a photograph, not only to the person portrayed but also for we the viewers. Barthes's statements have become aphorisms: "What I see indeed existed" (1981, p. 82); "the image is never metaphoric" (p. 78); "photography has something to do with resurrection" (p. 82). For Barthes, a photograph is alive. Even "the photograph of a corpse means that a corpse is alive *as a corpse*" (p. 79). If the photograph is alive, there is no vanishing point.

But at the same time, the photograph, taken now at some happy time in a friend's life, moves on to become eventually her *memento mori*. It is Barthes whose poetic persuasion convinces us that all photographs of people contain that tragedy as well as their potential for comfort.

The Making of the Image

A photograph of a person involves physics, chemistry, perhaps electronics, some skill in self-presentation, and a relationship between the subject and the photographer—technology and psychology. Identity work is central in the making. I refer to a photograph being made, rather than taken or shot. Acknowledgement must be made to a constructive dimension. It does not just happen. There is photographic activity going on. There is work for the creator and the subject, both.

An index of the element of impression management is given by the fact that some of us, women more than men, hate to have a photograph made. We righteously resent "being taken" unknowingly. We demand to have even a very quick chance to touch our hair and to sit up straight. We examine the results there and then, to see how we have come out. We fear that our impression is not good enough.

We know that it is important to follow the rules of the pose and show our appropriate self, our proper identity, in a creditable way, although at the same time it should be credible. In a family setting, we must appear healthy, happy, and handsome. The person with the camera holds serious power. They are in the position to create good identities of an individual or a whole family. That family album, that history will be kept and will form the very nucleus of the past for the present and the future—our past, present, and future.

After the first culling, printed photographs cannot be thrown away. They have a magical quality. To tear one up is not only to injure the subject but also to attack our relationship with them. In a sense, then, photographs have a quality of the *unheimlich*, the uncanny (Freud, 1985 [1919]), not least because they provide us with a kind of "double."

If we, at some level, understand their value to our identity, we must also appreciate the power of the photographer (Beloff, 1985). It is that power that is at the heart of all the discussion about the ethics of photographing, including the evils of intrusive newspaper pictures. The camera has the ability to make us for good or bad—and that is not limited to outward appearance. Included here are our social presence and our continued existence. A photograph becomes an externalization of memories of us. As we are on the little piece of paper, so we remain.

It is our awareness, not usually put into words, of the contradictions and imbalances here that provides the pathos of a photograph. Loved ones are present in their absence, though dead or distant. We see the trivial picture, and that is what is left of their wonderful part in our life and our existence—all that is left in our world. And yet we have that. The remains, we hope, will provide some solace. But Roland Barthes did not find the picture of his mother a solace; for him it simply reproduced the overwhelming tragedy of his loss.

Such an evocation of emotion can happen sometimes even when we have never known the subject, let alone have a relationship with them. Barthes illustrates the idea with the engaging *Ernest, Paris 1931.* We wonder what happened to Ernest. Is he still alive? He is

"It is possible that Ernest is still alive today: but where? how? What a novel!"

A. Kertész: Ernest. Paris, 1931

Figure 14.1 Kertesz, Ernest, Paris 1931. "It is possible that Ernest is still alive today: but where? how? What a novel!" From *Camera Lucida: Reflections on Photgraphy*, New York: Hill & Wang. Andre Kertez © Ministère de la Culture, France, by R. Barthes, 1981. Reprinted with permission.

Figure 14.2 Zille, Friedrichstrasse, Berlin, c. 1900. From *Heinrich Zille: Photographien, Berlin 1890–1910* (p. 92), by W. Ranke, 1979, Germany: Schirmer/Mosel. Photograph by Heinrich Zille.

here so innocent, so vulnerable. Was he tenacious enough to survive the 1939 war and the German occupation? He might have become a collaborator, a very bad man. In the picture, his naïveté is unaware of these possibilities.

Returning to the earlier contention of Benjamin, we must consider in this boy's image too some of the multitude of selves that are with us and form our background. We can see our partial innocence, our potential lost selves. No wonder there is "reflection" and there is "agitation."

This may apply even to less ingratiating images. Zille's (1979) man, taken about the turn of the last century, has not posed but has been unknowingly captured. That is his particular simplicity. Unlike Ernest, his life is there before us. A serious, poor workingman in the hurly-burly of a city street; he is unnoticed in it. With the mundane gesture of looking at the change in his pocket, he demonstrates the saying that money lives in cities. The clock stands as another particular symbol of city life and its regulation. The paradox is that his life in nearly over, and yet here we are a hundred years later, and he is available for inspection in various parts of the Western world. His physical death is unimportant. My gaze has an intrusive, voyeuristic quality. And the feeling has a personal resonance with me and perhaps others, in terms of our grandfathers and great-grandfathers as workingmen like him.

It is the voyeurism that is balanced by the serious attention. The latter term is a worthy locution. Among the torrent of millions of photographs produced every year; we avoid doing that nearly all the time to remain sane. Only a few earn that privilege.

Demonstrations of Frozen Memories

Consider photography at its most everyday and seemingly spontaneous, in the amateur snap and in the family album. Will we find here the reproduction of the most casual perception and memories? Occasionally we see people caught off guard and at random, but that is not the rule of the game. Jo Spence (1986; Spence & Holland, 1991) has made a full dissection of the family snaps and the meaning of domestic photographing, but we must note that family albums show a specific set of representations that depict us in our moments of celebration, in bloom. Thus we like to be seen and remembered. There are no off moments. Nick Waplington (1991) and John Billingham (1998), art photographers, have been brave enough to produce documents in art galleries and books that break that rule. They work to subvert the canon of family photography and show up the careful masking that we normally are permitted in front of the camera.

Human beings are all in the construction business, here creating particular personal and family narratives. The visual stories in our albums are an earnest part of that, not a trifling sideline. The fact that there is not a true story here but rather a demonstration of social custom—sometimes a cover for secrets and lies and also a valiant attempt at aesthetic production—does not detract from their interest or the power of their discourse.

In family albums, our histories are not only contained, but are validated by them and partly constructed for them. In such albums, the meaning for the family members is rich and complex, as much about what and who are not there as about what and who are.

There have been formal publications of some albums that demonstrate the concepts present for all of us. The publications may come about because the family members were or became famous, or because the context of the family has some significance. But for the purpose here, the critical issue is that the images show us individuals in life, who communicate with us, with whom we can empathize, and whose absence now evokes emotions of sadness and more than that, as we have seen, of melancholy. But at the same time, for most of us they also evoke the happiness of the past and enable us to relive our relationships with them and the good times when we existed to give each other pleasure.

The Camera of My Family

It is good to consider here a heightened case, although the basis is the same for all of us. A family and its members want to document their existence; in doing so they celebrate not only their experiences and achievements but also their love and respect for one another. But all glory is fleeting. In a few years, everyone and all things are gone. Noren (1976) has published the

Figure 14.3 Summer Bavaria, 1910. From *The Camera of My Family* (p. 79), by C.H. Noren, 1976, New York: Alfred A. Knopf. © Catherine Hanf Noren. Reprinted with permission.

summary album of the Wallach family, who first flourished in the town of Remagen in the Lower Rhineland. From formal studio portraits and the grandfather's work with a big wooden camera, we move to the clever, casual moments captured by a Leica.

They were Jewish, educated, and affluent, in business manufacturing textiles, particularly the embroidered ribbons and fabrics for traditional German folk costumes as they came to the fore again in the 1930s. In a black irony, we are told that it was their firm that had singlehandedly revived the moribund craft of *Dirndl* accouterments, and the curtain trimmings much favored by the National Socialist *Völkerische* fashion for leisure wear, which formed part of the interior design at Berchtesgaden. The Wallachs claim their identity as assimilated, middle-class, intellectual people in and through their photographic history.

The family Bible has been superseded by the photo album, but not all is change from austere facts to visual commentary. Births, or at least the social advent of babies, are recorded, with some details of socio-historical import. But there are now almost infinite possibilities for remembering and nostalgia that were inconceivable before the camera.

And what happened to them after that? Fritz, on the right, disappeared in the mountains one day in 1926. Two years later his bones were found; he had shot himself in the head. Oskar and Richard were murdered in concentration camps and have no graves.

Figure 14.4 Hitler with Wallach Curtains. From *The Camera of My Family* (p. 144), by C.H. Noren, 1976, New York: Alfred A. Knopf. © Catherine Hanf Noren. Reprinted with permission.

15. Juli
Top, from left to right surrounding Emilie and Samuel: Hede's husband, Arthur Gotthelf; Richard Strauss; Fritz Strauss; Oskar Strauss; and Grete's husband, Theo Loeb. Below: Hede, Oskar, Meta, Richard, Grete (she was to marry Theo Loeb the following year), and Fritz.
Top right: Fritz with his mother, Emilie, September 1926, shortly before he disappeared.

Figure 14.5 During 1914–1918. From *The Camera of My Family* (p. 27), by C.H. Noren, 1976, New York: Alfred A. Knopf. © Catherine Hanf Noren. Reprinted with permission.

In the Wallach collection we see evidence of civic duty, hard work, business enterprise, aesthetic values, family love and loyalty, and an innocence in a group who happened to have a Jewish background, in Germany in the first part of the last century.

Here are representations of impulsive identity work and spontaneous feeling. The reality is vanished, but the images remain. And so they become the memorial of the inexplicable wickedness that was to destroy their culture and to kill many of these men, women, and children.

In the Noren Wallach publication we have a single named family acting as the metaphor for a vast historical upheaval. The personal has indeed become the political. And the photographs become not just mementos, but tombstones too. As John Berger has argued (in Brody & Ignatieff, 1985), we learn to understand the recent past not just from the study of gigantic political movements; but we must also include the testimonies of the most intimate and sacred private.

People of the Twentieth Century

Remaining in Germany and in the earlier decades of the last century, it is useful to contrast these private images with the public archive of August Sander (1980), which paradoxically was intended for the political forum and yet enters our mind's eye as a series of unforgettable individual human beings.

Standing on the photographic Olympus, Sander (1876–1964) was a modest professional photographer working in Cologne, who between 1906 and 1935 set himself the task of producing a survey of German society, classified according to occupation, which he called *Menschen des 20 Jahrhunderts* ("people of the twentieth century").

The title was grand, but Sander worked in a simple style. In the city and traveling in the surrounding countryside, he chose children, women, and men to sit for him, posing themselves. They were intended to show us their occupational identities, but their individuality remains.

His work was anathema to the National Socialist Party. He was banned from continuing his great work. One must assume that his Germans were not all Aryan enough and his Party members not sufficiently convincing as *Übermenschen.* But the men and women still live for us. They have entered the visual history of Western culture.

"Here I stand. I can do no other," is what Sander must have wanted his sitters to say to, and for themselves, and that is what they did. We do not know exactly how they were invited to pose, but his serious commitment to his project and to their character surely communicated itself. The mood is one of solemn dignity. One cannot watch them with impunity.

It is to Sander's images that we can relate some of the pronouncements in John Banville's novel *The Untouchables* made by the simulated art historian and spy Victor Maskell, based on the real person Anthony Blunt. Maskell sneers at those who look for meaning in Poussin's work:

> "The fact is, of course, there is no meaning. Significances, affects, authority, mystery, magic—if you wish—but no meaning ... they simply are. Their meaning is that they are there ... this is the fundamental fact of artistic creation, the putting in place of something. Why did he paint it? Because it was not there." (Banville, 1997, p. 343)

They were not there in our visual history until Sander made their images.

In a discussion of memorials, we have here affect, authority, and mystery, entering our mind's eye, not to be forgotten. It was Sander's genius that created such beautiful, powerful pictures and his genius that allowed the people to appear with the full significance of their quality, their center.

Rundfunksekretärin. Köln, 1931
Secretary at a radio station
Secrétaire de station de radio
191

Figure 14.6 August Sander, Secretary at a Radio Station, 1931. The intellectual women were outside fashion. From *August Sander*, 2006. Cologne/London: August Sander Archvie/Portrait Gallery. © SK Stiftung Kultur, Cologne/DACS, London. Reprinted with permission.

They form part of the high-water mark of humanistic modernity, which does not lose sight of the single person, although its ideology placed them in community. Sander's community exists with strength. They are his partners in the production of their own *memento mori*. In their solemnity, I am tempted to say that they understood this. Their own authority overcomes that of biology and mortality, which otherwise seems to prevent our going beyond the paramount claim of our survival.

Here we may echo the question of the New York writer Walter Abish (1980). Those men and women and children are constructed at that time and place. They are absolutely German, yet one remains convinced that they are icons of humanity. And then a social psychologist also has to ask, "If Sander were among us again, would the participants of his survey have that same look?" That question is about more than the current sophisticated Rules of the Pose and that business of the placatory smile, which, after all, a professional photographer can prevent.

Figure 14.7 August Sander, Unemployed Man, 1928. This is what an unemployed man is supposed to look like. From *August Sander*, 2006. Cologne/London: August Sander Archvie/Portrait Gallery. © SK Stiftung Kultur, Cologne/DACS, London. Reprinted with permission.

Would they, or we, have that stillness? Would they or we take themselves, ourselves, so seriously? They would not have the certainty of their calling, their occupational identities—that we do know. Would they be as satisfied with their place in the hierarchy of status? Would they show the power of irony in their postmodern lives? Would they not show self-deprecation—the commonplace of today's adjustment? Would they, would we, be centered in that powerful way? We are not judges of our own time.

For me, Sander's people have no vanishing point. They will never be subsumed either by history or by art. They are still truly present. This is the rationalist, atheist afterlife.

References

Abish, W. (1980). *How German is it? Wie Deutsch ist es?* New York: New Directions.

Banville, J. (1997). *The untouchables.* London: Picador.

Barthes, R. (1981). *Camera lucida.* New York: Hill & Wang.

Beloff, H. (1985). *Camera culture.* Oxford: Blackwell.

Benjamin, W. (1973a [1934]). The author as producer. In his *Understanding Brecht.* London: NLB.

Benjamin, W. (1973b [1936]). The work of art in the age of mechanical reproduction. In his *Illuminations.* London: Fontana.

Berger, J. (1985). Afterword. In H. Brody & M. Ignatieff, 1985 Nineteen nineteen. London and Boston: Faber.

Billingham, J. (1998). *Ray's a laugh.* London: Scala.

Buck-Morss, S. (1995). *The dialectics of seeing: Walter Benjamin and the Arcades project.* Cambridge, MA: MIT Press.

Freud, S. (1985 [1919]). The 'uncanny.' In *The collected works of Sigmund Freud,* vol. l4, *Art and literature.* Harmondsworth: Penguin Freud Library.

McGrath, R. (2005). Waiting in the examination room. In C. Grant (Ed.), *The examination room.* Belfast: Exposed Photography. http://www.belfastexposed.com/tours/2005/tourgracat.html.

Noren, C. H. (1976). *The camera of my family.* New York: Knopf.

Sander A. (1980). *Menschen des 20. Jahrhunderts.* Munich: Schirmer/Mosel.

Spence, J. (1986). *Putting myself in the picture: A political, personal and photographic autobiography.* London: Camden.

Spence, J., & Holland, P. (1991). *Family snaps: The meaning of domestic photography.* London: Virago.

Waplington, N. (1991). *Living rough.* Manchester: Cornerstone.

Zille, H. (1979). *Photographien: Berlin l890–l900.* Munich: Schirmer/Mosel.

CHAPTER **15**

Art as Afterlife

Posthumous Self-Presentation by Eminent Painters

ROBERT WYATT

There is a persistent human desire for a kind of permanency, to stop or at least resist time, that may partly account for what compels individuals to make art. The works produced over an artist's career can be regarded as an expanded set of self-characteristics, an enduring *meta-self* that is larger than life. In addition to its potential for self-expression or its practical value as a source of income, it seems evident that the choice of painting as the medium of expression is rooted to some extent in the creation of a relatively permanent reification of the artist's intentions, and especially in its capacity to endure well beyond the artist's lifespan.

This chapter will consider paintings, and particularly self-portraits, by major artists as artifacts intended to project a sense of self beyond the death of the artist. Within limits, it is possible to make a reasonable study of *mental life* (Beloff, 1994) based on the products of a life, such as books, music, significant changes in public policy legislation or—in the present context—works of art. We may assume that the works discussed in this chapter represent accomplishment of the artists' intended ends, and the creation of a public legacy that provides the artists with something approaching immortality.

When considering the enormous creative output of major artists, we realize that the products of their emotional, psychological, and intellectual life must constitute, in terms of the time and effort involved in artistic production, the greatest portion of the sum total of their lives. Through the creation of a life's work, artists create a physical extension of themselves, constantly aware not only that contemporary consumers (galleries, critics, buyers) are looking at and judging their works, but also that people will continue to do so long after their death. Of the products of "mental life" available to us, paintings arguably represent one of the greatest opportunities for interpretation. In fact, a popular view of painting is that it is not just a means of recording events and things, but that it is an artist's interpretation of his or her experience—although this essentially "lay psychoanalytic" view of art may not be the current view of the majority of academics.

As a basis for reading a painting as a kind of *text*, although painting does not supply a syntax to assist our reading, there exists a standard of correctness that provides a common basis for making comparisons and judgments. This is the everyday, atheoretical understanding of mimetic representation: what people see, understand, and interpret when they look at a painting as a depiction of reality. In other words, a picture's content is immediately accessible to the viewer because it requires only recognition of the things depicted—a picture is quite literally worth a thousand words—whereas linguistic expression in a piece of writing and retrieval of a writer's intentions are limited to the reader's competence in the language. This is what Richard Wollheim (1984) calls "retrieval" through the semantic power of "transfer." To understand a picture of a dog, for instance, a person only must know what a dog is, not what the word *dog* means; a description in words is not necessary. Transfer also does not require perfect mimesis, that a picture be "realistic"; the depiction can use visual metaphors that stand for real things in the world, and that provide the viewer with the opportunity for the aesthetic experience—that is, if the viewer is what Wollheim (1984) calls a *willing* spectator.

Although Western culture is splendidly visual, academic analysis has ignored the visual evidence in favor of language, carried out for the most part by sociologists and psychologists. With visual data, analysis depends on the one hand on psychologists' work on perception, and on the other on fine art connoisseurship. Considerable groundwork was laid by *Kunstwissenschaft*, the German philosophical tradition of "art science" (Listowell, 1961). German art science gave us a technical term for empathy with regard to art: *Einfühlung*. Art science was carried on into the late twentieth century by Ernst Gombrich, and by psychologists such as Rudolph Arnheim, Richard Gregory and Richard Latto (Latto, 1995). There has also been significant progress in the understanding of visual systems employed by children (Willats, 1997), but an interdisciplinary dialogue among psychologists, discourse analysts, and fine art academics, not to mention artists, has yet to be fruitfully explored. Recent work by psychologists examining human perception may produce an expanded taxonomy for visual stimuli beyond that used to describe perspective. Until such a lexicon is developed, art discourse will rely to a large extent on a more or less psychoanalytic approach to the interpretation of images.

A basic premise of Freudian interpretation, and of fine art connoisseurship, is that no aspect of a presentation is random or meaningless. Halla Beloff says that a social psychology of any portrait would involve attention to the choice of pose, gesture, expression, costumes, and props, all of which provide information about the way the subject is to be understood and categorized as an individual who plays roles according to his or her own definition (Beloff, 1993). A work of art is not merely a record of persons, places, and events; an artist's intentions are largely if not solely aesthetic. In terms of painting, the formal aspects—the marks, the textures, the selection of colors, and various compositional devices such as how space is depicted—are part of our "evidence" for analysis and interpretation. These aesthetic aspects are additional to those that are natural or ethological, such as facial expression and gesture, and cultural indices such as dress and contemporary depictions of place.

It is reasonable to expect that analysis of this type necessitates familiarity with the specific technicalities of the medium being analyzed, so some background discussion of the concerns of painting as a medium of expression is in order. The surface of the painting is the aesthetic vehicle for making the artist's intentions available to us. Familiarity with the historical context of a painting, and knowledge of the artist's aesthetic concerns—what Wollheim (1980) calls our "cognitive stock"—permits deeper appreciation and assimilation of its nonverbal semantic properties. The formal aspects of the work, how the picture is actually made, provide the emotional power and efficacy of the image and enhance an everyday reading, even though the viewer may not be aware of the artist's reasons for making it look the way it does. Through the excitement and pleasure we find in these artistic effects, the tactile values and the intended meanings penetrate our everyday cognition, resonating with and stirring our emotions.

The psychologist Kenneth Gergen (1981) claims that the self is a set of "undifferentiated rousings" made less chaotic by our available linguistic resources, which are used to give us some "situational self-characteristics," and are all that constitutes our belief in selfhood. In other words, our sense of self is limited by our own ability to describe it in words. The self-portraits by major artists at the top of their game challenge such a language-centered view—they are, in the first instance, *visual* texts. Although we use words to describe them, the primary experience is a purely visual one; the pictorial representation of, say, a velvet sleeve is transferred in the same way as is the experience of a *real* velvet sleeve. The cognitive difference, if you will, between a real sleeve and the painted sleeve is where the artist's intentions, his *art*, and our aesthetic experience reside.

If we refer to the self-portraits by Rembrandt and other artists as a medium of communication, rather than solely as examples of an autonomous and sublime tradition of High Art, they can be viewed as a form of evidence for a highly developed sense of selfhood. Aesthetic theory aside, part of Rembrandt's apparent message to us, embedded in these superb objects, is a request to see him as a quotidian *self*. His success in conveying this message is remarkable, and four hundred years after his death we find ourselves in empathy with a real person: someone's son, an aging man, a businessman with concerns, ambitions, and anxieties that we recognize instantly or attribute to his self-portraits.

To the objection that this is the anachronistic attribution of a theory that Rembrandt, for example, could not have been aware of, Wollheim counters that an artist works under a particular theory of art whether or not he or she is aware of it or not. Although it has been argued that a concept of formal composition such as the gestalt of a painting's surface (Arnheim, 1974) was unavailable to an artist of Rembrandt's generation, it is also inconceivable that Rembrandt—who was supremely competitive and cognizant of the revolutionary work of Titian, for instance, and at least indirectly informed by the Renaissance compositional codes of Alberti and Leonardo—was unaware of the significant differences in effect that even subtle modifications in a painting's organization and surface would produce. A work of art demands careful attention and symphonic arrangement by the artist, the organizer of its composition, and an image's meaning is first conveyed by what strikes the eye (Arnheim, 1974). In some respects paintings are like persons, and first impressions are important; a painting is first of all a *surface*. To anyone with a practical familiarity with the medium, it is impossible to imagine Rembrandt's being unaware of the surface characteristics of his own work, or of the techniques of his looming antecedents and contemporaries. But, even without assuming such a competitive awareness, the daily practice of painting involves a consuming meditative, almost trancelike fascination with the medium and its effects in the surface of the painting.

One does not arrive at a technique as evolved as Rembrandt's without relentless attention to the physicality of the surface and constant attention to the gestalt of the developing image, although it is impossible that Rembrandt could have attended to his work with such psychoanalytical concepts in mind. However, to ignore the tactile qualities of a painting is to miss much of the point of painting, and although the primary objective of a painter such as Rembrandt may have been to portray his version of reality, it was done in a critical context that included awareness of the flickering "touch" of Titian's mature style. One cannot look at Titian's *The Flaying of Marsyas* without taking that touch into account or "feeling" how the marks in the painting's surface drive the sense of immediacy and vitality of the image. Titian's flickering brushmarks impart a live feeling to the surface. As we scrutinize the painting we empathize not only with the nominal subject of the painting, engaging as it is—poor old Marsyas, hanging upside down from that tree, having his skin removed—but empathy with Titian himself as he created this mythical scene. To take Wollheim's view, *we put our self into the painter's shoes.* The empathetic and immediate sense of "feel" from attending to the physicality of Titian's or Rembrandt's technique is what makes these works *work.* The transparent technique and illusionism of Rembrandt's predecessors was eclipsed by his radical concern with the painting's surface. If the painting can be viewed as a kind of body, the immediacy and physicality of paint serves as a concrete metaphor for the materiality of life.

Painting is a deliberate and methodical medium. Despite the clichéd idea of artistic self-expression, no one familiar with its processes, other than lay romantics, think of even the most subjective and immediate of paintings as a direct and spontaneous emotional outburst. Most of the apparently spontaneous paintings seen in galleries are the product of days, months, and even years of working, contemplation, and reworking. A painting, no matter how abstract or realistic or expressive, cannot pretend to be anything but a manipulated surface under the complete control of its maker, and in this respect it represents true self-expression. Early in the twentieth century, painting surrendered part of its claim to objective *truth value*—the core of a photograph's power as a recording of the *real*—and gained expressive potential through freeing itself from this restraint. Ironically, this new freedom was instantly suppressed under the emerging modernist regime, and painting had to rid itself of subjectivity and what Hans Belting calls the "stigma of the literary" (Hyman, 1998).

For the spectator, the experience of viewing a painting is twofold (Wollheim, 1984). In a painting we are at once aware of the depicted subject and the aesthetic aspects of the surface. This means that to understand a painting we cannot depend solely upon the natural routes for cognition exploited by photography, but must expand our analysis to include a vast range of artistic conventions and complex and idiosyncratic codes of representation. Some of these formal aspects may be intended to convey information not fully accessible by language, such as the experience of an emotional state, and some may have been invented by the artist—a kind of visual neologism, and the kind of inspired leap that most artists hope for.

Relative novelty of form is a salient characteristic of modernist expressionistic paintings that do not attempt to mimic everyday reality.

It is also important as well to keep in mind that the painter is also a spectator (Wollheim, 1984) at every juncture throughout the production of the image, which reinforces in us the attribution of intentionality (if not semantic significance) to every aspect of the image. Although it is clear that the interpretation of non-mimetic paintings is often restricted to a superficial and narrow reading by the limitations of language, as well as by the "cognitive stock" of the viewer (Wollheim, 1980), which includes access to the visual code of the artist. The appreciation of a painting is carried out against the background of natural, everyday seeing. The natural, universal way of "seeing-in" (Wollheim, 1980) provides the necessary standard of correctness for acquiring access and making judgments and sense of non-mimetic paintings. Once some purchase has been acquired on a thematicizing element, tactile or semiotic, in a specific visual code, retrieval of some or all of the artist's intentions becomes possible through further scrutiny. It is the nature of the medium that full retrieval of the intentions of the artist may not be possible, but, as in language, complete transparency is an ideal.

While recognizing the limitations of treating paintings as texts, we can immediately see that the intentions of Rembrandt and Picasso are quite different, in particular how they represented themselves and in their sense of self-importance. Rembrandt, on the one hand, presents a quotidian self of modest and certain mortality, while from the earliest stages of his career Picasso was obviously attempting to establish himself as a figure of heroic, even mythic proportions. By current standards, Rembrandt's self-portraits are reserved if dense visual texts. Rembrandt painted around 70 known self-portraits, in which he appears dressed in various costumes. Rembrandt's costumed self-portraits were possibly intended to display his talents to prospective patrons. Beloff (1990) supports her contention that these posed images by Rembrandt were used as a form of advertising to a public and to prospective customers: the emergent capitalists of The Hague. The representation of materialistic bourgeois values projected by the rich costumes and settings may have served Rembrandt quite well as a vehicle to display consummate skill that undoubtedly impressed his target clients. Rembrandt's self-portraits were made for sale. Beloff's analysis of these utilitarian aspects of Rembrandt's production provides a plausible way to understand them beyond the received acknowledgment of his genius in aesthetic terms.

Svetlana Alpers (1988) posits a similar theoretical conception of Rembrandt as a *pictor economicus* who commodified *himself* through the sale of his highly identifiable works. Richard Reid puts the idea rather more

Figure 15.1 Rembrandt van Rijn, Self-Portrait, 1669; oil on canvas, 86×70.5 cm. (Reproduced by permission of the National Gallery, London.)

sympathetically: "Rembrandt helped to make of selfhood a new kind of marketable product, such that, the more it is distinctive, the more it is a kind of mould, into which what makes a self is poured, so to speak, as a new form of niche marketing" (Reid, personal communication, 2006). Despite the costumes, or possibly even enhanced by them, an aging and very mortal Rembrandt gazes out of these pictures, and has done so for four centuries. Rembrandt's paintings prefigure the photographic self-portraits by the postmodern artist Cindy Sherman, in which she presents herself in various fictitious roles. Sherman certainly had Rembrandt's self-portraits in mind.

That said, it is important to recognize that if Rembrandt wished simply to advertise his talents, he could have chosen subjects that were not nearly so revealing psychologically, nor so unflattering. Pragmatic considerations, such as the unavailability of models or a desire to maintain close control over the subject of the work, really do not adequately explain his production of 70 self-portraits. Even if his aims are assumed to be pragmatic in the early stages of his career, it is just as reasonable to assume that, at some point, Rembrandt became aware that he was documenting his own mortality. One does not need to be a specialist in the interpretation of fine art to understand these images as a means to freeze time with an intention to speak to an unknown spectator and even beyond the grave, in a way that is quite different from the scope of the written word (or later, photography). This lay view of portraiture, as a means to freeze time and so achieve a kind of immortality—the "flip side" reality, so to speak, of Oscar Wilde's *Picture of Dorian Gray*—is so commonplace as probably to be considered banal by many art critics. But it is a fact that these images are naturally accessible and "readable" in an everyday manner to anyone, and with an "aesthetic remainder" that is the spectator's sensation of empathy with the artist.

Picasso, if we are to believe what he said about himself, has a message different from that of Rembrandt. His impact on art was enormous, and he created several of the seminal and greatest modern paintings, including the revolutionary *Les Demoiselles d'Avignon* and *Guernica*. It is hard to see him clearly; Picasso the man is subsumed by these great works, but it seems evident that part of his message is to remember him not only as a man, but a very special man—a hero of nearly supernatural sensibilities. Like Rembrandt, his artistic style was so original that during his own lifetime it was popularly considered to be the evidence of genius. Unlike Rembrandt, and just in case anyone missed that point, Picasso went to great lengths to reinforce the public attribution of genius to his work. There exists a large and increasing literature on his life and work, and even the more deprecatory analyses tend toward a grudging acceptance of him as a person of extraordinary powers. Becoming a worldwide household name in one's own lifetime, before the age of television, is certainly a mark of genius of a kind. But, self-promotion aside, Picasso was extraordinary in ways that ensure his position as *the* popular exemplar of Modern Art.

There are obvious differences between the styles of Rembrandt and Picasso; in fact, they exemplify the concept of artistic style. Picasso's self-portraits incorporate his radical schema in a clear attempt to fuse the identification of his projected persona with that of his highly idiosyncratic painting style. Picasso fuses his constructed self with an instantly identifiable artistic product, and his self-portraits play a very important part in this public presentation of artist as hero. The self-portraits provide a kind of rough guide for the reading of other works within his oeuvre. The apparent savagery and irony of his treatment of himself as a subject make the treatment of his other subjects somewhat more accessible to us, while providing a reinforcing tribute to himself as an unflinching if passionate dissector of appearances.

In his study of the early years of Picasso, Norman Mailer writes: "The radical shift in style that is approaching will come not only from the best of his impulses but also from the most calculating. Given the seriousness of his talent, his motives have always to be respected as aesthetic—yet, all the same, a part of his ambition has to be on edge at this time ... Can he still believe that he is the most exciting young painter in Paris?" (Mailer, 1996). Mailer quotes a previously untranslated account by Fernande Olivier, who writes of a study of herself that Picasso has hidden away from sight in a cupboard reserved for secret works. She describes this work as being classical in style, revealing a mastery in a genre altogether opposed to his new, public explorations. Olivier wonders if Picasso is really a "repressed person" who sees this "classical" type of painting as opposed to his desperate will to become the recognized leader of the modernist avant-garde.

Where Rembrandt shares with us the idea that here was a real person, occupying a real time and place that is accessible to ordinary minds, Picasso's self-portraits demand our acknowledgment that here was a special kind of person—one with supernormal ways of seeing reality beyond appearances. This claim became a commonplace among modernist artists and undoubtedly contributed to the current climate of popular skepticism toward any attempt to exalt artists and attribute such powers to them. The similarity between Picasso's projected self-image and Nietzsche's "artist-tyrant" is too obvious to be overlooked. "See how I saw myself," his self-portraits seem to demand, "Imagine what it must have been like to be me." What this requires, of course, is that we accept the idea of Picasso's subjective analysis of reality on faith, or on sufferance. Unlike the relatively objective reality projected by Rembrandt, Picasso's intentions are clearly to present a unique psychological perspective on the world. We should consider Picasso's oeuvre as a whole, as he undoubtedly did. Picasso's body of work was enormous, and it was produced over so long a life that it is important to realize that certain paintings probably represent fluctuations in Picasso's own sense of selfhood. Superficially similar paintings might reflect periods when he was doing no more than a parody of his own style. But, if we view the entire body of work not as the reified perceptions of an artistic genius but as material evidence of a highly differentiated self, we find ourselves in empathy with a very human being. The self that he painted, not only the self-portraits but his entire *oeuvre*, survives him as "Picasso." This extended "self," an enormous material meta-self, is the enduring, socially constructed aggregate of his combined biographical and artistic production.

Few painters have struggled to represent the self to the extent or in the way that the English painter Francis Bacon attempted. Arguably the supreme "outsider" artist, Bacon presents an essentially ironic and negative sense of personal immortality. It has been argued that Bacon sought to free the self from an artificially confining context (van Alphen, 1992), but there is the evidence in his paintings and his public and private statements to suggest that Bacon was convinced that the self was inseparable from the body. Picasso had many followers in terms of style, most of whom could never escape the category of "Picassoesque," but Bacon developed a radical style that no succeeding painter could hope to follow and be taken seriously (Hughes, 1990). Bacon's paintings invite a Freudian interpretation, but this does not necessarily focus solely on the artwork itself, which he may have desired; it also includes his self-conscious creation of a public persona. Bacon's paintings insist on the materiality, the brevity, and ultimately the pointlessness of existence, but at the same time he expresses this through one of the most traditional, permanent, and commodified of visual mediums—oil paint on canvas. Painting as a medium has a cultural importance related to its ability to endure. That Bacon was conscious of this is evident in his interviews with David Sylvester (Sylvester, 1987), even if he sometimes claimed to work against a sense of permanence through the employment of unstable materials.

Bacon took pains to protect some of his most fragile works under sheets of glass—the paintings using dust from his studio floor, for instance—despite his disclaimer that the glass was to provide a distancing barrier between the image and the viewer. Bacon also made reference to the erasing of a figure from a painting and expressed a concern that the white lead he employed would prevent the figure from reappearing, at least in his lifetime, as *pentimento* (Sylvester, 1987). This suggests that Bacon was very conscious that the potential lifespan of a painting was considerably longer than that of his mortal self. When asked why he would be concerned about his best works being destroyed, he replied, "For myself, I would like, if anything remains of mine when I'm dead, I would like the best images to remain" (Sylvester, 1987, p. 88). There is no doubt that his theme, the materiality and mortality of the flesh, and his disregard for the conventional sexual norms of his time (transgression is a major motif in his work, in both painterly and rhetorical terms) claim the high ground for posthumous interest in a major artist. In no sense could Bacon be considered innocent, nor would he wish to be, and he was clearly aware of the public persona he was creating through rigorous control of the public exposure of his work and enthusiastic impression management with regard to his public persona.

Art world fashions did not affect Bacon's oeuvre, and he consciously positioned himself outside historical trends and aesthetic, political, or social discourse as much as was possible, while operating successfully within the art world. Bacon was supremely conscious of the public persona he was constructing, and he was so concerned about the attributions made toward his work that he destroyed a large amount of it so that it could not leak out into the world. Bacon took pains to create the image of a completely spontaneous artist, creating his paintings through a concentrated impulse. At least he always maintained that he did so; the appearance of a body of preliminary sketches in 1998 may prove that he was not as impulsive and spontaneous as he always maintained. Bacon said:

> [T]here are two reasons for not destroying one's work. One is that, unless you are a rich man, you want, if you can, to live by something that really absorbs you to try to do. The other is that one doesn't know how far the will to make this thing hasn't got already leaked into it the stupidity, you may say, of immortality. After all, to be an artist at all is a form of vanity. And that vanity may be washed over by this rationally stupid idea of immortality. (Sylvester, 1987, p. 89)

If one applies Gergen's principle of how a self is constructed to Bacon's lifetime output, including his public utterances and extroverted, transgressive lifestyle, we can view his constructed public persona and "situational self-characteristics" as a large part of his real body of work—a fully reified and expertly managed set of highly differentiated "rousings" (Gergen, 1981). This may partly explain why Bacon seemed completely rational, even reasonable, when discussing the extremities of his highly unconventional life and work. If Bacon's entire body of work and his everyday life are considered to constitute a set of constructed self-characteristics, an aggregate meta-self, externalized to such a degree that it achieved celebrity status and enormous commodity value, it is arguable that this set subsumes any earlier version of self, even the private internal self. In the case of a cultural figure like Francis Bacon, you really *are* what you do. Further, if what you *are* is collected and protected indefinitely by the public institutions of high art, you have achieved a degree of immortality.

The suppression and destruction of early or unsatisfactory work is very common among artists as they achieve success and public visibility. This apparently reflects their desire to protect themselves from investigations into formative periods of their careers, and to suppress the evidence of early influences and failures. The myth of genius is that it appears in the world fully formed. It is reasonable to assume that this manipulation of an artist's work history is primarily a concern with how the work "fits" into a self-projected schema for public consumption. Sometimes, those interested in reinforcing this public perception carry out this manipulation after the artist's death.

A late modern legend centers on the anxious and paranoia-laden life and work of Mark Rothko, culminating in his suicide at the moment his work was about to be exhibited in a major museum and effectively marking the death of the American abstract expressionist movement. It seems too cynical to suggest, but nothing could have been better calculated for maximum public effect and attention, ensuring his historical position. Such concerns on the part of an ambitious artist should not be underestimated. His strict instructions regarding how a specific group of his paintings was to be presented suggest that, maybe unintentionally (but then again, maybe not), he was constructing a monument as much to himself as to the medium. If the paintings are such a part of an artist's self, how could it be otherwise? Rothko's concerns were the great achievements of great art—this is made clear in his formal statements—but Rothko exemplifies the proposal that, no matter what the nominal subject of the work of art or the apparent concerns with a painting's formal aspects, a real subject of these works is always the artist's self, a self that the artist is constructing for public consumption and for history's judgments. We can only speculate on how much Rothko's suicide involved his sense of history's pronouncements. Whether it was his desperate intention or not, and we should probably give him the benefit of the doubt, Rothko's suicide established forever the relationship between his painting and his own psychology. Interested parties have not overlooked the significance of this relationship (Hughes, 1990).

The concern with personal mortality and death is in itself not unusual. What is interesting is the compulsion in painters to develop a symbolic repertoire and make personal imagery clearly intended to be experienced, or *read,* by others. Furthermore, the painting tradition incorporates the idea of relative permanence, so it is apparent that this public reading is intended to be carried well beyond the artist's expected term of life. It is important to take into account the choice of painting as a medium, more so now when painting no longer occupies its traditional position in the hierarchy of practice and critical focus. At the moment, painting is a medium that only the most secure, reactionary, or avant-garde of artists will choose to employ. On an institutional level, the practical traditions of figurative painting are either considered obsolete or almost completely forgotten. The historical tradition, the inexhaustible potential for direct personal expression, and the relative permanence of the painted image may still, however, offer something for the individual artist.

Despite the determined and sustained challenge to traditional art forms by Marxist critics and theorists and the modernist repression of art of the self, it is apparent that commodification is not the sole rationale for a traditional art practice like painting. *Selbst-Kunst* emerged as an aesthetic category in German art criticism in the early 1920s; the term was coined for the work of painters such as Corinth, Beckman, Munch, and Kirchner (Hyman, 1998). The modernist and ultimately institutionalized avant-garde was successful in a temporary suppression of "self-art" but struggled, and ultimately failed, to negate art as a commodity. Ways were found to commodify the most fugitive of conceptual works of art, and current avant-gardes are enthusiastically packaging and marketing their products in ways that make the old studio–dealer relationships seem quaint (Herwitz, 1993). It is readily apparent that the commodification of "conceptual" art is no more complicated than the marketing of dance, music, or theater, and similar institutional structures are now in place to effect this. Unfortunately for painting, the dead hand of modernism still exerts its grip, and painting has not yet fully enjoyed the revived institutional interest in the new "self-art" seen in other contemporary art media, although there has lately been revived interest in painting among European artists. In an age of transient and fugitive artworks, not to mention the very idea of selfhood, painting's concreteness, durability, and potential for self-expression are increasingly attractive. Exhibitions such as the Saatchi Gallery's "Neurotic Realism" and "The Triumph of Painting" have highlighted the resurgence of self-art among British and European painters.

In addition to the necessity of producing a marketable commodity during an artist's lifetime, painting is also valued for its capacity to project its various types of aesthetic and rhetorical communication beyond the life of the maker, and especially for its capacity to *endure*. Artists themselves have been remarkably reticent and circumspect about these aspects of their production, which often appears to be at odds with the desire to project the self into the public sphere. Sometimes this appears to be no more than a genteel politeness, a concern to avoid the appearance of materialistic self-interest, which would disrupt the popular view of the artist as being at arm's length from worldly concerns. Others seem to resist what they perceive as any attempt to codify their work, in the possibly justified belief that this will reduce the work to mere semiotics. In many cases the concern for an artist's legacy is not apparent until the latest stages of a career, but any analysis of why a person chooses to paint is often met with discomfiture, contradictory responses, or denial.

Timothy Hyman, an author and art critic and a respected painter himself, is well placed to consider the reasons to choose painting as a medium of expression. His analysis of the oeuvre of Bonnard provides an articulate account of that artist's adventures into the "split between the person and the world." A common response by many artists to a request to explain their work is that they are primarily "visual" people and not comfortable with the use of words; the work must speak for itself. Hyman, however, is perfectly comfortable with the word, and he seemed an obvious choice to attempt such an explanation (Hyman, 1999).

Correspondence and an interview with Hyman made it apparent that he found it difficult fully to account for his own desire, or need, to paint. Hyman's work could be described as biographical, a perfect example of *situational self-art*. When asked the blunt question, "Why paint?" Hyman gave what he admitted was a set of contradictory responses. On one hand,

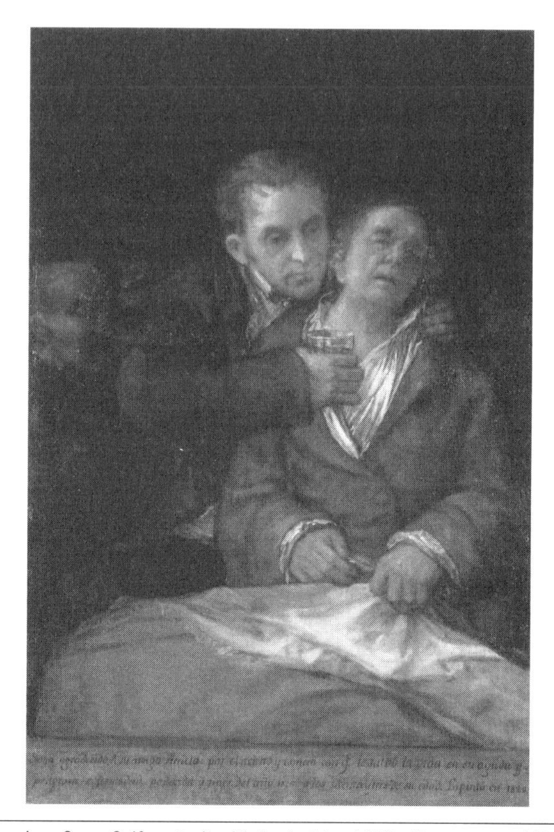

Figure 15.2 Francisco Goya, Self-portrait with Dr. Arrieta, 1820; oil on canvas, 117×79 cm. (Reproduced by permission of the Institute of Arts, Minneapolis.)

he regarded his painting as a necessary *psychic unloading*, a catharsis. On the other hand, he regarded it as *bearing witness*, the artist acting as an aesthetic mediator between the world and the viewer, which is probably the way the concept of art is most widely understood.

Psychic unloading may not require a spectator other than the artist himself, but if painting is viewed as a kind of therapy, then a spectator is probably necessary to complete the communicative loop; otherwise, such an activity suggests an unhealthy isolation. The last works of Goya, the so-called Black Paintings made in complete isolation and deafness toward the end of his life, come to mind and have been used as evidence of his descent into insanity. Hyman suggests that the final output of Goya may be an example of "psychic unloading," but he does not agree with a description of his own art as mere therapy, which leaves us with the idea of "bearing witness" to life and the world. To be seen to bear witness requires a spectator other than the artist himself. Setting aside the subject of the painting, the

Burke's body was given over to the anatomist Alexander Monro III to dissect publicly. Like Karrer's, Burke's articulated skeleton survives and is in the Anatomical Museum of the University of Edinburgh. A few years after the execution of Burke, the anatomy act of 1832 was passed, ensuring a sufficient legal supply of bodies for dissection to the growing anatomy schools of London and Edinburgh and discouraging the practice of body theft.

Another notable example of a specific corpse is the remains of an enlightened subject of a dissection, the political writer and philosopher Jeremy Bentham (1748–1832), whom we can meet to this day at the end of the South Cloisters of the main building of University College, London (Hurwitz & Richardson, 1987). Bentham, who was a supporter of the movement behind the passing of the Anatomy Act of 1832, stipulated in his will that after his death his body should be publicly dissected by his friend, Dr. Thomas Southwood Smith, as the topic of lectures on anatomy: "The object of these lectures being ... first to communicate curious interesting and highly important knowledge and secondly to show that the primitive horror at dissection originates in ignorance" (Marmoy, 1958, p. 80). Bentham further gave directions annexed to his will for the creation of his "auto-icon," as he called it, ordering that his skeleton was to be articulated in a seated position in his usual chair "in the attitude in which I am sitting when engaged in thought," clothed in one of his own suits, holding his favorite cane, and enclosed in a portable case. He also requested that his figure be surmounted by his own head, preserved by a drying process according to the reported practice of the native tribes of New Zealand. Bentham's preserved head survives, but his friend Dr. Southwood Smith found that it lacked expression, and so it was replaced by a wax head made after portraits of Bentham taken in life.

Late twentieth century parallels to Bentham are the man and woman whose bodies were donated to be dissected and digitally photographed after their deaths and made available on line. The National Library of Medicine's *Visible Human Project* is composed of images that capture the body through a variety of processes including magnetic resonance imaging (MRI), computed tomography (CT), and cryosectioning. The body can be seen in extremely fine cross-sections or it can be entirely reconstructed, viewed in three dimensions and at different anatomical depths, and rotated in three-dimensional space. The cadaver is thus resurrected electronically and from a myriad of possible viewpoints. The female body was that of an anonymous 59-year-old woman who died of a heart attack. The male body was that of 39-year-old convicted murderer who died by lethal injection in Texas in 1993, continuing the long tradition of the bodies of executed criminals serving anatomy. The difference was that this was a voluntary contribution, in that the man had willed his body to science before his execution. The documentation and virtual dissemination of these bodies through the National Library of Medicine's *Visible Human Project* and through the other projects based on its data sets is a further example of the survival on the World Wide Web of the body after death.

A final remembrance of the specific corpse may be seen in the religious services that sometimes accompanied the interment of the remains following a dissection. In sixteenth-century Rome, doctors and students escorted the corpse to burial and contributed to payment for a mass to pray for the soul of the executed criminal whom they had just anatomized (Carlino, 1994, pp. 122–125). The practice, in one form, has survived in modern times. Following cremation, an ecumenical service of thanksgiving and remembrance is held each year for relations and friends of those who have donated their bodies to the London medical schools.

References

Albinus, B. S. (1747). *Tabulae sceleti et musculorum corporis humani.* Leiden: J. & H. Verbeek.

Amerson, L. P., Jr. (1969). Marco d'Agrate's San Bartolomeo: An introduction to some problems. In M. L. Gatti Perer (Ed.), *Il Duomo di Milano: Congresso internazionale, Milano, Museo della scienza e della tecnica, 8–12 settembre 1968*, vol. 1 (pp. 189–206). Milan: La Rete.

Amerson, L. P., Jr. (1975). The problem of the écorché: A catalogue raisonné of models and statuettes from the sixteenth century and later periods. Dissertation Abstracts International.

Ball, J. M. (1928). *The sack-'em-up men: An account of the rise and fall of the modern resurrectionists.* Edinburgh & London: Oliver & Boyd.

Bidloo, G. (1685). *Anatomia humani corporis.* Amsterdam: The widow of J. van Soemeren, the heirs of J. van Dyk, and Henry and the widow of T. Boom.

Bignamini, I. & Postle, M. (1991). *The artist's model: Its role in British art from Lely to Etty.* Nottingham, UK: Nottingham University Art Gallery.

Brackett, J. K. (1992). *Criminal justice and crime in late Renaissance Florence, 1537–1609.* Cambridge: Cambridge University Press.

Brock, C. H. (Ed.). (1983). *William Hunter 1718–1783, a memoir by Samuel Foart Simmons and John Hunter.* Glasgow: University of Glasgow Press.

Browne, J. (1681). *A compleat treatise of the muscles.* London: T. Newcombe.

Bryant, J. (1991). Thomas Banks's anatomical crucifixion: A tale of death and dissection. *Apollo, 133*(352) (n.s.), 409–411.

Camper, P. (1821). *The works of the late Professor Camper, on the connexion between the science of anatomy and the arts of drawing, painting, statuary.* (T. Cogan, Trans.). London: J. Hearne.

Carlino, A. (1994). *La fabbrica del corpo: Libri e dissezione nel Rinascimento.* Turin: Einaudi.

Casserius (1627). *Tabulae anatomicae.* (D. Bucretus, Ed.). Venice: E. Deuchinum.

Cazort, M., Kornell, M., & Roberts, K. B. (1996). *The ingenious machine of nature: Four centuries of art and anatomy.* Ottawa: National Gallery of Canada.

Cheselden, W. (1733). *Osteographia, or the anatomy of the bones.* London: n. pub.
Choulant, L. (1962 [1852]). *History and bibliography of anatomic illustration.* (M. Frank, Ed. & Trans.). New York & London: Hafner.
Colombo, R. (1559). *De re anatomica libri xv.* Venice: N. Bevilacqua.
Coppola, E. D. (1957). The discovery of the pulmonary circulation: A new approach. *Bulletin of the History of Medicine, 31*, 44–77.
Edgerton, S. Y., Jr. (1985). *Pictures and punishment: Art and criminal prosecution during the Florentine Renaissance.* Ithaca, NY: Cornell University Press.
Haskell, F., and Penny, N. (1988) *Taste and the antique: The lure of classical sculpture 1500–1900.* New Haven: Yale University Press.
Hurwitz, B., & Richardson, R. (1987). Jeremy Bentham's self image: An exemplary bequest for dissection. *British Medical Journal, 295*, 195–198.
Jenty, C. N. (1758). *The demonstrations of a pregnant uterus of a woman at her full time.* London: privately published.
Kemp, M. (Ed.). (1975). *Dr. William Hunter at the royal academy of arts.* Glasgow: University of Glasgow Press.
Kemp, M., & Wallace, M. (2000). *Spectacular bodies: The art and science of the human body from Leonardo to now.* London: Hayward Gallery.
Kornell, M. (1996). The study of the human machine: Books of anatomy for artists. In M. Cazort et al. (Eds.), *The ingenious machine of nature: Four centuries of art and anatomy* (pp. 43–70).
Krumbhaar, E. B. (1922). The early history of anatomy in the United States. *Annals of Medical History, 4*, 271–286.
Lambert, S. W. (1952). The initial letters of the anatomical treatise, "De humani corporis fabrica", of Vesalius. In S. W. Lambert, W. Wiegand, & W. M. Ivins, Jr. (Eds.), *Three Vesalian essays to accompany the Icones anatomicae of 1934* (pp. 3–24). New York: Macmillan.
Lind, L. R. (Ed. & Trans.). (1959). *Jacopo Berengario da Carpi: A short introduction to anatomy (Isagogae breves).* Chicago: University of Chicago Press.
Maclise, J. (1851). *Surgical anatomy.* London & Philadelphia: John Churchill and Blanchard & Lea.
Mantel, H. (1998). *The giant, O'Brien.* London: Fourth Estate.
Marmoy, C. F. A. (1958). The "auto-icon" of Jeremy Bentham at University College, London. *Medical History, 2*, 77–86.
Meyer, A. W., & Wirt, S. K. (1943). The Amuscan illustrations. *Bulletin of the History of Medicine, 14*, 667–687.
National Library of Medicine, *Visible human project.* www.nlm.nih.gov/research/visible/visible_human.html.
Norman, J. M. (1986). *The anatomical plates of Pietro da Cortona.* New York: Dover.
O'Malley, C. D. (1964). *Andreas Vesalius of Brussels, 1514–1564.* Berkeley & Los Angeles: University of California Press.
Paterson, S. (1766, August 20–22). *A catalogue of the remaining part of the stock in trade, of Mr Robert Withy, of Cornhill, print-seller ... consisting of a great variety of prints ... among which are several curious anatomical pictures prints and models, of Dr. Charles Nicholas Jenty: which will be sold by auction, by Samuel Paterson at Essex-House, in Essex-Street, in the Strand.*
Petrioli, G. (1741). *Tabulae anatomicae.* Rome: A. de Rubeis.
Paulson, R. (1989). *Hogarth's graphic works.* 3rd rev. ed. London: Print Room.

Platter, F. (1961). *Beloved son Felix: The Journal of Felix Platter a medical student in Montpellier in the Sixteenth Century.* (Seán Jennett, Trans.). London: F. Muller.
Punt, H. (1983). *Bernard Siegfried Albinus (1697–1770) on 'human nature': Anatomical and physiological ideas in eighteenth century Leiden.* Amsterdam: Israël.
Richardson, R. (1987). *Death, dissection and the destitute.* London & New York: Routledge & Kegan Paul.
Roberts, K. B., & Tomlinson, J. D. W. (1992). *The fabric of the body: European traditions of anatomical illustration.* Oxford: Oxford University Press.
Rodari, F. (Ed.). (1996). *Anatomie de la couleur: L'invention de l'estampe en couleurs.* Paris: Bibliothèque Nationale de France.
Russell, K. F. (1954). The *Osteographia* of William Cheselden. *Bulletin of the History of Medicine, 28*, 32–39.
Russell, K. F. (1959). John Browne, 1642–1702: A seventeenth-century surgeon, anatomist, and plagiarist. *Bulletin of the History of Medicine, 33*, 393–414, 503–525.
Sibson, F. (1844). On the changes induced in the situation and structure of the internal organs, under varying circumstances of health and disease; and on the nature and external indications of these changes. *Transactions of the Provincial Medical and Surgical Association, 12*, 307–574.
Sibson, F. (1869). *Medical anatomy: Or, illustrations of the relative position and movements of the internal organs.* London: John Churchill & Sons. [The Wellcome Library catalogue notes that the "Index catalogue of the Library of the Surgeon-General's Office indicates that 7 fasciculi were produced from 1855–1869."]
Valverde, J. de. (1556). *Historia de la composición del cuerpo humano.* Rome: A. Salamanca and A. Lafrerij.
Vesalius, A. (1543). *De humanis corporis fabrica.* Basel: J. Oporinus. [The plates are handily reproduced in J. B. de C. M. Saunders & C. O'Malley, *The illustrations from the works of Andreas Vesalius of Brussels.* New York: Dover, 1973.]
Wolf-Heidegger, G. (1944). Vesals Basler Skeletpräparat aus dem Jahre 1543. *Verhandlungen naturforschenden Gesellschaft in Basel, 55*, 210–234.
Wolf-Heidegger, G., & Cetto, A. M. (1967). *Die anatomische Sektion in bildlicher Darstellung.* Basel & New York: S. Karger.

CHAPTER 17
Representing Trauma
The Case for Troubling Images

RICHARD READ

Perhaps there are as many means of representing the trauma of violent death aesthetically as there are kinds of death and trauma, but in this essay I will write about the relative merits of only four, which I categorize roughly as transcendence, acting out, denial, and working through. Since it should not be assumed that everyone knows what the psychological process of working through entails, I will start by reiterating the received view that if traumatic experience is not dealt with successfully, then "neurotic" patterns of behavior are likely to appear, together with a continued experience of being retraumatized by memory. Thus, children, for example, who are still traumatized tend to represent their experience as graphic and exact re-creations of the traumatic incident, while those who have come away from the trauma are more likely to represent it in symbolic form. An adult witness to the collapse of the Twin Towers in what is now glibly referred to in the abbreviation "9/11," to offer another example, may graphically remember the strange visual beauty of that event, but, in denying the carnage it entailed, may develop otherwise unaccountable physical ailments as substitutes for more a conscious apprehension of its horror. These are examples in which working through has not occurred.

A positive example, conveying the "feel" of working through, or rather the state of mind of a secure person about to be confronted by the process of working through, is perhaps nowhere better conveyed than in this paradoxically fertile metaphor of deathly threat from Shakespeare's *Richard the Second:*

... yet again, methinks,
Some unborn sorrow, ripe in fortune's womb,
Is coming towards me, and my inward soul
With nothing trembles ...
(Shakespeare, *Richard the Second*, act II, scene 2, ll. 9–12)

The womb metaphor lends some living kind of psychic shape and potentiality to the deathly threat it conveys.

Technically, of course, working through is a psychoanalytic concept entailing processes that are more complex and complete. It is a specific psychotherapeutic technique employed after unconscious material has been raised or rather interpreted by the analyst, and is defined as such by Laplanche and Pontalis:

> Process by means of which analysis implants an interpretation and overcomes the resistances to which it has given rise. Working-through is taken to be a sort of psychical work which allows the subject to accept certain repressed elements and to free himself from the grip of mechanisms of repetition. It is a constant factor in treatment, but it operates more especially during certain phases where progress seems to have come to a halt and where a resistance persists despite its having been interpreted.
>
> From the technical point of view, by the same token, working-through is expedited by interpretations from the analyst which consist chiefly in showing how the meanings in question may be recognized in different contexts. (Laplanche & Pontalis, 1988, p. 488)

The last three words are relevant to the process of this essay and especially its conclusion, but I should state from the outset what is probably already obvious: to engage with a work of art is clearly different from engaging in psychotherapy. A work of art does not react to us as dynamically as a therapist or analyst does. Perhaps it can do no more than trigger inner processes that through our own agency may proceed on any number of courses, and yet works of art often embody the processes of their own manufacture in ways that suggest trajectories of change in our feelings that are perhaps a lot more than random, and perhaps even especially meaningful when the processes of artistic manufacture bear directly on death.

My four categories will be illustrated by encounters with a loose assortment of past and present works of art and literature concerning death that have contributed to my thoughts on the representation of trauma. As far as art and literature are concerned, I have thought about the relations between words and images in the past in terms of datable, theoretical equivalences,[1] but here I am concerned with emotional processes that verbal and visual structures of quite different kinds might hold in common across large tracts of space and time. To this end, I hope a travel theme throughout the narrative of this essay will turn out by the end to be apt.

Transcendence

It was in June that a postgraduate student, newly arrived from America to the Australian faculty of art where I teach, gave a paper on her chosen topic of disturbing images in contemporary American art. Her work was mainly studio-based but, perhaps to satisfy her sense of what "art history" required, she included a few old works among contemporary ones she wanted to address.

At one point she brought up two slides, one of which I instantly recognized because I had seen the real Roman monument it captured only a couple of months before. It featured some of the four thousand skeletons of friars brought down from the Quirinal to the Cappuccini chapels beneath Santa Maria della Consolazione in three carriage loads from 1628 to 1631, to which additions were made from bodies of the brethren until as late as 1870. There are many ossuaries of this kind around the world, particularly at Paris (emulating the Roman one), a big one at Sedlec, Czechoslovakia, and a spectacular one at Palermo, of which Peter Robb has written:

> Earthly power, sex, religion and professional status were even more rigidly distinguished than in the world of the living. ... The entire casts of Tolstoy's Balzac's and Dickens's novels seemed to have been dried out and stacked away vertically in their disintegrating dress uniforms, their rotting ball gowns, their dusty frock coats, rows and rows of the upper strata of nineteenth century society, rigorously grouped in their Darwinian or Marxist categories. (Robb, 1996, p. 88)

The Roman ossuary could hardly be more different from this Sicilian microcosm of society, for the disarticulation of individual skeletons into promiscuously batched types of bone ensured an effect of almost total impersonality. Hundreds of skulls are piled up together and pinned back by wire netting into an architecture of alcoves in which only the occasional grinner beneath a cowl, with a scythe in its hands, remains intact to personify the abstract figure of Death. A clock made of real arm and finger bones signifies the inexorable passage of time, while everything else answers to the *memento mori* motto erected in one of the chapels:

Where you are now so once were we,
Where we are now you soon shall be.

Perhaps this spectacle of so many human remains should make it my most macabre example, but it does not come across like that to me at all. What had struck me, as I mentioned at the seminar, was the disposition of the most curvilinear bones—ribs and radii and ulnae—into patterns that swerved around the formal borders of the walls in a manner that seemed to emulate the most frivolous Rococo drawing rooms. Why should the builders of a mass grave have aspired to an elegantly whimsical effect? I am so godless that it took a good while for the penny to drop: for an ardently Christian community, the prospect of the life everlasting is so real that death is naught but a joke, a mild velleity, polite enough for everyone to share. It is perhaps difficult to describe transcendence of individual death in this instance as a psychological process. It might tend to surprise most of us because we are no longer harnessed in the shared religious rituals that gave the former beholders (over many centuries) their consolation, yet in the light order given to graphic remnants of decay we may still intuit value, even though it depends, from the nonbeliever's point of view, on displacement of reality to a fictional "better world."

Acting Out

I think I went on about the above at length because I was subliminally trying to avoid the other slide that the postgraduate student was showing us on the screen and that a colleague slyly invited me to comment on. It was an art photograph by Joel-Peter Witkin called, pretentiously enough, "Le Baiser" ("The Kiss"), a title that I suppose alludes ironically to common knowledge of Rodin's sculpture of the same name. In stark contrast to that tender sculpture, Witkin's photograph consists of the greasy head and matted hair of the corpse of an elderly man that had been severed down the middle and opened out so that the sides of the face were locked together in an everlasting "French" kiss. At the invitation to comment, I think I blurted out something like "If the slide on the right (of the Roman chapels) signifies the triumph of life over death, then this one stages the paradoxical impossibility of death triumphing over death." I instantly saw how clever it was, how "ahead of the game" it must have seemed in whatever art world it was first exhibited. Hegel called all art a trick because it confers the illusion of life upon resolutely dead materials. Well, no one would be fooled for a moment into thinking that this figure was alive. Rather, the lips twisted round upon themselves merely underlined the unrelenting factuality of death. I also saw the radical economy by which so glib an intervention could break so many taboos at once—fetishism in the care lavished on the silvery-antique quality of the negative, same-sex desire, geriatric narcissism, and, of course, necrophilia. It also entails Romantic transvaluation in the Christian tradition in which a part reads as whole, low as high, specific as universal. And if a literal corpse is at odds with the high-art allusions to Bosch, Goya, Velasquez, Miró, Botticelli, and Picasso that Witkin points to in his work, then these still perfectly prepare his work for discussion in the hypermarket of academic programs such as ours. One could say a lot more in this cerebral vein, but as the image sank in a little, a completely different kind of response began to assert itself, and I asked, no doubt sententiously: "Are there ethical issues with this image?"

The postgraduate student showing us the slides instantly knew what I meant, because she said she thought that the artist had sought permission of his subject before he died. This turns out to have been wishful thinking on her part. One Web site states:

> Witkin's greatest artistic accomplishment may be the deal he was able to work out with a hospital morgue in Mexico City, which allowed him to sift through its daily supply of anonymous corpses picked up from the streets and cavalierly manipulate them into "art." (Germano Celant, quoted in Wilson, 2000)

This unsolicited manipulation of the dead worries me, but intellectual and ethical considerations felt beside the point compared to the visceral feelings of horror that set in over the next 24 hours. It was like feeling locked into a schizophrenic double bind whose only hopeful outcome was the possibility that the horror of the remembered image might gradually fade from memory. Later on I told the student, who seemed perfectly normal and kind, about my reaction, but she only seemed pleased that one of her disturbing images was doing its job, though later she seemed to convey the impression that her project was "getting" to her, rather than fulfilling the promise of Witkin's Web site that "Through his imagery, we gain a greater understanding about human difference and tolerance" (Witkin, n.d.a).

I do not, of course, assume that everyone who sees Le Baiser will have the same response to it that I did. Another photograph by Witkin ("Story from a Book," 1999) that featured an intact version of the same head did not make me turn a hair. I admit that, like many people, I am susceptible to violent imagery and tend to avoid live footage of executions on television these days. But I can sit through most of *Reservoir Dogs* because I know it isn't real, and I am certainly not as bad as a friend of mine who even cries at advertisements on TV (but perhaps that borders on pathology).

As I was recovering from the trauma, I wondered whether I was getting "square" or had missed something valuable about Witkin's photograph.

Though it didn't help to alleviate my feelings of violation, I cast around for some intellectual framework that might prove useful to the student and shed some positive light on the image by finding a place for it in some broader scheme of things. Since I had just finished a book on the English art critic Adrian Stokes, it was natural that a theme from his later writings should spring to mind.

Stokes's taste was formed by his experience of Italian Renaissance art, but toward the end of his life he tried very hard to find a justification for what he felt was the violent impact of the wide range of contemporary art that came before him as a trustee of the Tate Gallery in the 1960s.

The theory he came up with is interesting. Simply put, the lack of wider symbolism in what he regarded as the stark factuality, anomalous juxtapositions, "issness," and "concrete thinking" of contemporary art was itself symbolic of an absence of wider symbolism in the surrounding environment (Stokes, 1978, vol. 3, pp. 167, 175–184). The violent dislocations or all-over impact of contemporary art helps to reconcile us to the deathly shocks and dislocations that everywhere confront us in everyday life and so renders them more bearable. This theme is so pervasive in Stokes's later writings that it is difficult to pin it down to any one passage, but the following is interesting to contemplate with Witkin in mind:

> An emptiness, a destruction, has been exhibited as such. So called anti-art has had an important place in pioneering. A chance conglomeration might amplify the ceaseless meaningless shocks from the juxtaposition to which urban life is subject. That the shock of juxtaposition ... in contemporary art has become a requirement prior even to the often very evident poetry desired and discovered in the process, is perhaps illustrated by the fact that the power of an antiquated *trompe l'oeil* imitativeness has served as an avant-garde method in Surrealist hands when used to transmit the shock of unexpected conjunctions. (Stokes, 1978, vol. 3, p. 316)

Quaint as it now seems, Stokes was thinking of nothing more gruesome than Dada, Surrealism, Pop, and Abstract Expressionism, whose shock effects were fresher then than now.

Compare Witkin working at the limits of his tolerance at the Mexico City morgue, which he too seems to register as a general state of contemporary being:

> He told Sand of his horror upon discovering a drawer full of bodily fluids with severed arms, legs, eyes, penises and little children floating around in them. "Because the bureaucracy is so incredibly corrupt, no one had said 'get this stuff out of here.' No one had the balls to do it. That time I did say, 'Why am I doing this?'"

But Witkin's divine mission prevailed over his outrage, and he liberally utilized the drawer's contents. "I did have the belief that there was a purpose to my being there," he concludes, "that I could make something beautiful" (quoted in Wilson, 2000, p. 3).

Perhaps if I were one of the hermaphrodites, dwarfs, amputees, androgynes, or various other kinds of outcasts that Witkin has recruited as subjects for his photographs—and I suspect this helps to explain the awards that academies have showered on him—if I had lost an ear or was just obese, then perhaps I might turn to Witkin and his art to feel "OK" about myself, but I am not sure I would be flattered by the comparison with a mutilated corpse or give permission to be photographed as one. What, in any case, does his justification for his choice of sitters have to do with his attitude toward what is delivered to the public? "When you really want to say something to someone, you grab them, you hold them, you embrace them. That's what happens in this still form" (Witkin, n.d.b)—by which he means his photographs. That's fine for the clasper, as fine as his thinking, "My work shows my journey to become a more loving, unselfish person" (Witkin, quoted in Wilson, 2000, p. 2), but what about the claspee? Might it not be tantamount to secondary trauma? First the sitter gets it: now for the spectator. What annoys me is that, for all his sympathy, particularly for himself, Witkin never seems bothered by this possibility, however easy it might be to underestimate the courage of his stand against the denial, intolerance, and hypocritical prudishness that reign in certain sectors of his native cultural establishment. Then again, my concerns about secondary trauma might seem trivial to those who have sustained war conditions for many years, or long-term torture, or the brutal murder of loved ones. Yet it may be exactly such people who—afterward—are most vulnerable to the retraumatization of their memories by such images; and, though it might take a separate essay to justify, I think it could be argued that the allegedly high-minded self-consciousness of Witkin's photographs makes them potentially more traumatic than those that emerged from Abu Ghraib, though for whom they would be so is a vexed issue indeed.

For all their differences, Stokes and Witkin both clearly espouse redemptive theories of art, which I seemed to remember had been roundly challenged in the 1990s. The most trenchant objections came from Leo Bersani in *The Culture of Redemption* (1990), whose arguments against Melanie Klein's theory of psychological reparation are summed up as follows:

> Theories of the restitutive or redemptive power of cultural forms … give us extraordinarily diminished views of both our sexuality and our cultural imagination. … Sexuality is consecrated as violence by virtue of the very definition of culture as an unceasing effort to make

> life whole, to repair a world attacked by desire. A fundamentally meaningless culture thus ennobles gravely damaged experience. Or, to put this in other terms, art redeems the catastrophe of history. … Claims for the high morality of art may conceal a deep horror of life. And yet nothing perhaps is more frivolous than that horror, since it carries within it the conviction that, because of the achievements of culture, the disasters of history somehow do not matter. Everything can be made up, can be made over again, and the absolute singularity of human experience—the source of both its tragedy and its beauty—is thus dissipated in the trivializing nobility of a redemption through art. (Bersani, 1990, p. 22)

This paragraph has been enormously influential, I suspect, but what is to replace redemption? According to Bersani, it is an art that reenacts the way in which "the human subject is originally *shattered into* sexuality," which he extends first to masochism and then to narcissism, which reenacts

> a primitive but immensely significant move from fragmented objects to totalities, a move taking place at this stage as a form of self-reflexiveness. It is as if a certain split occurred in consciousness, a split that paradoxically is also the first experience of self-integration. In this self-reflexive move, a pleasurably shattered consciousness becomes aware of itself as the object of its desire. (Bersani, 1990, p. 36)

In thinking what kind of art might satisfy such principles in representing "the object of desire" as "the very experience of ébranlement or self-shattering" (Bersani, 1990, p. 36), the theory appears to work brilliantly on a work such as Francis Bacon's Portrait of George Dyer in a Mirror (1968; reproduced in Russell, 1979, p. 136, Fig. 66)), where the morphed image of the lover's head flicking round in conversation generates such momentum that it splits asunder in the mirror's sharp and ravenous reflection of it. Bacon's pictorial butchery can be far more gruesome than this, of course, and paint has long and often asserted its identity with every visceral fluid and substance, but whatever the organic modifications his paint submits to, it is never contiguous with the subject matter it kills or reanimates in the way Witkin's photographs are. Painting shares this ultimate refusal of the actual with literature.

The limitations of Bersani's purely erotic "take" on art emerge in what seems at first a much closer match with literature: the title story of Denis Cooper's *Wrong* (1992), a collection of fiction that provided a focus for literary studies of trauma in the 1990s. A gay cruiser in New York meets his end in a penthouse bondage suite before continuing his inconclusive wanderings as a ghost:

> It started out with a spanking. Slaps to the face, which George wasn't so wild about. His asshole swallowed in something's enormity simply enough. More slaps. Fred's breaths grew worse, a kind of storm knocking down every civilized word in its path.
>
> George was hit on the head. 'Shit!' Again. This time he felt his nose skid across one cheek. His forehead caved in. One eye went black. Teeth sputtered out of his mouth and rained down on his chest. He died at some point in that. (Cooper, 1994, p. 69)

The limitations of the erotic significance of Bersani's attachment to *ébranlement* or self-shattering are exposed here, for the value of the passage, it seems to me, depends on the strict *occlusion* of the eroticism. The understatement ("wasn't so wild about") of the victim's experience before his seat of consciousness disintegrates around him makes the murder's sadistic pleasure conspicuous only by its utterly unthinkable, so all the more horrific, absence. The occlusion is sustained by author, rather than the murderer, taking over the victim's point of view at "some" indeterminate "point" of death. Bersani's thesis seems too narrow for the cathexis entailed. Yet the risk is the same as in Witkin's *Le Baiser*. Destructiveness cleaves so closely to the matter-of-fact sequence of events that violent acting out threatens to lead nowhere. It sticks in the mind, but that is all it does.[2]

Denial

Oddly enough Cooper's character, bent on suicide, prophetically rules out the following scene before his death:

> The World Trade Center was not what he'd hoped. It wasn't like he could fall off. Big slabs of glass between him and his death. No matter where he turned his thoughts were obvious. The city looked like a toy, a space-age forest, a silvery tray full of hypodermics. He wanted one fresh perception, but … (Cooper, 1994, p. 65)

Perhaps the crudest means of representing traumatic death is terrorist massacre, or for that matter antiterrorist war, in which the aim of drawing attention to innocent suffering is lost in a spiral of revenge. Consider reports of young Chechnyans after the Moscow siege, claiming that if only the Russian people understood the sufferings of Chechnya, they would prevent the authorities from inflicting them.

In one sense terrorism works. Psychological surveys taken well before the Bali bombings suggested that 50% of Australians were unhappier than they were before the New York tragedy, a figure that dropped from 93%

one week after its occurrence. Over the first weekend in America, on the other hand, sales of violent videos soared.

In broaching denial as a means of representing trauma, I interpret M. Night Shyamalan's recent film *Signs* (Touchstone Pictures, 2002) as Hollywood's early response to and clunky denial of the threat posed by al-Qaida to American life and values. My gist is that the crop circles left by alien landings in the film are perfect euphemisms for debris from the Twin Towers—flattened corn plants free of blood and gore, neatly arranged and without the acrid smoke that drifted over New York City for months. It is the exact antithesis of a pre-9/11 disaster movie such as *Independence Day,* in which city-sized flying saucers darken the skies of metropolitan centers before obliterating their tallest buildings (the Twin Towers are explicitly referenced) with vertically descending beams of glamorously sublime destruction. *Signs,* by contrast, dissipates audience anxiety about America's enemies by successfully overpowering the alien invaders with nothing more complex than a baseball bat and a glass of water! Having denied the awesome menace of an incomprehensibly evil enemy, the paternal hero and lapsed priest, played by Mel Gibson, puts his dog collar back on so that, in a crudely symmetrical response, one fundamental religion is vanquished by another. *Signs* dramatizes denial as a possible defense against the trauma of mass carnage.

I do not want to suggest that everything about the film is bad. There are several unusually interesting moments—for example, when the viewer is momentarily identified with the alien intruder, being nailed out of the house as unwanted voyeur or put supine on the floor to look up at falling water that is about to turn it into a pile of steaming giblets. My favorite character is the television set. At one juncture, the children mysteriously claim that every channel is showing the same program—an impossibility except when mass tragedies like the Twin Towers are shown. At first one thinks the uniformity of channel is an alien intervention, but it turns out only to be global coverage of their landings. Perhaps the trope of TV sameness will recur as an emblem of shocks to the collective fantasy life of the film and television industry. In opposition to the prior public ideal of broadcasting, the current aim of narrowcasting through cable means that few sets will ever show the same program at the same time. A fear posed by coverage of the 9/11 kind, which the choreographed bombing of Baghdad tried to reverse, was that the communally witnessed spectacle shown on almost every television in the world would establish an unpremeditated focus of public attention at the heart of diversified private consumerism. The derangement of normally flawless continuities of presentational hierarchy and etiquette, in which presenters strained at the chaotic indications on their headsets to comprehend the enormity of the visual events transpiring behind them (especially when viewers saw the second plane crash before the presenters did), provided a reference point for oppositional politics symbolically threatening "the system" from within. At a time when television is less and less about shared consciousness (Derby Day and the Queen's Christmas speech on the BBC) and more and more about localized distraction (the DVD set beside the post office queue or above the dentist's chair), the symbolic trope of imagery shared across rival channels potentially mitigates denial by seeming to offer a form in which the significance of collective tragedies can be apprehended. My general point, however, is that like "acting out," "denial" is a primitive form of defense, whereas "transcendence" may not be, and "working through" is not.

Working Through

After the postgraduate seminar in June, I stopped off on my way back from a conference in the United Kingdom to accompany some friends to the "Tuttonormale" exhibition of contemporary art in the grounds of the Villa Medici on the hillside of the Pincio district overlooking Rome. The brief of this fabulous exhibition was to bring the bustling modernity of a major city into creative rapport with the privileged seclusion of an ancient garden that was normally closed to the public. Each artist mounted his or her work in one of the rectangles of the formal garden, behind the villa, internally divided by low hedges, umbrageous trees, and gravel paths. All I knew in advance about Georgina Starr's installation, *Inside Bunny Lake Garden*, was the single sentence on the exhibition handout sheet:

> This British artist has reconstructed a secret children's playground in an area of the garden, representing the final scene from the film *Bunny Lake Is Missing*, which tells the story of the murder of an innocent young girl.

The installation occupied one rectangle of the formal garden, bounded by gravel path, low hedges, and trees. It consisted of a square of blank walls without an entrance but with a couple of brightly colored ladders for visitors to climb up and look down within upon a scene of fictional child murder where plastic toys, playground equipment, an abandoned record player with a record still spinning, and a shallow grave littered the interior. In one sense, the stroller in the tranquil garden was assaulted by the stark brick walls and the eerie clues of death and departure within the secret garden. But by way of compensation for sensory deprivation and frustrated curiosity was the melancholy warmth of an infinitely relaxing song whose ambient sound did not at first seem to belong the installation but was finally the means of bearing in its force upon the visitor. From the precarious ladder at the top of the wall one looked down into the interior where playground equipment, abandoned toys, a shallow grave, and a vinyl disc revolving on a children's plastic record player provided eerie signs of recent occupation, like a landlocked version of the abandoned *Marie Celeste* (see http://www.pinksummer.com/pink2/art/str/wks001en.htm).

Sinister perplexity gave way to empathy only when I sat down at some distance from the walled garden, distractedly attending to the melancholy strain of what I later discovered was Tim Hardin's "Misty Roses" rerecorded by 13-year-old Ben Walford and amplified beyond the walls of the installation. (It was supposed to be coming from the plastic record player inside the walls.) On my return to Australia, I was consumed with curiosity about the work and wanted to see the film it was based on: Otto Preminger's 1965 *Bunny Lake Is Missing,* which, far from being on general video release as I had expected, could only be secured on two dusty 16-mm reels sent over from the National Film Archive of Australia. It is an excellent film noir about the abduction of a little girl whose existence hindered her uncle's incestuous involvement with her mother. Its final scene corresponds in many ways to the view down into the installation, but the girl did not die as the little grave in the installation suggested she had. And where was the plangent music? Good though it was, it was much dated and intent on producing a different range of emotions. Far from explaining the installation, it only deepened its mystery.

For me, instead, the peculiar structure of its feelings was mirrored by an unlikely analogy with, of all things, William Wordsworth's "The Solitary Reaper" (1807), a poem suggested to its author by an equally remote source: a sentence in a manuscript tour of Scotland written by a friend, which ends, "Passed a female who was reaping alone; she sung in Erse as she bended over her sickle, the sweetest human voice I ever heard: her strains were tenderly melancholy, and felt delicious, long after they were heard no more" (Thomas Wilkinson, Tours to the British Mountains [1824], quoted in Bloom et al., 1973, p. 184 n.).

What I think the contemporary installation and the Romantic poem share is a cognitive dissonance between an emotional affect and its unknown cause, a cause that generates a productive shearing of temporal and spatial relations and sets the mind racing toward the discovery of a larger and more inclusive equilibrium. Writing of Toni Morrison's novel *Beloved* (1989), Peter Nicholls employs Freud's concept of belatedness to illuminate a disruption in the traditional notions of causality. The excessive character of trauma requires a second event to release its traumatic force, but the second event presents itself as the cause of the first, and its retroactive logic forms the past in retrospect, as "the original site ... comes to be reworked" (John Forrester, quoted in Nicholls, 1996, p. 54). Earlier I opposed Stokes's redemptive theory of art and Bersani's theory of identity born of autoerotic self-shattering, but now I would insinuate an element that reconciles but changes them: the work they call out of the spectator not to "put Humpty Dumpty together again," so to speak, or to find pleasure in the shattered disarray of his parts, but to make something new from them; "the effect of the present on the past is to cause a repetition of the 'event' within which something new is taking place" (Andrew Benjamin, quoted Nicholls, 1996, p. 54). From Stokes's point of view, it is as if the lack of symbolic integration in the dislocations of contemporary art might prepare us for richer and wider integration, dislocations that Bunny Lake engenders as process rather than product by the rift between the confining walls and the expansive music. Equally, from Bersani's point of view, so long as the art continues to work on us effectively, there is none of the premature, stereotypically sententious closure with which overtly redemptive images (such as peace-dove symbols?) content us. I think this is so because Bunny Lake's compound of images and sounds is more troubling than traumatic. But why and how?

In answer to a personal inquiry, Georgina Starr has told me that her interest in the film derived from viewing it as a terrified eight-year-old alone with her adopted sister who, it later transpired, was never to recover from the traumatic circumstances of her life before adoption.[3] It strikes me, however, that neither this personal tragedy, nor its fictional refraction in the film, nor any of the child murders in England that inform the public dimension of the installation are really what it is "about." The haunting effect of the music, whose words seem so asinine in cold print—"Flowers often cry but too late to find / Their beauty has been lost with their peace of mind"—would not be so moving if one hadn't been perplexed beforehand: What's inside the wall? Where is the child? What happened in the film and in this garden?

Likewise, the "foreign" Erse language in which the Solitary Reaper's song is heard, plus the fact that we cannot hear its melody, ensure that, in search of an explanation, a series of radically incompatible possibilities passes in review before the reader's imagination without any of them proving adequate to explain the enduring emotional impact of the "the Vale profound … overflowing with the sound":

Will no one tell me what she sings?
Perhaps the plaintive numbers flow
For old, unhappy, far-off things
And battles long ago,
Or is it some more humble lay,
Familiar matter of to-day?

Could the differences be greater between alternative explanations of the causes for a strain of feeling? Yet none of them takes precedence.

To revert to Starr's work, the feeling expressed by Ben Walford's version of "Misty Roses" is quite different if one listens to it apart from the installation. Then it is a love song set in the present, not a dirge of melancholy resignation that is perhaps the best the bereaved could ever hope to feel about a tragic loss. If I am right, or merely plausible, then both the poem and the installation might entail the richly simultaneous reaction upon each other of an early and a late stage of mourning that would normally be experienced at widely separated times.

Let me not be misunderstood. I'm not attempting to yoke the works of Starr and Wordsworth together as "great art," but rather to suggest that there may be something similar about the emotional operation of their structures. Certainly, the rhetorical structure of the poem provides more guidance to the subsequent modulation of initial feeling. In this it is more like the therapeutic definition of working through, and offers itself as a retrospective commentary on the less directive installation, though the song there offers very oblique commentary too. But in either case, the dissonance between "affect" and speculation upon its causes lowers our emotional defenses so that something foreign lodges in the center of the self (Nicholls, 1996, p. 57)—something that, loosed from the gruesome specificity of Witkin's portraits, collects kindred future instances to itself of "sorrow, loss or pain / That has been, and may be again." Hence the appeal to imaginative memory: "The music in my heart I bore, / Long after it was heard no more."

Though neither poem nor installation may provide the choric resonance adequate to representation of a really collective tragedy such as the Holocaust, terrorist atrocity, or devastating war of retaliation, troubling images of this kind enlarge empathy by triggering a personal sense of working through larger than the single referenced occasion. Though much would depend on the constitutions of particular communities of response, it seems to me that the value of troubling images is that they transform and enlarge our feelings rather than perpetuate the trauma displaced by transcendence, repressed by denial, or merely repeated as secondary trauma in representations of violent acting out. Clearly my earlier complaints about Witkin's photograph Le Baiser place it in this category. In that case, it is not just the pornography of depicted violence that stuns or hardens the observer's psyche. Rather, it is the sure sense that the maker intended such damage as is inflicted on us that deepens its morbidity, and it is deepened again by the hypocritical art-speak in which the artist seeks to deny that intention with false and self-congratulatory claims to high-minded altruism.

Acknowledgment

I wish to acknowledge the value of comments on earlier versions of this essay kindly offered by Peter Nicholls, Andrew Relph, and Janet Sayers.

Notes

1. See Read (1989, 1998). I should say that for the most part I stand by these different exercises.
2. Compare Stokes (1978, vol. 3, p. 289): "When snatches of the environment are abstracted into art, we must stomach in such unexampled closeness the fact that what we clasp permits no other reverberation of itself."
3. Nevertheless, the sense that *Inside Bunny Lake Garden* is an apparatus for producing unanswerable questions resonates with a passage from the artist's autobiographical essay on "sisters, brothers, sons and daughters" in her book *The Bunny Lakes* (2002), where she makes an implicit contrast between her sister's irrevocable sense of loss and her own unsatisfied but dynamic quest for explanation:

   > "My sister never knew of any specific reason why she was orphaned. She had been rejected, and that is all she was really sure about. In all of her actions she seemed to be testing her new family to the limit. But was not she just plainly asking, 'How much do you really want me?' When things got really bad I was always questioning why. Had this happened because her mother had abandoned her? Was she out for revenge or retribution for this early betrayal? Had we been a really shit family? Or, was she aiming for total self-destruction because she did not think she was worth anything more? ... My sister, I think, thought that the only proper place for her was as a rejected child, and no matter what, that would be the destination she would strive to reach again, until the day she realised she was truly wanted."

References

Bersani, L. (1990). *The culture of redemption.* Cambridge, MA: Harvard University Press.

Bloom, Harold, et al. (Eds.). (1973). *The Oxford anthology of English literature: Volume 2, 1800 to the present.* New York: Oxford University Press.

Cooper, D. (1994). *Wrong.* London: Serpent's Tail.

Laplanche, J., & Pontalis, J. B. (1988). *The language of psychoanalysis.* London: Karnac.

Nicholls, P. (1996). The belated postmodern: History, phantoms and Toni Morrison. In S. Vice (Ed.), *Psychoanalytic criticism: A reader* (pp. 50-74). Cambridge: Polity.

Read, R. (1989). "A name that must be looked after": Turner, Ruskin and the verbal-visual sublime. *Word and Image*, *5*(4), 315–325.

Read, R. (1998). "Art Today": Stokes, Pound, Freud and the word-image opposition. *Word and Image*, *14*(3), 227–252.

Robb, P. (1996). *Midnight in Sicily: On art, food, history, travel & Cosa Nostra*. London: Harvill.

Russell, J. (1979). *Francis Bacon*. London: Thames & Hudson.

Starr, G. (2002). *The Bunny Lakes*. London: Emily Tsingou Gallery.

Stokes, A. (1978). *The critical writings of Adrian Stokes*. (L. Gowing, Ed.). London: Thames & Hudson.

Wilson, C. (2000). Joel-Peter Witkin. Retrieved 17 September 2006, from http://archive.salon.com/people/bc/2000/05/09/witkin/index.html.

Witkin, J.-P. (n.d.). Joel-Peter Witkin *and* Story from a book (manipulated photograph). Paris, 1999. Retrieved 17 September 2006, from http://www.edelmangallery.com/witkin.htm.

Witkin, J.-P. (n.d.). Joel-Peter Witkin. Retrieved 17 September, from Retrieved 17 September 2006, from http://www.zonezero.com/exposiciones/fotografos/witkin/jpwdefault.html.

Contributors

Judith Allsop is a professor of health policy at the University of Lincoln and a professor emerita at London, South Bank University. She has written widely on health policy, complaints in health care settings, the health professions and health consumers. Recent publications include *The Regulation of the Health Professions* (Saks, 2002) and *Speaking for Patients: Health Consumer Groups and the National Policy Process* (Baggott and Jones, 2005), funded by the Economic and Social Research Council.

Halla Beloff was formerly chair of social psychology at Edinburgh University. At some risk to her respectablity as a social psychologist, Dr. Beloff's research gradually moved into an analysis of fine art works, principally photography, considered as visual texts. She is active with the British Psychology Society and is currently a committee member of the Scottish Arts Council. Dr. Beloff's work has always been influenced by the ideas of members of her family. She is author of several books including *Camera Culture* (Blackwell, 1985)

Joanna Bourke is professor of history at Birkbeck College, London, and author of seven books, including *Dismembering the Male: Men's Bodies, Britain and the Great War* (Reaktion Books); *An Intimate History of Killing* (Granta); and *Fear: A Cultural History* (Virago). She is currently working on a book about rapists in the nineteenth and twentieth centuries.

Lauren Breen is completing her doctor of philosophy (community psychology) at Edith Cowan University. Her research interests include grief and bereavement, and she is especially interested in the ways in which a person's context influences his or her grief experience. She previously held the position of an associate lecturer in the School of Psychology, Edith Cowan University (2001-2004), and as a member of team, received an Australian Award for University Teaching in 2003.

Deirdre Drake is a lecturer in psychology at Edith Cowan University, where she teaches in the postgraduate forensic psychology program and in developmental psychology. Her doctoral thesis investigated older adults' views on the distribution of inheritance. Her current research interests include adult development and aging, and the intersection between psychology and law, particularly in the civil and family law areas.

Bridget Fowler is a professor at the University of Glasgow. She specialises in the sociology of culture with particular reference to art and literature. Her long term interest is the ideas of Pierre Bourdieu, whose theory she has taken up in two books, *The Alienated Reader* (Harvester Wheatsheaf, 1991) and *Pierre Bourdieu and Cultural Theory: Critical Investigation* (Sage, 1997). She is currently working on *Obituary as Collective Memory* to be published by Routledge.

Camilla Herbert is consultant clinical neuropsychologist with the Brain Injury Rehabilitation Trust and Sussex Partnerships NHS Trust. She has worked in post acute and community brain injury rehabilitation settings since qualifying as a clinical psychologist in 1988 and has a particular interest in working with families and also in the assessment of capacity.

Jenny Hockey is professor of sociology at Sheffield University. Trained as an anthropologist, she has published extensively on death, dying and bereavement. Her most recent book relevant to her contributed chapter is *Death, Memory and Material Culture* (Berg, 2001) coauthored with Elizabeth Hallam.

Glennys Howarth is director of the Centre for Death and Society at the University of Bath. Dr. Howarth has been researching and writing in the field of death, dying and bereavement for almost twenty years. She is coeditor and founder of the journal *Mortality* and editor (with Oliver Leaman) of *The Encyclopedia of Death and Dying* (2001) and author of *Death and Dying: A Sociological Introduction* (Polity Press, 2006).

Kathryn Hughes reviews for *The Guardian* newspaper and teaches life writing at the University of East Anglia. Her biography, *George Eliot: The Last Victorian* (1998) won the James Tait Black Memorial Prize for

Biography. Her most recent work is *The Short Life and Long Times of Mrs. Beeton* (2006).

Carolyn Harris Johnson is a social worker of twenty-five years experience. She devised and implemented the first Community Based Corrections Sex Offender Treatment Program in Western Australia. Her masters of arts research on familicide and disputed custody and access has been published by University of Western Australia Press in the book *Come With Daddy* (2005). She is completing her PhD at the University of Western Australia extending her research on spousal homicide and familicide.

Leonie Kellaher is emeritus professor in the Cities Institute at London Metropolitan University. Her research has taken an anthropological and social policy approach to the organizational, material and built environments people occupy—in life and in death. She is coauthor of *The Secret Cemetery* and has been coinvestigator with Jenny Hockey on the project Environments of Memory.

Monique Kornell is a freelance scholar with an interest in the study of anatomy by artists and anatomical book illustration. She has published articles on anatomical drawings and prints from the sixteenth to eighteenth centuries and was cocurator of *The Ingenious Machine of Nature: Four Centuries of Art and Anatomy*, an exhibition of prints and drawings organized by the National Gallery of Canada in 1996.

J. John Lennon holds the Moffat chair in travel and tourism business Development, Glasgow Caledonian University. He worked on tourism and travel projects in Fiji, United States, Egypt, Nepal, Romania, Poland, Germany, Czech Republic, Singapore, Ireland, Russia and the United Kingdom, and is an independent policy advisor to Visit Scotland. He is author of seven books and numerous articles and reports.

Margaret Mitchell is an associate professor at the School of Law and Justice, Edith Cowan University, Perth, Western Australia. She is the director of the Sellenger Centre for Research in Law, Justice and Policing and editor of *The Aftermath of Road Accidents* (Routledge 1997) and *Police Leadership and Management in Australia* (Federation Press, 2006).

Moira O'Connor is senior lecturer at the School of Psychology, Edith Cowan University. Moira teaches social psychology, community psychology and environmental psychology. Her research interests center around health, with a focus on women's health, palliative care, psycho-oncology, and bereavement. Recent projects include an exploration of interdisciplinary teams in palliative care; an examination of GPs' attitudes to palliative care and an evaluation of a domestic violence organization.

David Prendergast is senior researcher in social policy and ageing, Social Policy and Ageing Research Centre, Trinity College, Dublin, currently working on the subject of ageing in Ireland. In 2005 he published *From Elder to Ancestor: Old Age, Death and Inheritance in Modern Korea* (Global Oriental, 2005). David has since collaborated with Dr. Bill Adams on research into the history of international conservation and with Jenny Hockey and Leonie Kellaher on changing rituals of mourning in the United Kingdom.

Richard Read is associate professor of art history at the University of Western Australia. He has published in major journals on the relationship between literature and the visual arts, nineteenth- and twentieth-century European and Australian art and contemporary cinema. His book, *Art and Its Discontents; The Early Life of Adrian Stokes* (2003) was joint winner of the 2003 Art Association of Australia and New Zealand best book prize in art history.

Gerard Sullivan is associate professor at the University of Sydney. Much of his work has been in gay and lesbian studies, access and equity in the provision of social services, and comparative sociology. He teaches and writes on research methods and contributed significantly to *The Encyclopedia of Death and Dying* (Howarth & Leaman, 2001).

Robert Wyatt is lecturer in painting in the School of Fine Art, The Glasgow School of Art. He is also a painter himself, with a practical interest in the analysis of how images work and why they are made. He is author of *Trouthunting: The Pursuit of Happiness* (Stackpole 2004). He curated the exhibition *Like a Shadow: Representations of Death in Art* at Glasgow School of Art, an exhibition mounted in partnership with the Fourth International Conference on Death, Dying and Disposal held in Glasgow in 1998, and contributed commentary on death and art to Howarth and Leaman's *Encyclopedia of Death and Dying* (2001).

Index

O

P

R

S

T

V

W

Z